The Lincoln Assassination
Conspiracy Trial
and Its Legacy

ALSO BY FREDERICK HATCH

*Protecting President Lincoln:
The Security Effort, the Thwarted Plots
and the Disaster at Ford's Theatre*
(McFarland, 2011)

The Lincoln Assassination Conspiracy Trial and Its Legacy

Frederick Hatch

McFarland & Company, Inc., Publishers
Jefferson, North Carolina

LIBRARY OF CONGRESS CATALOGUING-IN-PUBLICATION DATA

Hatch, Frederick, 1945– author.
   The Lincoln assassination conspiracy trial and its legacy / Frederick Hatch.
     p.   cm.
   Includes bibliographical references and index.

   ISBN 978-0-7864-9498-9 (softcover : acid free paper) ∞
   ISBN 978-1-4766-1699-5 (ebook)

   1. Lincoln Assassination Conspiracy Trial, Washington, D.C., 1865.
2. Trials (Conspiracy)—Washington (D.C.)—History—19th century.
3. Military courts—United States—History—19th century. 4. Lincoln, Abraham, 1809–1865—Assassination. I. Title.
KF223.L47H38 2015
345.73'02524—dc23
                                                    2014044430

BRITISH LIBRARY CATALOGUING DATA ARE AVAILABLE

© 2015 Frederick Hatch. All rights reserved

No part of this book may be reproduced or transmitted in any form or by any means, electronic or mechanical, including photocopying or recording, or by any information storage and retrieval system, without permission in writing from the publisher.

On the cover: *top row left to right* Michael O'Laughlen, Mary Surratt, Lewis Powell (also known as Lewis Payne), Dr. Samuel Mudd; *bottom row* Samuel Arnold, Edman Spangler, David E. Herold, George A. Atzerodt; *bottom image* execution of the conspirators, scaffold in use and crowd in the yard, seen from the roof of the Arsenal (all images from Library of Congress except Mary Surratt image is from National Archives)

Printed in the United States of America

McFarland & Company, Inc., Publishers
  Box 611, Jefferson, North Carolina 28640
    www.mcfarlandpub.com

To the memory of
Dr. Richard Dyer Mudd
(1901–2002),
grandson of Dr. Samuel A. Mudd,
and a tireless crusader for justice

Die höchste Tugend, wie ein Heiligenschein,
Umgibt des Kaisers Haupt, nur er allein
Vermag sie gültig auszuüben:
Gerechtigkeit!—Was alle Menschen lieben,
Was alle fordern, wünschen, schwer entbehren,
Es liegt an ihm, dem Volk es zu gewähren
Doch ach! Was hilft dem Menchengeist Verstand,
Dem Herzen Güte, Willigkeit der Hand,
Wenns fieberhaft durchaus im Staate wütet
Und Übel sich in Übeln überbrütet?
Wer schaut hinab von diesem hohen Raum
Ins weite Reich, ihm scheints ein schwerer Traum,
Wo Missgestalt in Missgestalten schaltet,
Das Ungesetz gesetzlich überwaltet
Und eine Welt des Irrtums sich entfaltet.

Johann Wolfgang von Goethe,
Faust, Part II, Act I

The highest virtue like an aureole
Circles the Emperor's head; alone and sole,
He validly can exercise it:
'Tis justice!—All men love and prize it;
'Tis what all wish, scarce do without and ask;
To grant it to his people is his task.
But ah! What good to mortal mind is sense,
What good to hearts is Kindness, hands benevolence,
When through the state a fever runs and revels,
And evil hatches more and more of evils?
Who views the wide realm from this height supreme,
To him all seems like an oppressive dream,
Where in confusion is confusion reigning
And lawlessness by law itself maintaining,
A world of error evermore obtaining.

Table of Contents

Acknowledgments — ix
Preface — 1
Introduction — 4

1. The Crime — 9
2. Judges, Jury and Accused — 29
3. Military Justice — 43
4. Prosecution — 55
5. Defense — 66
6. Witness or Defendant? — 83
7. Verdict — 101
8. Justice? — 121
9. History's Long Shadow — 145

Summation — 171
Afterword — 173
Appendices:

    I. Opinion of the Attorney General Regarding Suspension of the Writ of Habeas Corpus *by Edward Bates* — 177

    II. The Constitution of the United States of America, Analysis and Interpretation — 182

III. Opinion of the Constitutional Power of the Military to Try and Execute the Assassins of the President *by Attorney General James Speed*	190
IV. Digest of Opinions of the Judge Advocate General of the Army *edited by Major W. Winthrop, USA*	206
V. Instructions for the Government of Armies of the United States in the Field *by Francis Lieber*	210
Chapter Notes	213
Bibliography	222
Index	229

Acknowledgments

A great many people, both those associated with major historical and academic institutions, as well as many private individuals involved in their own investigations of the same, and associated studies, have contributed to this book. To try to name them all, or to rate the nature and degree of the assistance they provided, would be impossible. However, there are among the legions of those who have, both knowingly and unknowingly, aided in the development of the researches which led to this book, certain persons and organizations which cannot be allowed to remain anonymous. It is not intended that in naming these, the author fails to acknowledge and feel the greatest respect and gratitude for all the others.

Listed alphabetically, I wish to give my special thanks to the following individuals: David R. Barbee, John C. Brennan, Joan L. Chaconas, Roy Z. Chamlee, Jr., Arthur T. Downey, William C. Edwards, Louis Fisher, Joseph George, Jr., James O. Hall, William Hanchett, Michael W. Kauffman, Steven G. Miller, Dr. Richard D. Mudd, Richard E. Sloan, Edward Steers, Jr., Laurie Verge, Sandra Walia, and Frank J. Williams.

Likewise, the staff, past and present, of the following institutions: Georgetown University, Washington, D.C.; Library of Congress, Washington, D.C.; Lincoln Museum at Ford's Theatre, Washington, D.C.; National Archives, Washington, D.C.; National Park Service, Department of the Interior, Washington, D.C.; Surratt Society, Clinton, MD; University of Arizona, Tucson; University of California at Los Angeles; University of Southern California, Los Angeles; University of Texas, Austin.

Preface

The brutal murder of Abraham Lincoln, America's greatest and most beloved leader, shocked and grieved the people of his time, and it can be said that the echo of that fatal shot has reverberated across the centuries since. America's sixteenth president is possibly the most recognizable figure in all our history. His impact upon his country continues to grow and develop. Our interest in the man and his time also grows and evolves.

Aware of the countless books, articles, poems, plays, motion pictures, television programs, and even depictions of Lincoln in the crass displays of advertising, the public, despite its saturation in Lincolniana, remains ready, even eager, to know more. Lincoln stands at the forefront of our history and has indelibly penetrated our psychology. One may fairly ask, what more is there to say about him that has not already been dealt with countless times? But the search for something new continues, for Lincoln's life and accomplishments are an inexhaustible fountain.

Lincoln was a complex man. While he lived, it gradually became known that he was not only multifaceted but also a reserved and private man, always careful in crafting the image of himself that he presented to his contemporaries. This skill went well beyond the natural-born politician's ability to be many things to many people, instead suggesting a man absorbed in the process of exploring himself, a man of mystery, both to the people of his own time and to their descendants.

This book delves into the darker side of our understanding of Lincoln and his time. It was a time of unprecedented crisis, a crisis so fundamental and troubling that it overshadows all other problems in American history, no matter how challenging those other crises have been and are. Lincoln's belief that the very existence of his country and the solution to the huge and complex challenges he faced in dealing with the crisis, called for unprecedented measures, measures which created the paradox that in order to save and preserve the land of liberty, those very liberties must be set aside, however temporarily. The effects of that decision, like ripples on a pond's surface, continue through American history and are very much evident in our own time. The dilemma that faced Lincoln continues down to the present and will persist into the imaginable future.

This book is not a comprehensive history of the trial of the conspiracy suspects, but rather an examination of whether the military had jurisdiction and whether the rights of the accused were violated. Many sources, both original and recent, have been used to describe the case for the prosecution and for the defense. This includes background material on the crime itself, the investigation and arrest of the suspects, the people involved, and the issues at stake, as seen by the people of the time and by later generations. In addition, American history has been examined, both before and since the Lincoln case, to see when and how military law has been used as a substitute for civilian law. The Founding Fathers of America, and the nature of the Constitution they wrote, have been consulted to show how some of the strengths of that document can also become weaknesses, depending on how it is interpreted. Lincoln's actions are compared with those of other American leaders, both before and after his time, down to and including the current controversy over the so-called War on Terror, with its questions about prisoners being tried by the military. The crimes themselves are not minimized, and many would support the sentiment that the more terrible the crime, the more cruel, the more powerfully aroused the grief and anger, the more harsh should be the punishment. Whatever the reader feels about that is for him to decide. This book is not a plea for compassion or mercy for those responsible for some of the most heinous crimes in American history. Neither is it intended to minimize or denigrate the contributions and sacrifices of those who have served and are serving in the armed forces. We must never fail to acknowledge their dedication to serving America. The debt we all owe them, past and present, can never be repaid. It is no disrespect of their service to suggest that in some cases they should not have been involved.

This book asks whether justice was truly served, both a century and a half ago and over the years since. Were the precedents set then wise and not likely to lead us away from the concept of justice?

The debate which arose regarding some of the actions of the Lincoln administration, and in the wake of Lincoln's assassination, have an all-too-familiar sound. As I wrote this book, it became my belief that what started out as an examination of historical events in the remote past has a very contemporary application. As the issues raised then were never adequately resolved, and the questions never satisfactorily answered, so they have also failed to be properly addressed in our time.

The subject of this book is the Lincoln assassination conspiracy trial, but it is also an examination of the larger issue, that of the expansion of executive power and the stretching, and even dismissal, of the constitutional safeguards against encroachments on our liberties. We fail in our duty to history and to our own time, if we do not make the connection and recognize the danger.

Some may say that this account is biased, that it is lacking in objectivity. Honesty requires an acknowledgment that the opinions expressed here are weighted toward questioning the commonly accepted interpretation of the events described here. While objectivity should ever be the goal of the historian, there are times when it is necessary to lean in the opposite direction in order to bring about a righting of the scales, when the majority has been overly tipped the other way. Those who have accepted that the Lincoln assassination trial was legal and that the convictions and punishments meted out were just need to consider the other side of the argument, and especially to reflect upon the consequences of the accumulation of power by the executive, weakening the concept of a balance of power intended by the Constitution.

Our Founding Fathers did not answer the question of how to establish and preserve liberty, and neither shall we. The reader may not agree with this analysis of Lincoln's acts and how his contemporaries dealt with the crisis growing out of those acts, but it is enough that the modern reader be aware of the danger, and being aware, seek to do something about it.

Introduction

Law is the foundation of civilization. Indeed, without law there can be no civilization. Of course, as law is an invention of man, it is, and must be, flawed, as its inventor is flawed. The great contest, then, is not between law and lawlessness, but rather the effort to let law work as it is supposed to, as an instrument for justice. Justice is not naturally occurring. Like law, it is an invention of man. Law and justice are not synonymous. If there can be no justice without law, it is not always true that there is no law without justice. Human history is filled with examples of laws which do not foster justice. Every society wants law, but not every society is willing to try to achieve justice.

The United States of America is unusual, perhaps even unique, in that it was intended to be a just society. Mechanisms were created to try to being about and to nourish and develop the concept of justice. In their quest for liberty, and in the belief that Americans could free themselves from the spoilers of justice—ignorance, prejudice, greed, lack of equality, lack of opportunity, oppression, intolerance, the failure to try to apply the law fairly and evenly to all—our Founding Fathers created institutions whose purpose was to do battle with those ancient barriers to life, liberty, and the pursuit of happiness. They also challenged human nature itself in creating law and the concept of justice with enough flexibility both to adapt itself to changing times and conditions and yet to uphold and preserve those ideas and ideals which they felt could be, and would be, valued for all time and experience to come.

The Founding Fathers did not achieve their purpose. They knew they would not and suspected that their descendants would never achieve the realization of perfect justice. As we said, justice is a creation of man, therefore it is as flawed as man is. But if man is flawed by nature, he also possesses the idealism to want to achieve, and to try to achieve, the realization of that which can scarcely be defined, but which can never entirely be relegated to the great dumpster labeled "impossible." One could say that the story of America is that of a people who denied the impossible, who refused to believe, again and again, that might does not make right, and, however impossible it may seem and however often it might collapse in failure, the idea that right makes might is so powerful that it cannot be allowed to be abandoned. If America is not the perfect society envisioned by its founders, Americans are still not prepared to say that it cannot be.

The Civil War of 1861–1865 was the greatest crisis that has, and probably ever shall, challenge America. Economic, political, or natural disasters can severely strain the fabric that holds the nation together, but unlike in hard times before and since, the fabric was ripped in two, and desperate people sought to pull it back together by any means possible. Americans fought each other with all the ferocity they have ever shown foreign enemies. For both sides, for all involved, the stakes were as high as possible and unprecedented measures were the order of the day. Under such conditions concerns for the future are often laid aside. People become so involved with their immediate problems that they cannot, or choose not to, consider what effect the actions of today can or will have on tomorrow.

Law is for cool heads. Laws that are made in desperate times by desperate people often prove to be unwise, incapable of standing in the light of day once the crisis is past. Recognizing this, one is tempted to say that in such times, when emotions are strong and passions high, actions whose results are incapable of being undone should not be taken. It strikes the reader of history, especially when considering the cases of the Lincoln assassination conspiracy suspects, the German saboteurs during World War II, or the War on Terror after September 11, 2001, that the high feelings of the moment produced a rush to the gallows or the electric chair or lashing out at perceived enemies abroad when cooler, calmer thinking and feelings might have spared lives. Of course, lives lost cannot be recalled, but neither can time spent incarcerated or harshly treated. Even in times of strained rationality, law and order must be served. We cannot say that justice cannot be done in times of crisis. That generalization is too sweeping. But is it not reasonable to suggest that justice, the concept behind the term, is more likely to be accomplished at a safe distance from the fires of passion?

The U.S. Constitution was deliberately designed to require compromise as the cornerstone of government, whether on local, state, or national levels. Checks and balances were created as safeguards against emotional outbursts or disproportionate ascendancy of political ideals. This kind of government requires time and reason to be allowed to prevent hasty or unsound doctrines, whether of the left or right, to override the built-in safeguards which are our defenses for liberty and justice. The most important of these safeguards are the constitutional amendments collectively called the Bill of Rights. These are the strongest and surest protections Americans have against encroachments upon their liberty and justice. Take them away and we still have a rich and powerful nation, but we can no longer claim to have a free and just one. The Founding Fathers were not perfect, and, like us, they could not always anticipate future events. When they slipped into the Constitution the still little-known provision that habeas corpus could be suspended under certain circumstances, they left what amounts to a ticking time bomb, waiting to undo all their attempts to safeguard their and their descendants' liberties. America cannot be a land of liberty and justice some of the time. Either it is or it is not. I will show how this problem has again and again done damage to our most cherished possessions, liberty and justice.

A great people, having announced to the world their passion for justice and right, must not and cannot abandon the fine-sounding words and ideals when the chips are down. Law and order can and will be served no matter what the circumstances. Justice and right need tolerance to help them stand against the harsh winds of aroused passions. Human nature can be advanced as an explanation for the failure of justice and right to prevail, but excuses are never a satisfactory substitute for the failure of a people to live according to their announced ideals.

The America of today bears little resemblance to the creation of its founders. It has grown enormously in physical size and complexity, and, like other great and powerful nations of the past, has been beguiled by a multiplicity of temptations into dangerous waters far from its original ideals and purposes. Unlike most other nations, though, the United States of America was founded on ideas. It is a nation which did not evolve naturally by chance, but was deliberately created by its inhabitants, justifying their actions through their devotion to the idea of liberty. To those founders, the phrase "liberty and justice for all" was not just window dressing. The Founders were worldly men who recognized that human beings are often weak, short-sighted, prejudiced, emotional creatures, easily tempted to be swept along by the passions of the moment into setting aside, or even abandoning, the ideals of their forefathers. This is no less true of our time than it was of Lincoln's.

It is greatly to be regretted that our most revered leader, Abraham Lincoln, allowed basic concepts of liberty and justice to be suspended, even if only temporarily, setting the precedent not to be forgotten by his successors. The questions raised at the trial of those accused of conspiring to assassinate Lincoln were not adequately answered at the time, and, like the seeds of unwanted weeds blown into the garden by storm winds, have taken root and have posed danger to the tree of liberty. If we value that which was so carefully planted and cultivated by the Founders, we must be relentless in seeking to identify and root out those harmful and unwanted varieties. Lincoln was as devoted to liberty and justice as any American who ever lived, but the suspension of basic liberties and rights troubled him even as he set his signature of approval to the documents allowing it to happen. He believed it was necessary, in a time of grave crisis, to preserve the nation. But it worried him, as it should have, and as it should worry all of his descendants.

The issues raised here are not new, and whatever we think today about the actions of those in times long past, we must acknowledge that we have no power to go back and right a wrong. The past is what created the present. Our ancestors were not endowed with superhuman wisdom and had no way of peering into the future. They, like us, were powerless to undo the errors of previous times. They, like us, could not see what perils and opportunities the future might hold. And they, like us, could not know how our descendants will behave when faced with problems and perils perhaps unknown in all previous history.

The value of history, the reasons for studying our past, are twofold. We study the past in order to discover who the people were whose actions—or inactions—brought about our world as we know it. This is a very important thing for us to know, for it leads to our other reason for the study of history: the use of the past as a guide to the future. In examining the problems and pitfalls of bygone times, as well as the accomplishments and triumphs of our predecessors, we can learn and relearn their lessons. We can discover how to avoid the errors and to try to create the conditions and opportunities which will shape a future in which our descendants will prosper, and perhaps feel gratitude for us, for our wisdom and abilities.

We must be willing to disentangle ourselves, to some extent, from the troubles of the moment. We must foster the ability to imagine a future not bound by our errors and short-sightedness. We must try to leave behind something of value, which can serve us by offering to our future opportunity, wisdom, and hope. We cannot know whether our efforts will provide such advantages for the future, but we must make the effort, if for no other reason than to try to give our descendants reasons to praise, more than to damn, their predecessors.

1

THE CRIME

On April 14, 1865, the president of the United States, Abraham Lincoln (1809–1865), was assassinated. His friends and supporters had long feared such a thing, and Lincoln had received many warnings. This was the first time in the history of the United States that a president, the chief of state, the leader of the government, the commander-in-chief of the armed forces, had been murdered. Adding to the shock was the fact that the Union states were in the midst of celebrating the rapidly approaching end of the long, difficult, and very bloody Civil War. Lincoln, the long-suffering war president, had already turned his attention to the peace process, the reconstruction of the Union, the reuniting of the states to return as rapidly as possible to the way it had been before. His was a call for a compassionate peace, "with malice toward none, with charity for all"; and his purpose, "to bind up the nation's wounds ... to do all which may achieve and cherish a just, and a lasting peace, among ourselves, and with all nations."[1]

In the midst of the rejoicing of the people of the Union, as they proclaimed their admiration for the man who had brought them all through the worst trial the nation had ever had, the man whose heart had remained true and whose hand had remained firm, perhaps more than anyone else's could have, suddenly, brutally, had been struck down. Shock, grief, anger, fear, uncertainty welled up within them, along with other emotions less easily defined. Out of this mass of feeling congealed a demand for vengeance. To punish those responsible for this great atrocity became the sworn duty, the relentless obsession, the overwhelming resolve of the people and their representatives.[2]

From the very first, while news of the president's assassination was still spreading, even while Lincoln still lived, Secretary of War Edwin M. Stanton (1814–1869) seized control of the investigation, interviewing witnesses, sending orders far and wide, personally writing press releases, and directing the hunt for the assassination conspirators. It was taken for granted that this crime came under the jurisdiction of the military, in spite of the fact that no law then existed designating the assassination of the president as a federal crime, let alone as an offense against the United States military.[3]

The dictatorial power assumed by Stanton was cloaked in legality. A little known clause in the Constitution read, "The privilege of the writ of habeas corpus shall not be suspended, unless when in cases of rebellion or invasion the public safety may require it."

Habeas corpus, Latin for "you have the body," as used in the law, means to bring a person being held before a court. A writ is an order requiring a person to carry out an act. Thus, a writ of habeas corpus is a legal order to produce a prisoner before a court. The significance of this is fundamental in democratic nations, for it means that no one can be arrested and held without coming before a court, where the prosecutors must present their case against the defendant, who has the right to a defense. Such a writ does not say anything about the guilt or innocence of the person being held, only whether due process of the law is being observed.

The great English authority Sir William Blackstone (1723–1780) stated that habeas corpus was the most celebrated writ in English law. The Judiciary Act, passed by the U.S. Congress in 1789, enabled the federal courts "to grant writs of habeas corpus for the purpose of an inquiry into the cause of commitment" to custody. Beginning with a proclamation of May 10, 1861, Lincoln had suspended the writ, authorizing federal authorities to arrest people without warrants and hold them without trial, or to try them by military courts or commissions. These measures were restrained and local at first, but soon were extended over virtually the entire country, North as well as South. No one knows how many were arrested, but they numbered in the thousands. At first, the arrests were administered by Secretary of State William H. Seward (1801–1872), through the State Department. After Edwin M. Stanton became secretary of war in early 1862, he took over the process from Seward. Curiously, although some politicians, especially Democrats, denounced Lincoln's policies and called him a dictator, the majority of the public in the North accepted the suspension of the writ as a necessary wartime measure.

Although Lincoln had been uneasy about assuming such power as suspending the writ placed in his hands, he defended the policy as essential for the successful prosecution of the war, and always regarded it as a purely

1. The Crime

temporary action. He asked, "Must a government, of necessity, be too strong for the liberties of its own people, or too weak to maintain its own existence?" To those who said that only Congress had the power to suspend the writ, Lincoln replied, "The Constitution itself, is silent as to which, or who, is to exercise the power, and as the provision was plainly made for a dangerous emergency, it cannot be believed the framers of the instrument intended, that in every case, the danger should run its course, until Congress could be called together, the very assembling of which might be prevented, as was intended in this case, by the rebellion."

When Congress passed the Habeas Corpus Act of March 3, 1863, Lincoln's policies gained legislative approval, even though the Congress did not make it

Once thought to be the last photograph taken of the president, this photograph is now believed to have been taken on February 5, 1865, two months before the assassination (Library of Congress).

clear exactly where the power of suspension ultimately lay. To this day no such clarification has ever been made. Lincoln's assumption of the power to suspend habeas corpus can be considered the single most important act any president has ever taken to increase the power of the executive.

The great majority of arrests were for acts deemed to be in aid of the rebellion, such as blockade running, desertion, and draft dodging. Suppression of newspapers, though it did happen, was relatively rare, and one could not make a convincing case that the Lincoln administration was attempting to stifle dissent.

Lincoln's suspension of the writ of habeas corpus was part of John Wilkes Booth's motives for committing the crime. In his "To Whom It May Concern" letter, written in November 1864, Booth said,

> When a country like this spurns justice from her side, she forfeit's [sic] the allegiance of every honest freeman, and should leave him untrammeled by any fealty so ever, to act, as his conscience may approve.... I love justice, more than I do a country that disowns it.

One of the most learned and prestigious legal authorities in American history was Joseph Story (1779–1845). A professor of law at Harvard University and one of the founders of the Harvard Law School, Story served as an associate justice of the United States Supreme Court from 1811 to 1845. On the question of suspension of the writ of habeas corpus, Story wrote, "It would seem as the power is given to Congress to suspend the writ of habeas corpus in cases of rebellion or invasion, that the right to judge, whether exigency had arisen, must exclusively belong to that body." British jurist Albert Venn Dicey (1835–1922) stated that habeas corpus acts "declare no principle and define no rights, but they are for practical purposes worth a hundred constitutional articles guaranteeing individual liberty."[4]

The writ of habeas corpus has existed in English law since the twelfth century. The British parliament passed the Habeas Corpus Act in 1640, following with the Habeas Corpus Act of 1679, regularizing the procedures for issuing the writ. In American history, suspensions of the writ were rare prior to the Civil War. The Continental Congress had directed the military to disarm and arrest citizens of Queens County, New York, who had not supported the American Revolution, stating "Those who refuse to defend their country should be excluded from its protection and be prevented from doing it injury."[5]

Without the protection provided by the writ of Habeas corpus, in the emotionally charged conditions of April 1865, the United States military was allowed to assume police power over civilians on a nationwide scale, leading to the arrest and detention of thousands of Americans, whose fundamental legal rights were regarded as suspended. Without the necessity of filing official charges, without specifying the nature of their "crimes," without reference to laws or systems of law, denying their right to a defense before a lawfully ordained court, it appeared to some Americans that their country could no longer be called the land of liberty and justice.

Feeding the public reaction to the calamity of the murder of the president and attempted murder of the secretary of state, many religious leaders throughout the nation showed no mercy for anyone suspected of aiding the assassins. Ministers, noting that the shooting of Lincoln had taken place on Good Friday, preached in their Easter Sunday sermons cries for vengeance, for retribution, often so feverishly as to amount to near hysteria. "God has permitted the thing to be [so that] the hearts of all loyal people may be filled with hatred for treason." "In avenging the blood of the martyred Lincoln [people will] root up even the smallest fiber of treason from the soil." As these quotes show, it was widely assumed that the assassination had to be the work of the Southern rebels.[6]

It was widely believed that the rebels had plotted to assassinate many of the leaders of the government. Papers found in a hotel room implicated several of the assassin's fellow conspirators. The simultaneous attack on Secretary Seward, taking place at the same time as the assassination of Lincoln, established early on that there was a conspiracy. Soon rumors arose that there were, or had been, plots to kill General Ulysses S. Grant (1822–1885), Secretary Stanton, Vice President Andrew Johnson (1808–1875), Senator Charles Sumner (1811–1874), Chief Justice Salmon P. Chase (1808–1873), and possibly others. It was eventually established that Johnson had been included among the conspiracy's intended victims, but no credible evidence was produced to substantiate threats against the other leaders. It would later be charged that the elaborate multiple funerals of Lincoln were arranged by Stanton in order to encourage the idea that the Southern rebels were responsible, that Lincoln's murder was part of the Rebellion.[7]

In the midst of traumatic events, as the nation's sorrow and grief mixed with anger and a demand for vengeance, with huge armies still contending with each other on far-flung battlefields, it became necessary to undertake an investigation of the great crimes, and to determine the possibility of a conspiracy of vast proportions. In addition to his responsibilities of managing the War Department, whose personnel and scope of operations had swelled enormously during the war, Secretary Stanton now assumed the direction of the investigation, arrest of suspects, and the management of the trial and punishment of those believed to be responsible. In spite of such daunting responsibilities, few at the time doubted Stanton's capacity to shoulder such burdens.[8]

Edwin McMasters Stanton was described as being "haughty, severe, dominating, and often rude.... He hated disloyalty and had no patience with critics of his administration." Stanton's assumption of power and responsibility on the night of the assassination was described by his assistant, Charles A. Dana (1819–1897):

> Mr. Stanton alone was in full activity.... He ... dictated orders, one after another.... All these orders were designed to keep the business of the government in full motion until the crisis should be over. It seemed as if Mr. Stanton thought of everything, and there was a great deal to be thought of that night. The extent of the conspiracy was, of course, unknown, and the horrible beginning which had been made naturally led us to suspect the worst. The safety of Washington must be looked after. Commanders all over the country had to be ordered to take extra precautions. The people must be notified of the tragedy. The assassins must be captured. The coolness and clearheadedness of Mr. Stanton under these circumstances were most remarkable.

Stanton would not attend the trial of the conspiracy suspects, leaving the details and management of the trial to Judge Advocate General of the Army Joseph Holt (1807–1894). Stanton's control from behind the scenes and his influence was well known and felt by all.[9]

Born in Steubenville, Ohio, on December 19, 1814, to a Quaker physician and the daughter of a Virginia planter, young Stanton was delicate and asthmatic, suffering his first seizure at age ten. He would be troubled by poor health all of his life. When his father died, the twelve-year-old Edwin had to leave school to work in a bookstore, where he continued his education in available moments. In 1831 he entered Kenyon College in Gambier, Ohio, but lack of money again forced him to leave school. He then worked in a bookstore in Columbus, Ohio. Studying law with Daniel L. Collier, a family friend, he passed the bar exam in 1835, even though underage. His capacity for work, as well as his brilliance, which impressed all who knew him and awed even his bitterest enemies, showed itself early. In 1837 Stanton was elected county prosecutor of Harrison County, Ohio. Becoming a partner of U.S. Senator Benjamin Tappan (1773–1857) made Stanton a rising star in Democratic Party politics.

On December 31, 1836, Edwin Stanton married Mary A. Lamson (1815–1844). Their first child, a daughter named Lucy, died in 1841. There is a story that Stanton's grief was so severe he had the child's remains disinterred and kept them in his room. Though Stanton was always an emotional man, there nevertheless remains a good deal of doubt about this story. In the early spring of 1844 Mary died suddenly. The grieving man was heard to cry out as he searched his house by night for his vanished wife. Tragedy seemed to single him out again and again. His brother Darwin committed suicide in 1846. These losses caused him to grow even more withdrawn and serious than he had already been, but they did not break him. He had a young son to raise, Edwin Lamson Stanton (1842–1878). His enemies would later use rumors based on his personal tragedies to suggest that he was mentally unbalanced.

Stanton applied himself to the hard work which was beginning to earn him a reputation as one of the leading lawyers of his time. Moving to Pittsburgh in 1847, he kept ties with Ohio, and also with Harrisburg, Philadelphia, and Washington. His loyalty to the Democrats won his support for the Mexican War, though his asthma prevented him from serving in that conflict. Supporting the Free-Soil movement in 1848, Stanton returned to the Democratic fold for the campaign of 1852, but his opposition to slavery was weakening his old political loyalty.

The first meeting of Stanton and Abraham Lincoln did not suggest that they would later develop a satisfactory relationship. Lincoln had been hired as one of the attorneys in the *McCormick v. Manny* case, a patent infringement dispute. In the fall of 1855, Lincoln arrived in Cincinnati where the case was to be heard, unaware that he had been retained only should the case be heard in Illinois. Seeing Lincoln, Stanton said to Manny, "What did you bring that d——d long-armed ape up here for? He does not know anything that can do you any good." Lincoln overheard the remark, and did not forget it.

Establishing himself in Washington, Stanton practiced mainly civil and constitutional law, also spending a prolonged period in California evaluating land claims. Characteristically, he was not afraid to risk making himself unpopular in order to accomplish his duty. Returning to Washington, he defended his friend Daniel Sickles (1819–1914), on trial for shooting Philip Barton Key (1819–1859), son of Francis Scott Key (1779–1843), for having an affair with Sickles's wife. Stanton's brilliance saved Sickles, who went on to serve in the Civil War. It was the first time in America that a defense of temporary insanity was successfully employed. Along with his professional status, Stanton's personal life flourished again with his marriage to Ellen Hutchinson (1830–1873), on June 25, 1856.

Faced with the deepening crisis of a dividing Union and threatened civil war, President James Buchanan (1791–1868) reorganized his cabinet. His new secretary of state, Jeremiah S. Black (1810–1883), urged him to name Stanton attorney general. The Senate confirmed Stanton unanimously and he took office on December 27, 1860. Joining with Black and Secretary of War Joseph Holt, Stanton urged Buchanan to take a strong stand against the secessionists, criticizing the president behind his back for failing to take Stanton's advice. Buchanan didn't go as far as Stanton urged him to go, but the Black-Holt-Stanton pressure did influence the president. By the end of his brief tenure as

Secretary of War Edwin M. Stanton assumed powers far exceeding any previous war secretary (Library of Congress).

attorney general, Stanton's concern for the Union moved him to inform opposition leaders in Congress about cabinet deliberations.

Sitting out the first several months of the Lincoln administration, Stanton was highly critical, referring to the "imbecility" of the new leaders. Originally approving of the appointment of General George Brinton McClellan (1826–1885) to command the Union forces, Stanton became friendly with the general. He was serving as legal advisor to Secretary of War Simon Cameron (1799–1889) when he was named to be Cameron's successor.

Although Stanton was a Democrat, he was well known for his strong pro–Union feelings, as well as for his capacity for hard work and honesty. The War Department, which Stanton took over early in 1862, had been plagued by scandal and corruption. Millions of dollars had been wasted, and the Union armies were doing badly. Stanton immediately got to work, assuming powers which no previous secretary of war had ever held, particularly the authority, under Lincoln's suspension of the writ of habeas corpus, to make arbitrary arrests, to hold persons in prison for lengthy periods without filing charges against them, and to search and seize property without warrants. His personal style in dealing with subordinates caused much friction. He installed bells in the War Department offices so he could quickly summon clerks and even generals to his office. As can be imagined, high-ranking officers resented being treated like house servants. In addition, while receiving his many visitors, "Stanton seldom sat down, but stood before a high desk as the crowd passed before him and one by one presented their requests or complaints, which were rapidly disposed of." However high-handed his actions, Stanton did strengthen the idea of civilian supremacy over military leaders, a principle which he did not apply to habeas corpus and military trials of civilians. The new secretary of war was careful to cultivate the friendship of powerful members of Congress, especially Senators Benjamin F. Wade (1800–1878) and Zachariah Chandler (1813–1879), of the Joint Committee on the Conduct of the War. Stanton even went so far as to urge the Ohio legislature to reelect Wade, earning the senator's gratitude.

Now that he was inside the administration, Stanton had to change his mind about some things, especially his opinion of General McClellan. The two men were formerly friends, but it wasn't long before Stanton's new ideas about him and his strategy earned him the scorn of the general.

It also became necessary for Stanton to change his mind about the president. Now that he was working so closely with Lincoln, seeing him daily, Stanton was in a far better position to observe and get to know the man. Although they often disagreed on methods, they shared a common goal, and that, their strong devotion to the Union, was the factor which overrode all other considerations. Of Lincoln, Stanton wrote, "Mr. Lincoln was never a good projector and frequently not a good manager; but his intuition was wonderful. He was one of the best of men to have by the side of a projector or manager.... Usually his mind was as free from bias as any I ever knew, and it was a genuine pleasure to consult him on new matters." Lincoln often praised his secretary of war and stood by him. When one seeker of favors had taken a presidential request to Stanton, and was refused with Stanton's comment that the president was a damned fool, Lincoln replied, "Did Stanton say that? Then it must be true, for Stanton is usually right." When the post of chief justice of the Supreme Court became vacant in 1864, and Stanton's friends urged Lincoln to give it to him, Lincoln replied that he would make the appointment if anyone could be found for the War Department who could match Stanton's performance.

Leonard Grover (1835–1926), manager of the National Theatre in Washington, described an incident which occurred in his theatre. Lincoln had gone to see a play, as he often did, and Stanton followed, apparently hoping to discuss some important business and perhaps secure presidential agreement on some point. At first, Lincoln spoke briefly with Stanton, then responded only with monosyllables, and finally only with nods. When Lincoln, absorbed in the play, no longer seemed to be paying any attention to Stanton, the secretary took the president by the lapels and turned Lincoln toward himself to regain that attention. "Mr. Lincoln responded to this brusque act with all the smiling geniality that one might bestow on a similar act from a favorite child, but soon again turned his eyes to the stage.... Finally, impressed with the futility of his efforts, Mr. Stanton arose, said good night, and withdrew." This little incident tells us much about the easy familiarity of the relationship between Stanton and Lincoln. It also shows that, as long and as hard as he worked, Lincoln could not keep up with Stanton. Probably no one could.

Stanton was late for the cabinet meeting of April 14, 1865. He had labored hard on a detailed plan for the reconstruction of the Southern states and was anxious to have it approved by the president and other cabinet members. Frederick Seward (1830–1915), sitting in for his father, the secretary of state, who had been seriously injured a week before in a carriage accident, remembered that Stanton's plan was in general agreement with Lincoln, though Navy Secretary Gideon Welles (1802–1878) recalled it as being a much more controversial plan, which Stanton was forced to modify.

Ford's Theatre was the scene of the assassination. A very popular venue, it had been rebuilt after an 1863 fire and was quite luxurious for the time (Library of Congress).

That evening, after having dinner at his home, Stanton paid a call on the injured William Seward, staying to talk with other callers. Returning home, he was serenaded by people celebrating the impending end of the war. He made a short speech to them and then retired for the evening, it being just after ten o'clock. As Stanton was preparing for bed a messenger arrived with news that Seward had been murdered. Coming down stairs half-dressed, the secretary of war could not credit the report, since he had visited Seward that very evening, but others coming bearing tales of assassination, not only of Seward but of Lincoln as well. Reports of a mysterious man hiding in the shadows near Stanton's house were made, and he was cautioned not to go out. Ignoring the danger, Stanton hurried to the Seward home, and found it in chaos. Five men had been brutally attacked, including both Seward and his son Frederick, who initially were not expected to live. Arriving at the Petersen House around eleven o'clock, Stanton immediately took charge.

As Stanton waited among dignitaries and ordinary people who had

This photograph of Ford's Theatre was taken in 1865, probably just before the assassination. The play advertised in the bill at left, *The Octoroon*, was to have opened on April 15 (courtesy Surratt House Museum/MNCPPC).

crowded into the small room, beside the bed, listening to the labored breaths of Lincoln, he thought of his son James, who had died at age nine months in 1862, fighting to breathe as Lincoln was doing. Accounts differ as to Stanton's reaction to Lincoln's death, but most agree that he appeared profoundly stricken with grief, and when the end came he said something very nearly like the often quoted remark "now he belongs to the ages."[10]

Although he did not attend the trial of the conspirators, Stanton was very much involved behind the scenes. He personally described the measures which were to be taken to secure the prisoners, such as balls and chains, imprisonment aboard naval vessels, and, most controversially, the placing of heavy canvas hoods over their heads, padded to prevent communication. The details of the trial he left to Judge Advocate General Joseph Holt, his old friend from their days together in Buchanan's cabinet.

As Stanton tried to conduct an investigation of the president's assassination he had been frustrated, for no one present at Petersen House could take shorthand. General Christopher C. Augur (1821–1898) stepped out of the front door and asked for a stenographer. Albert Daggett, watching from the balcony of the house next door, immediately thought of his friend James Tanner (1844–1927), who had just returned home from attending the play at the National Theatre. Tanner was soon sitting opposite the secretary of War, taking down testimony.

Born in Richmondville, New York, in 1844, Tanner, like many of his contemporaries, had rushed off to the great adventure of war. As a member of Company C, 87th New York Volunteer Infantry, he was promoted to corporal shortly before the second battle of Bull Run. There, on August 30, 1862, he was struck in the left ankle by a shell fragment, which passed through and hit his right leg below the knee. Carried away on a blanket, his head hanging down at one end, he could see his feet dangling at the other end of the blanket, held on only by shreds. Both legs were amputated about four inches below the knees. His many months of convalescence were difficult, his survival at times uncertain. Gradually, he learned to use artificial limbs with the aid of a cane.

Enrolling in Ames's Business College in Syracuse, New York, Tanner soon mastered shorthand, learning the Pitman method, then called "standard Phonography." Moving to Washington, Tanner became an employee of the War Department's Ordnance Bureau on December, 1, 1864. He supplemented his salary by transcribing the notes of the U.S. Senate reporters, and was able to find modest lodgings across the street from Ford's Theatre, next door to the Petersen House, the house where Lincoln died.

Supplying his own pencil and paper, as well as making use of the sheets upon which another had tried to take testimony, Tanner worked steadily through the night. "In fifteen minutes," he later wrote, "I had enough down to hang Wilkes Booth, the assassin, higher than ever Haman hung" (Esther 8:7). Tanner described how he had frequently to stop when reports came in or whenever Stanton issued orders. Finishing the taking of testimony by 1:30 a.m., Tanner labored for five more hours transcribing his notes into longhand. When he was finished, he entered the back room and observed the final moments of Lincoln's life. He was a keen observer, and his accounts of that night, though not published for many years, are among the best.[11]

Among the many messages Stanton sent that night was one calling for the return to Washington of his chief of War Department detectives. Lafayette Charles Baker (1825–1868) was born in Stafford, New York. Family legends linked the Bakers to Revolutionary War hero Ethan Allen (1738–1789). As for many Americans of that day, the frontier beckoned to the Bakers, and the family moved westward, settling in southern Michigan. Lafayette, however, returned to New York by 1848, then moved on to Philadelphia about 1850, seeking business opportunities. It may be that his father's puritanical attitudes pushed him out of the nest early.

Marriage to Jennie Curry of Philadelphia in 1852 could not forever cause Baker to forswear his wandering ways and desire for adventure. His brother Milo had gone to California for the gold rush, and Milo's letters were an irresistible temptation. The long passage to San Francisco was interrupted by an adventure which saw Baker pursued by Central American natives, using a disguise to elude them.

San Francisco during the gold rush days was a lawless town whose population had skyrocketed in only a few years from a few hundred to tens of thousands, all looking for the quick and easy way to wealth. Baker joined the vigilantes, volunteer lawmen who worried very little about due process. Another member of the vigilantes at this time was theatre manager and actor Junius Brutus Booth, Jr. (1821–1883), older brother of John Wilkes Booth. Baker's activities as a lawman did not prevent him from also achieving a reputation as a claim jumper.

By 1861, Baker, like most of the opportunists in California in those days, had failed to achieve wealth and power. Seeing in the nation's troubles a greater opportunity than the gold rush had offered, he would at last achieve—for a time, at least—his life's ambition. Arriving in Washington, Baker played upon the extremist radical feelings of Congressman William D. Kelley (1814–1890) of Pennsylvania, a Republican then just beginning his nearly thirty years in the House of Representatives. Kelley arranged an introduction for Baker to General Winfield Scott (1786–1866), commanding general of the army. Baker always had a plan. Knowing Scott was vain and proud as well as super-patriotic, he played upon those attributes to win the general's admiration. Offering his services as a spy, Baker embarked on a mission behind rebel lines, even to the Confederate capital itself.

Using his considerable powers of observation, and displaying his legendary cunning to deceive the Confederates, Baker reached Richmond and was able to survey its defenses, learning much about the strength and capabilities of its defenders. Arrested on suspicion of being a spy, Baker claimed to have bluffed his way through, deceiving Confederate President Jefferson Davis (1808–1889) himself, whom he said he met several times.

Returning to Washington, Baker impressed General Scott with the success of his mission, which resulted in Baker being appointed a detective for the State Department. Impressing his new employer, Secretary of State William H. Seward, with his patriotism and zealous devotion to hard work, Baker found that his star continued rising.

At this time, early in the war, the intelligence collecting for the Union was done mainly by two rival agencies. The Army of the Potomac employed the celebrated detective Allan Pinkerton (1819–1884), who reported to General George Brinton McClellan (1826–1885). Baker headed the other service, reporting first to Seward, then, after some reorganization, to the new secretary of war, Edwin M. Stanton. Confusion was promoted as agents of one spy operation got in the way of the other, and more than once agents were embarrassed to find they had arrested a colleague. Similar problems plagued the Confederate clandestine services. Baker would later complain that many of the sins attributed to him and his detectives were actually the work of those not in his employ.

Setting up his Washington headquarters at 217 Pennsylvania Avenue, Baker received the honorary rank of colonel, a rank which was made official in June 1863. Once established, Baker reached out for more power. Though at first he had a budget of only $65,000 a year with about thirty detectives, he formed connections with local authorities far and wide, setting up branch offices of his "National Detective Bureau," as he called it. His men would ride roughshod over rights of liberty and property. Always resourceful, Baker pioneered the use of photographs in his files to aid in the identification of suspects. Not content with domestic operations, he sent his agents over the border to spy on suspected Confederate sympathizers in Canada.

In interrogating his prisoners, Baker was ruthless. Suspects were held in the dingy confines of the Old Capitol Prison, deprived of sleep, denied legal representation, forced to sign falsified confessions, frightened and intimidated until they cracked. Although Baker did perform useful services for the Union cause, such as cracking down on the corruption and pilfering of agents and contractors, he was never above helping himself to some ready money at the same time.

Stanton, seeking to manage the huge war effort, probably had little time to devote to the supervision of Baker. Impressed that Baker could deliver results, Stanton supplied the funds and looked the other way as Baker's empire grew. When Baker arrested Louisa P. Buckner for smuggling quinine, the fact that her uncle was Postmaster General Montgomery Blair (1813–1883) of the very influential Blair family, saved her from lengthy imprisonment, but not from scandal. In this case, at least, Baker's victim was, in fact, guilty. Stanton was not the only official who protected Baker from the many protests of his enemies. President Lincoln echoed his war secretary's desire not to hinder Baker when he told protesters, "Rascal catchers have their own ways. We must let them do their job."

The people of Washington, too, had cause to be grateful to Baker and his men for their suppression of gambling, bounty jumping, drunkenness, smuggling, thievery and every sort of fraud. Baker's men seemed to be everywhere, battling the frailties and follies of the people of the wartime capital.

Baker's cousin Joseph Stannard Baker (1838–1912) left a vivid description of Lafayette. "He had small deep set eyes. He did not carry himself erect with head up like most of the Bakers. When not directly addressing one, his head was always inclined forward, his eyes on the ground, and his shoulders slightly stooping. He was about five feet nine or ten inches in height and weighed about 170 to 180 pounds. Every motion he made was quick and gave one the impression of nervous restlessness. Even when sitting at his desk unoccupied, he was either drumming with his fingers, making rapid erratic marks with his pencil, or tapping his feet restlessly upon the floor. His personal courage was very marked—in fact, he acquired the reputation of a daredevil wherever he went. I have seen him in many positions of extreme anger, but never noticed the slightest indication of fear. In desperate situations, he always reminded me of a cat ready to spring upon its prey."

Early in 1863, Baker was able to convince Stanton and Lincoln that his capabilities could be increased if he was given a military command. Military men all the way up to U.S. Army Chief of Staff Major General Henry Wager Halleck (1815–1872) strongly opposed the granting of such status to Baker, for whom he had only contempt. With his customary resourcefulness, Baker discovered that an act of Congress had authorized the raising of a battalion of cavalry to operate

Lafayette C. Baker, head of the War Department's detective bureau. Baker's detectives led the party of soldiers who captured and killed John Wilkes Booth (Library of Congress).

within the District of Columbia. Securing an order from Lincoln, Baker was named colonel of the First District of Columbia Cavalry, which the professional military men soon began calling "Baker's Rangers." With his cousin Stan now a captain and doing much of the hard work of training the troops, Baker managed to arrange for his men to have only the best of housing and equipment, such as the new Henry repeating rifles. Headquarters for the cavalry was established in a sparsely populated area, half a mile east of the Capitol building, that was soon referred to as "Camp Baker." The hard look of Baker's features must have been greatly enhanced by his tailored colonel's uniform, complete with golden epaulets. He would impress his men with his ability to empty a sixteen-shot Henry rifle in ten seconds. No one doubted Baker's reputation as one of the deadliest, most dangerous men in America.

By April 14, 1865, Baker was at the height of his powers. It was quite natural for Stanton, faced with the task of hunting down the assassins who had killed the president and seriously injured the secretary of state, to send for his chief of detectives. Baker, in New York at the time, hurried back to Washington and stepped into a chaotic scene. Military and civilian parties were competing with each other to find the assassins, with little coordination or effect. Baker would later take credit for bringing organization to the hunt, but at the time, his main concerns were to see that large rewards were offered and to make sure that he received an important share of both the money and the glory.[12]

Another officer who chased after the fleeing assassins, James Rowan O'Beirne (1838–1917), provost marshal of the District of Columbia, received orders from Stanton, who said, "You are relieved from all other duty at this time and directed to employ yourself and your detective force in the detection and arrest of the murderers of the president and the assassin who attempted to murder Mr. Seward, and make report from time to time."

O'Beirne was a highly respected and trustworthy man. He was born at Ballach, County Roscommon, Ireland, on September 25, 1838. When the American Civil War began, O'Beirne was quick to enlist, holding the rank of private in Company I of the 7th New York Militia. His initial service lasted only from April 26 to June 3, 1861. Moving to Washington, D.C., O'Beirne enlisted again, this time for a two-year commitment, in Company C, 37th New York Volunteer Infantry, called "The Irish Rifles." He was promoted to second lieutenant on July 9, 1861, first lieutenant on August 9, and captain on November 4, 1861. At the battle of Fair Oaks, Virginia, May 31–June 1, 1862, O'Beirne was cited for "gallantly maintain[ing] the line of battle until ordered to fall back." At Chancellorsville, Virginia, on May 3, 1863, O'Beirne was wounded in the lung, right leg, right knee, and forehead. He was mustered out of the service at New York City on June 22, 1863, only to rejoin the Veteran Reserve Corps on July 24. He was promoted to major on May 12, 1864. By the spring of 1865 Major O'Beirne was provost marshal of the District of Columbia. A provost (pronounced "provo") Marshal is an officer in charge of military police. On the night of the crime, O'Beirne escorted Vice President Andrew Johnson to the Petersen House for his visit to Lincoln's deathbed.

A search of Booth coconspirator George Atzerodt's (1835–1865) room at the Kirkwood House had produced a map of southern Maryland. With eight of his detectives, O'Beirne took a steamer from Washington to Chapel Point, near Port Tobacco, in Charles County, Maryland. They learned that David E. Herold (1842–1865), about three weeks before the assassination, had told people he knew he would be leaving the country. O'Beirne learned Atzerodt lived in the area and his mistress feared that he was involved in crime. Joining forces with seven hundred men of the 8th Illinois Cavalry, six hundred of the 22nd Colored Troops, and one hundred from the 16th New York Cavalry, O'Beirne and his detectives searched the Zekiah Swamp. In spite of fatigue that forced all the others to rest, O'Beirne and one of his men continued the search, crossing the Potomac River, and continuing on through the night as far as King George's Court House, Virginia, before returning to Chapel Point.

O'Beirne was developing leads which might have enabled him to locate assassination conspirators Booth and Herold, but he was ordered to continue the search on the Maryland side of the Potomac River. Lafayette Baker had organized a small force of cavalry to chase the assassin and his coconspirator, and Baker did not want competition from O'Beirne. O'Beirne did receive $2,000 of the reward money and congratulations from Stanton, who conceded, "You have done your duty nobly and you have the satisfaction of knowing that if you did not succeed in capturing Booth, it was, at all events, certainly the information which you gave that led to it."[13]

To encourage the capture of the conspirators, the U.S. government offered and paid rewards totaling $105,000: $75,000 for the capture of John Wilkes Booth and David Herold, $25,000 for the capture of George A. Atzerodt, and $5,000 for the capture of Lewis T. Powell (1844–1865), the attacker of Secretary Seward.

General Christopher C. Augur issued the first reward on April 15, 1865. His notice stated, "A reward of ten thousand dollars ($10,000) will

War Department, Washington, April 20, 1865.

$100,000 REWARD!

THE MURDERER

Of our late beloved President, ABRAHAM LINCOLN,

IS STILL AT LARGE.

$50,000 REWARD!

will be paid by this Department for his apprehension, in addition to any reward offered by Municipal Authorities or State Executives.

$25,000 REWARD!

will be paid for the apprehension of JOHN H. SURRATT, one of Booth's accomplices.

$25,000 REWARD!

will be paid for the apprehension of DANIEL C HARROLD, another of Booth's accomplices.

LIBERAL REWARDS will be paid for any information that shall conduce to the arrest of either of the above-named criminals, or their accomplices.

All persons harboring or secreting the said persons, or either of them, or aiding or assisting their concealment or escape, will be treated as accomplices in the murder of the President and the attempted assassination of the Secretary of State, and shall be subject to trial before a Military Commission and the punishment of DEATH.

Let the stain of innocent blood be removed from the land by the arrest and punishment of the murderers.

All good citizens are exhorted to aid public justice on this occasion. Every man should consider his own conscience charged with this solemn duty, and rest neither night nor day until it be accomplished.

EDWIN M. STANTON, *Secretary of War.*

DESCRIPTIONS.—BOOTH is 5 feet 7 or 8 inches high, slender build, high forehead, black hair, black eyes, and wears a heavy black moustache. JOHN H. SURRATT is about 5 feet 9 inches. Hair rather thin and dark; eyes rather light; no beard. Would weigh 145 or 150 pounds. Complexion rather pale and clear, with color in his cheeks. Wears light clothes of fine quality. Shoulders square; cheek bones rather prominent; chin narrow; ears projecting at the top; forehead rather low and square, but broad. Parts his hair on the right side; neck rather long. His lips are firmly set. A slim man. DANIEL C. HARROLD is 22 years of age, 5 feet 6 or 7 inches high, rather broad shouldered, otherwise light built; dark hair, little (if any) moustache; dark eyes; weighs about 140 pounds.

GEO. F. NESBITT & CO., Printers and Stationers, cor. Pearl and Pine Streets, N. Y.

One of several different posters issued in the wake of the assassination. The rewards offered were huge sums of money by contemporary standards. Such posters inspired many would-be treasure hunters (Library of Congress).

be paid to the party or parties arresting the murderer of the president, Mr. Lincoln, and the assassin of the Secretary of State, Mr. Seward, and his son." On April 16, General Lafayette C. Baker issued another reward of $10,000, "for the arrest and conviction" of the assassins. On April 20, Secretary of War Edwin M. Stanton issued his reward notice: "Fifty thousand dollars reward will be paid by this department for the apprehension of the murderer of the president. Twenty five thousand dollars reward will be paid for the apprehension of Atzerodt, one of Booth's accomplices. Twenty five thousand dollars reward will be paid for the apprehension of Herold, another of Booth's accomplices." Another well-known reward poster, issued on April 20 and also signed by Stanton, offered $50,000 for "the murderer of our late beloved President," "$25,000 for the apprehension of John H. Surratt, one of Booth's accomplices," and another $25,000 for Herold. In addition to government rewards, state and local authorities and private organizations were offering rewards, bringing the grand total to at least $200,000, a huge sum in the money of 1865.

Stanton placed two of his subordinates in charge of deciding to whom the rewards should be paid, and how much was to be received by each claimant. Judge Advocate General Joseph Holt and Adjutant General Edward Davis Townsend (1817–1893) examined all applications for reward money, a process lasting three months. The deadline, January 1866, was set for the filing of claims. This was a difficult process, with many claimants hoping for much more than they ultimately received. Finally, the War Department handed the question of rewards over to Congress, with the House of Representatives' Committee on Claims member, Giles Waldo Hotchkiss (1815–1878), New York Republican making the final recommendations. The committee's initial recommendation called for $17,500 each for L.C. Baker and Everton J. Conger, a Baker detective who was one of the leaders of Booth's captors. These amounts were later reduced, as were the claims of army telegrapher Samuel H. Beckwith (1839–1916).[14]

On the night of the assassination, Stanton sent the following bulletins to inform the nation of what had happened. The messages bore his name and were identified as official bulletins from the War Department.

> Last evening, about 10:30 p.m. at Ford's Theatre, the president, while sitting in his private box with Mrs. Lincoln, Miss Harris and Major Rathbone, was shot by an assassin, who suddenly entered the box and approached behind the president. The assassin then leaped upon the stage, brandishing a large dagger or knife, and made his escape in the rear of the theatre. The pistol ball entered the back of the president's head and penetrated nearly through the head. The wound is mortal. The President has been insensible ever since it was inflicted and is now dying.
> About the same hour an assassin (whether the same or another) entered Mr. Seward's home and under pretense of having a prescription, was shown to the Secretary's sick chamber. The Secretary was in bed, a nurse and Major Seward with him. The assassin immediately rushed to the bed, inflicted two or three stabs on the throat and two in the face. It is hoped the wounds may not be mortal: my apprehension is that they will prove fatal. The noise

alarmed Mr. Frederick Seward, who was in an adjoining room and hastened to the door of his father's room, where he met the assassin, who inflicted upon him one or more dangerous wounds. The recovery of Frederick Seward is doubtful.

Stanton's information was confused. The assassin, Lewis T. Powell, known by his alias "Payne," first struggled with Frederick Seward, then with army nurse George Foster Robinson (1832–1907), and with another of Secretary Seward's sons, Augustus Henry Seward (1826–1876). On his escape, Powell encountered another man, State Department messenger Emerick W. Hansell (1817–1893). In all, five men were wounded, three of them seriously (William Seward, Frederick Seward, and Emerick Hansell), though, miraculously, all five survived and recovered.

The second bulletin followed about two hours after the first.

The President still breathes, but is quite insensible, as he has been ever since he was shot. He evidently did not see the person who shot him, but was looking on the stage as he was approached behind.

Mr. Seward has rallied and it is hoped he may live. Frederick Seward's condition is very critical. The attendant who was present was stabbed through the lungs, and is not expected to live. The wounds of Major Seward are not serious. Investigation strongly indicates J. Wilkes Booth as the assassin of the president. Whether it was the same or a different person that attempted to murder Mr. Seward remains in doubt.... Every exertion has been made to prevent the escape of the murderer.

The final bulletin read simply,

Abraham Lincoln died this morning at 22 minutes after seven o'clock.

Stanton also released to the press that the assassination of the president and attempted assassination of the secretary of state had been part of a rebel plot to kill the highest authorities of the Union government. He specified that the conspiracy had been directed by the chief officers of the Confederate government.[15]

Hundreds of suspects were arrested and imprisoned, some for prolonged periods, with no charges formally filed against them and little or no due process observed. Stanton and his assistants, wrapping themselves in bands of mourning and pro–Union patriotism, had their hands full sorting out those who appeared to be genuinely involved in the conspiracy from those who did not. In a relatively short span of time, they would decide upon whom to prosecute, what kind of a trial it would be, and what laws would govern.[16]

2

Judges, Jury and Accused

It was perhaps the greatest trial in American history. Seven men and one woman faced charges of "combining, confederating, and conspiring together ... to kill and murder ... Abraham Lincoln ... President of the United States of America, and Commander-in-Chief of the Army and Navy thereof; Andrew Johnson, now Vice-President of the United States aforesaid; and Ulysses S. Grant, Lieutenant-General of the Army of the United States." The specification went on to say the defendants were "incited and encouraged thereunto by Jefferson Davis, George N. Sanders, Beverly Tucker, Jacob Thompson, William C. Cleary, Clement C. Clay, George Harper, George Young, and others unknown ... who were then engaged in armed rebellion against the United States of America."[1]

The charges and specifications, and a great deal of the organizing of the trial, was done by Judge Advocate General of the Army Joseph Holt (1807–1894), who also headed the team of prosecutors, which included John A. Bingham (1815–1900), and Colonel Henry L. Burnett (1838–1916). The names of Confederate officials which Holt added to the defendants in custody were, aside from Davis, all members of the Confederate underground organization in Canada. John Wilkes Booth (1838–1865) had been to Canada in the fall of 1864, and John H. Surratt, Jr. (1844–1916), was known to have escaped there. These facts, together with the testimony of several witnesses, provided a link between Booth's ring of conspirators and the Confederates.[2]

The trial was conducted by the army, under military law, in spite of the fact that none of the defendants were serving in either the U.S. Army or the Confederate Army at the time, and despite the civil courts of Washington, D.C., scene of the crime, being open and functioning.

President Andrew Johnson (1808–1875) issued an order on May 1, 1865, calling for the appointment of a military commission, consisting of nine military officers, and that the defendants be tried before the commission, Judge Advocate General Holt being designated to prosecute. The president's order mentioned that the court should "avoid unnecessary delay." The officers named to the commission were Major General David Hunter (1802–1886), the senior officer who would preside; Major General Lewis Wallace (1827–1905); Brevet Major General August V. Kautz (1828–1895); Brigadier General Albion P. Howe (1818–1897); Brigadier General Robert S. Foster (1834–1903); Brevet Brigadier General Cyrus B. Comstock (1831–1910); Brigadier General Thomas M. Harris (1817–1906); Brevet Colonel Horace Porter (1837–1921); and Lieutenant Colonel David R. Clendenin (1831–1895). General Comstock objected that he felt the commission did not have jurisdiction to properly try this case, and when he publicly voiced his opinion Colonel Porter agreed with him. Comstock and Porter were both excused, and were replaced by Brevet Brigadier General James A. Ekin (1820–1891) and Brevet Colonel Charles H. Tompkins (1830–1915).[3]

Joseph Holt, appointed judge advocate general, the head of the army's legal branch, by President Abraham Lincoln on September 3, 1862, directed the prosecution of the conspirators, and brought upon himself a lifetime of controversy.

Born in Kentucky on January 6, 1807, Holt was educated at St. Joseph's and Centre Colleges and practiced law in Elizabethtown and later in Louisville, Kentucky. A highly successful attorney and newspaper editor in Kentucky and Mississippi, Holt's active role in Democratic Party politics obtained for him an appointment as commissioner of patents, followed by appointment in 1859 to be postmaster general. Sudden changes in President James Buchanan's (1791–1868) cabinet in the last weeks of his administration saw Holt named secretary of war, an office which he held from January 18 to March 4, 1861.

A highly accomplished lawyer, Holt was perfectly capable of refusing to approve the results of military commissions for legal reasons. His decisions, collected in book form after the war, were highly influential. Lincoln considered Holt for attorney general when that office fell vacant in 1864, but Holt declined the appointment. Promoted to brigadier general on June 22, 1864, Holt headed the new Bureau of Military Justice.

Major General David Hunter, president of the Military Commission, was born in Washington, D.C., on July 21, 1802. He graduated from the United States Military Academy, West Point, New York, in 1822. Promoted to first lieutenant in 1828, he was stationed at Fort Dearborn, near Chicago, which was then a frontier post. By 1833 he was a captain and had patrolled the plains as far as the Rocky Mountains. Leaving the army in 1836, he tried his hand at real estate speculation in Chicago. Returning to the army in March 1842, Hunter became a paymaster with the rank of major. During the Mexican War, Hunter was chief paymaster to Brigadier General John Ellis Wool (1784–1869). Following the war, Hunter served in army posts in New Orleans, Washington, Detroit, St. Louis, and on the frontier. He was one of the officers who escorted President-Elect Abraham Lincoln on his journey from Springfield, Illinois, to Washington in 1861. In Buffalo, New York, Hunter suffered a dislocated shoulder when the crowds pressed too closely.

David Hunter, the president of the military commission, sought to keep the trial going and was impatient with the attorneys, especially the defense lawyers. Some observers described him as drowsy (Library of Congress).

On May 14, 1861, Hunter was appointed colonel of the 3rd U.S. Cavalry, and was promoted to brigadier general only three days later. Seriously wounded at the First Battle of Bull Run, he became a major general of volunteers on August 13, 1861, and was named second in command to Major General John Charles Frémont (1813–1890) in Missouri, assuming command when Frémont was relieved on November 2. Becoming commander of the Department of the South in March 1862, headquartered at Port Royal, South Carolina, Hunter issued an order emancipating the slaves in his area, which President Lincoln, for political reasons, had to rescind. Hunter raised the First South Carolina Volunteers, the first Union regiment of black soldiers. Assuming command of the Department of West Virginia in May 1864, Hunter's men advanced into the Shenandoah Valley, doing much damage to Confederate communications and supply lines, but they were forced to withdraw after a fight with General Jubal Anderson Early's (1816–1894) forces at Lynchburg, Virginia. Hunter's withdrawal left the way clear for Early's raid, which brought the rebels within a few miles of Washington. Criticized for his retreat, Hunter took a leave of absence.

Having served as president of the military court which tried Brigadier General Fitz John Porter (1822–1901) in late 1862, Hunter's availability and experience, and above all, his loyalty to Secretary of War Stanton, bought him the presidency of the military commission to try the Lincoln assassination suspects. Hunter, and certain other members of the court and prosecution team, were attended throughout by guards, to insure their safety and prevent any disruption of the proceedings. Passes for reporters were issued, bearing Hunter's signature, once it was decided to conduct the trial openly. Conducting the trial with a tight rein at first, as it wore on through the very hot summer, Hunter was seen to close his eyes for long periods and was thought by some to be asleep. He became irritable with delays and sought to keep the trial moving. Hunter had to endure the criticism of those papers hostile to the prosecution. The New York World, on June 2, 1865, described him thusly: "what part of him is not fool is knave." Hunter agreed with his fellow commissioners, voting to convict, but he was one of five who signed a petition to commute Mary Surratt's sentence from death to life imprisonment.

Civil War general, territorial governor, diplomat, and a member of the military commission, Lew Wallace is perhaps best known today as the author of the novel *Ben-Hur* (Library of Congress).

A major general of U.S. volunteers, Lew Wallace is best known today as the author of Ben-Hur, published in 1880 and subsequently made into several dramatized versions, first for stage and later for motion pictures. Wallace's life was that of a romantic adventurer. He was born in Brookville, Indiana, on April 10, 1827, son of David Wallace (1799–1859), a Whig politician who served as governor of Indiana from 1837 to 1840. A law career was decreed for Lew, but he rebelled, showing an early interest in adventure, as well as artistic inclinations. When war broke out with Mexico in 1846, Wallace raised his own company of volunteers. Campaigning in Mexico was a great adventure for young Wallace, but also involved danger and hardship. Missing the major battles, he did experience one minor skirmish, and toured the battlefield of Buena Vista shortly after the battle.

Returning to the law to earn a living, Wallace became interested in politics, but not the Whig politics of his father; he became a Democrat. His marriage to Susan Elston (1830–1907) in 1852 brought him social position and economic help in his effort to make something of himself. The first of his novels, The Fair God, a story of Hernan Cortes's (1485–1547) conquest of Mexico, was written in the mid–1850s, but had to wait twenty years for publication.

When the Civil War began in 1861, Wallace immediately volunteered, hoping for action right away, but Indiana's governor Oliver H.P.T. Morton (1823–1877), prevailed upon him to become the state's adjutant general, in which capacity he helped to raise six regiments. Becoming colonel of one of these regiments, Wallace proved both effective and popular with his men. The rapid expansion of the army brought him quick promotions, first to brigadier general, then to major general. At the Battle of Shiloh in April 1862, Wallace's division was out of position for the main battle, and had to march for miles, being slowed down by contradictory orders. His enemies would claim for years afterwards that he had ducked the fight. Politics kept him from further combat command, though he was on hand to prevent the capture of Cincinnati in 1862, and later, as commander of the Middle Department, he threw together enough troops to slow down Confederate General Jubal Early's invasion of Maryland, helping to prevent the capture of Washington at the battle of Monocacy, Maryland, on July 9, 1864.

As a member of the military commission trying the Lincoln assassination suspects, Wallace passed the hot days of listening to the testimony by making drawings of the defendants. Later, he painted a picture of them meeting together. Wallace followed the arguments of the prosecutors and found no difficulty in voting to condemn the prisoners, even refusing to sign the petition for clemency which several of his fellow judges submitted in behalf of Mary Surratt.

There is no evidence that Wallace was a mere tool of the prosecution. He considered himself a man of honor, and the record of his life shows an independent thinker who made up his own mind. His service on the commission led to his appointment as president of the commission which tried Captain Henry Wirz (1823–1865), commander of the Confederate prison camp at Andersonville, Georgia.

August Valentine Kautz was born in Ispringen, in the German state of Baden, on January 5, 1828. Kautz and his family immigrated later that year to the United States, finally settling in Georgetown, Brown County, Ohio, in 1832. Kautz attended school there until his enlistment in the army on June 8, 1846. After seeing action in the Mexican War, Kautz obtained an appointment to West Point, graduating in 1852. Serving in the 4th Infantry in Oregon and Washington territories, Lieutenant Kautz fought Indians, being wounded in 1855 and again in 1856. In 1857 he tried to be the first to climb Mount Rainier in Washington Territory, but did not succeed. Promoted to captain at the beginning of the Civil War in 1861, Kautz was assigned to the 6th Cavalry and took part in the Peninsular Campaign in 1862. He was made colonel of the 2nd Ohio Cavalry in September 1862, and his next command was at Fort Scott, Kansas, followed by Camp Chase, Ohio. Commanding the 1st Cavalry Brigade, Kautz fought at Monticello, Kentucky, on June 9, 1863, then participated in the pursuit and capture of Confederate brigadier general John Hunt Morgan (1825–1864). After service in east Tennessee at the siege of Knoxville, Kautz was promoted to Brigadier General on May 7, 1864, and commanded a cavalry division of the Army of the James. After operations in and around Petersburg, Virginia, Kautz, promoted to major general, commanded the 1st Division, XXV Corps, and on April 3, 1865, his troops entered Richmond.

Returning to Washington on May 4, Kautz was dismayed to learn he had been appointed to be a member of the military commission to try the assassination suspects. Applying to General Ulysses S. Grant (1822–1885) to be relieved of this assignment so he could marry Charlotte Tod, daughter of Ohio governor David Tod (1805–1868), he was turned down. Kautz worried his way through the trial, but he also made notes in his diary, which offer us a revealing look at what at least one of the mostly silent judges thought of the trial. Kautz was initially so out of touch that he was very surprised to find, when the prisoners were brought into court, that "one of them was a woman." He also felt the secrecy, which at first kept the proceedings closed to the press and public, to be quite unnecessary. When General Thomas M. Harris objected to allowing Senator Reverdy Johnson (1796–1876) to appear before the court as a lawyer for the defense, over the issue of Johnson's objection to taking a loyalty oath, Kautz wrote that Harris's objection was "ill advised," but regretted that "Johnson did not do us the honor to appear before us again after this insult to his dignity. He did the other members [of the commission] great injustice if he supposed they united with Genl. Harris in his ill-advised objection."

After long sessions at the trial, Kautz, unable to be with Miss Tod and worried about their relationship, spent much time with other officers, being especially fond of General Philip Sheridan (1831–1888). The court met from 10 a.m. until 6 p.m. or even later, with a break for lunch, which was served to the commissioners in an adjoining room. Army ambulances took the commissioners to and from their places of residence, with guards to protect them. The weather in May and June of 1865 was, in Kautz's understatement, "very warm." The commissioners seemed bored and sometimes short-tempered. Anti-administration papers referred to them in unflattering terms, calling Kautz, "good natured" and "harmless," "who knows as much of the nature of a legal proposition as the horse he had killed by useless hard riding."

Robert Sanford Foster was born in Vernon, Jennings County, Indiana, on January 27, 1834. Foster worked as a tinner in Indianapolis before the war. He became captain in the 11th Indiana regiment, joining the 13th Indiana as a major ninety days later. Receiving further promotions, Foster served in the Shenandoah Valley in 1862, the Peninsula and Suffolk, Virginia, campaigns of 1862–63, and the siege of Charleston in 1863. At the siege of Petersburg, Virginia, in 1864, Foster commanded first a brigade, and then a division.

Serving as one of the investigating officers, questioning suspects, Foster was instrumental

Robert S. Foster helped investigate the crime before the trial. While he assisted in building the case against Mrs. Surratt he also signed the petition to spare her life (Library of Congress).

in building the case against Mary Surratt. He was also suspicious of witnesses Louis J. Weichmann (1842–1902), Anna Surratt (1843–1904), and Honora Fitzpatrick (1846–1896). Named to the court, Foster said little throughout the trial. He was one of the five members who signed the petition to commute the sentence of Mrs. Surratt.

Having been in the audience at Ford's Theatre on April 14, 1865, Brigadier General Thomas Maley Harris, a witness to the assassination, was nevertheless appointed a member of the Military Commission.

Born in Wood County, Virginia (now Ritchie County, West Virginia), on June 17, 1817, Harris studied medicine and went into practice, first at Harrisville, then Glenville, Virginia. Helping to organize the 10th West Virginia Infantry, Harris became colonel of the regiment in 1862. After opposing Confederate general Thomas J. "Stonewall" Jackson's (1824–1863) campaign in the Shenandoah Valley, Harris and his West Virginians operated on home territory and were part of George Crook's (1820–1890) forces opposing Jubal A. Early's attempt to capture Washington, and served under Philip Henry Sheridan in the Shenandoah Valley. Harris, now a brigadier general, commanded a division at the third battle of Winchester, Virginia, in September 1864. Transferred to the Army of the James, Harris's men took part in the siege of Petersburg, Virginia, and in blockading the final retreat of the Confederates at Appomattox Court House.

Appointed to serve on the Military Commission, Harris attracted attention early in the trial when he objected to the presence of Reverdy Johnson as one of the defense lawyers. After a heated oratorical battle with Johnson, Harris withdrew his objection. As a physician, Harris was especially interested in the medical testimony, being inclined to believe that Lewis Powell might be insane. Harris did not vote to save Powell, however. Taking a hard line, Harris also refused to sign the petition on behalf of Mary Surratt.

Albion Parris Howe was born in Standish, Maine, on March 13, 1818. He graduated from West Point in 1841, and became an instructor there. After service in the Mexican War, Howe alternated between posts in the East and on the western frontier. During the Civil War he participated in the Peninsular Campaign, being promoted to brigadier general in 1862. He was in the battles of Fredericksburg, Chancellorsville, and Gettysburg. In charge of the office of the inspector of artillery in Washington from 1863–66, he was brevetted major general by the end of the war.

Brevet Brigadier General Cyrus Ballou Comstock was born in West Wrentham, Massachusetts, on February 3, 1831. A West Point graduate in 1855, he served in the Army Corps of Engineers, Department of the Tennessee, on the staff of Grant, both in the West and after Grant's promotion to lieutenant general. He received brevet promotions for meritorious service in the capture of Mobile, Alabama, and at the battle for Fort Fisher.

Horace Porter was born in Huntingdon, Pennsylvania, on April 15, 1837, and attended Harvard University and West Point, graduating in 1860. His Civil War service included chief of ordnance, Army of the Potomac; chief or ordnance, Department of the Ohio; chief of ordnance, Army of the Cumberland; and aide-de-camp to Lieutenant General Grant.

David Ramsay Clendenin was born in Little Britain, Lancaster County, Pennsylvania, on June 24, 1830. After attending Knox College in Galesburg, Illinois, graduating in 1854, he taught school. Joining the Washington Clay Guards of the District of Columbia at the beginning of the Civil War, he rose from private to lieutenant colonel, serving in the 8th Illinois Cavalry by the end of the war.

James Adams Ekin was born in Pittsburgh, Pennsylvania, on August 31, 1819. His occupation before the Civil War was builder of ships and steamboats. Serving in the Quartermaster Corps throughout the war, in Pennsylvania, Indiana, and Washington, D.C., he was brevetted a brigadier general in 1865.

Charles Henry Tompkins was born at Fort Monroe, Virginia, on September 12, 1830. He attended West Point, serving in the Quartermaster Corps, with the 2nd U.S. Cavalry, the 5th U.S. Cavalry, the 1st Vermont Cavalry, and the 1st Veteran Army Corps. He was brevetted a brigadier general in 1865.[4]

James A. Ekin, a member of the military commission, signed the petition to commute Mrs. Surratt's punishment to life in prison (Library of Congress).

The Washington Arsenal prison building and south side of prison yard (courtesy Surratt House Museum/MNCPPC).

Holt tried to impose several restrictions on the trial. He wanted it to be held in secret, with no full record to be made available to the public. Stanton, along with many in the government and army, favored keeping the court's proceedings secret, but he left the decision to Holt. Weighing the desire to enlist popular opinion behind the government against the need to limit publicity of certain controversial activities by the government, Holt gave in to the public's interest. Holt further wanted to hold defense council arguments to only five minutes, but also bowed to public pressure. These requirements, especially the secrecy requirement, were soon removed after considerable objections, especially from the press, and other influential people.[5]

The trial was held at the old U.S. Arsenal, located on Greenleaf's Point, in the southwest portion of Washington, where the Eastern Branch (Anacostia River) joins the Potomac. The site has been a military post of one sort or another since the late eighteenth century. Pierre Charles L'Enfant (1754–1825), who planned the city of Washington, indicated Greenleaf's Point as a good place for a fort, the first of which was established in 1794. Fort Humphreys was built in 1803, but was blown up in 1814, during the War of 1812, when British forces occupied Washington. It was rebuilt in 1817, with workshops added for the making of military supplies, and the name "Washington Arsenal" became official. The construction of a federal penitentiary was begun in 1826 and completed by 1831. With brick walls twenty feet high and a cellblock containing 160 cells, each seven by three and a half feet, the prison was formidable, but it soon became necessary to expand the facilities. The arsenal was known as the District Penitentiary until 1862, when all prisoners were transferred to the prison at Albany, New York.

The remains of John Wilkes Booth were buried under the floor of a storeroom at the arsenal on April 27, 1865. Soon, it was decided to hold the trial at the arsenal. When the former prison chapel proved unsuitable, a room which had been part of the deputy warden's quarters was selected. Even this room was small, being only 27 by 40 feet. A door into what had been the women's cellblock was added, so the defendants could be held there and moved between their cells and the courtroom with a minimal security risk. The prisoners were seated behind a railing, along the west side of the room, with a guard between each one. The Military Commission, composed of nine army officers, sat at a table on the north side, with another table for the reporters facing it. The witnesses sat facing the commission, between two tables. The defense lawyers occupied smaller tables toward the east end of the room. Members of the public could crowd into the remaining space along the south side of the room, the lucky ones occupying a few chairs. As the trial was held in the late spring and early summer, the heat in this crowded room was stifling.[6]

The trial opened at 10 o'clock on the morning of Wednesday, May 10, 1865. The accused, extracted from the hundreds of suspects arrested, were informed of the commission's makeup, asked if they had any objections to the members, and read the charges and specifications against them. All the defendants pleaded not guilty, and were allowed to secure attorneys. By the following day legal representation was introduced. Frederick Stone (1820–1899) and Thomas Ewing, Jr. (1829–1896) represented Dr. Mudd; Frederick A. Aiken (1837–1878) and John W. Clampitt (1839–1906) represented Mrs. Surratt; William E. Doster (1837–1919) and Walter S. Cox (1826–1902) represented Atzerodt; General Ewing also agreed to represent Spangler. Next day saw the completion of the defense team, with Frederick Stone representing Herold, Ewing and Cox representing Arnold and O'Laughlen, and Reverdy Johnson for Mrs. Surratt.[7]

The eight defendants put on trial had at least one thing in common: they were all sympathizers with the cause of Southern independence. None

The Washington Arsenal from the north side. The trial took place in the far left of the building. The prison yard, where the execution took place, is on the far right. Most of the building was torn down in 1867 (courtesy Surratt House Museum/MNCPPC).

of them were anywhere near wealthy, though they ranged from impoverished to what then represented middle class. One indisputable link they all shared was an association of some sort with the assassin, John Wilkes Booth, an association which none of them denied.

Samuel Bland Arnold, thirty years old, was a native of Georgetown, D.C., and had attended Georgetown College (today Georgetown University). A boyhood friend of Booth, Arnold, returning home after service in the Confederate Army, was unemployed when his old friend, now a famous actor, invited him to join in a conspiracy to kidnap the president of the United States. Minimizing the risks while promising fame and fortune, Booth had no trouble recruiting Arnold. Booth made Arnold the custodian of one of his horses and of weapons and equipment for use in their plot.[8]

George Andrew Atzerodt, twenty-nine years old, had been born in Thuringia, now a part of Germany, and came with his family to America in 1844. Atzerodt and his brother operated a carriage repair business in the Potomac River town of Port Tobacco, Maryland. Capable at handling boats, Atzerodt served the Southern cause by ferrying spies across the river. Assigned by Booth to assassinate Vice President Andrew Johnson, Atzerodt lacked the nerve to carry out the act.[9]

David Edgar Herold, twenty-two years old, was born in Washington, D.C. His father was a clerk at the Navy Yard, rising to the position of chief clerk. David attended Georgetown College for three years, studying to be a pharmacist, and held responsible positions with at least three Washington drugstores. Meeting Booth as early as 1863, Herold seems to have come under the actor's spell. He began to exhibit frivolous behavior and act childishly. He also spent more time in the woods of southern Maryland. It is possible that Herold was becoming involved with the Confederate cause. A loyal and trusted member of Booth's conspiracy, Herold fled south with the assassin and was in Booth's company when captured.[10]

Samuel Alexander Mudd, aged thirty-one years, was born in Charles County, Maryland, into a long-established and large family. He attended St. John's College in Frederick, Maryland, Georgetown College, and Baltimore Medical College (now University of Maryland), graduating in 1856. He married Sarah Francis Dyer (1835–1911) in 1857. They had nine children. Dr. Mudd at first denied having met Booth previous to the night of the assassination, but later admitted having dealings with the actor in the fall of 1864. He steadfastly maintained his innocence of any involvement in the assassination conspiracy.[11]

Michael O'Laughlen, twenty-five years old, was born in Baltimore, Maryland. His family lived across the street from the Booths, and Michael became friendly with John Wilkes Booth as a child. Returning home after service in the Confederate army in 1862, Michael worked with his brother in the produce and feed business in Washington. Recruited by Booth in the summer of 1864, O'Laughlen and Arnold, involved in the kidnap conspiracy, apparently took no part in the assassination conspiracy.[12]

Lewis Thornton Powell, twenty-one, was born in Alabama and grew up in Florida. Despite his youth, he was a veteran of many battles as a Confederate soldier. After serving with Colonel John Singleton Mosby's (1833–1916) Rangers, he joined Booth's conspiracy at the beginning of 1865. Given the assignment to assassinate Secretary of State William H. Seward (1801–1872), Powell left five men wounded, including the secretary.[13]

Edman Spangler, thirty-nine years old, was born in York County, Pennsylvania. Spangler had known the Booth family since childhood, and had helped to build the Booth family home, Tudor Hall, in Bel Air, Maryland. He began working for theatre manager John Thompson Ford (1829–1894) in 1853, employed at the Holiday Street Theatre in Baltimore, moving to Washington when Ford opened his theatre in 1863. Booth gave Spangler the task of tending his horse behind the theatre on the night of the assassination. As he was required as a scene shifter inside, he asked young Joseph Burroughs to watch the horse.[14]

Mary Elizabeth Surratt, aged about forty-two years, was born Mary Elizabeth Jenkins in Prince George's County, Maryland, in 1823. Although coming from a Protestant family, she attended a Catholic school in the 1830s, and became a devout convert to the Church of Rome. She married John Harrison Surratt (c.1813–1862) in 1840. Their three children were Isaac Douglas Surratt (1841–1907), Elizabeth Susanna Surratt (1843–1904), and John Harrison Surratt, Jr. (1844–1916). Mary's husband inherited property in southern Prince George's County and built a tavern there in 1852. The little community which grew around the tavern became known as Surrattsville (now named Clinton). Her son Isaac joined the Confederate forces in Texas and John, Jr., left school to help his mother manage the tavern after the death of Mary's husband. John, Jr., also served the Southern cause as a courier. Financial difficulties moved Mary to rent out the tavern and take up residence in Washington, where she managed a boardinghouse. It was to this house that John, Jr., brought his friend John Wilkes Booth. In the weeks preceding the assassination of Lincoln, Booth visited the Surratt house often, and conferred with John Surratt and sometimes with Mary. Her arrest and trial became a cause for controversy which is still debated to this day.[15]

These eight people were formally charged with conspiracy to kill the president, and were put on trial. Mary's son John Surratt avoided arrest for a time, and thus was not tried together with his mother and the other suspects. The trial itself, and the punishments imposed, continues to be the subject of inquiry and uncertainty down through the years, as we shall see.

3

MILITARY JUSTICE

> Self defense is as clearly the right of nations as it is the acknowledged right of men, and that the American people may do in the defense and maintenance of their own rightful authority against organized armed rebels, their aiders and abettors, whatever free and independent nations anywhere upon this globe, in time of war, may of right do.
> —John A. Bingham

> If that jurisdiction do not exist ... however fully the recorded evidence may sustain your findings, however moderate may seem your sentences, however favorable to the accused your rulings on the evidence, your sentence will be held in law no better than the rulings of Judge Lynch's courts in the administration of lynch law.
> —General Thomas Ewing, Jr.[1]

The question of the jurisdiction of the court which tried the eight accused of conspiring with John Wilkes Booth to kill the president is a fundamental one. The controversy was recognized at the time, and large portions of the arguments of both the defense lawyers and prosecutors were given over to addressing the issue. The decision to try the defendants before a military commission originated with Secretary of War Edwin M. Stanton. Fearing to risk a trial in a civilian court, where stricter standards regarding evidence would be in effect, and with the possibility of appeals dragging out after the trial, Stanton and army Judge Advocate General Joseph Holt overrode the uncertainty of Attorney General James Speed (1812–1887), prevailing upon Speed to agree and even to defend the military trial in his official opinion.

Born in Farmington, Kentucky, on March 11, 1812, James Speed attended St. Joseph College in Bardstown, Kentucky, graduating in 1828. Working as a clerk in the county courts for the next two years, he studied law at Transylvania University in Lexington, Kentucky. In 1833 Speed was admitted to the bar and began his practice in Louisville. His political career began with his election to the Kentucky State Legislature in 1847, but his strong opposition to slavery limited his success. After his defeat in his effort to be a delegate to the Kentucky constitutional convention in 1849, he returned to the practice of law. From 1856 to 1858 Speed taught law at the University of Louisville. He served in the state Senate from 1861 to 1863, and also was active in organizing pro–Union Kentucky troops for the war.

As the brother of Joshua Fry Speed (1814–1882), James Speed became a friend of Abraham Lincoln around 1841. After Speed left the Kentucky Senate, Lincoln appointed him U.S. Attorney General, and Speed held that office from December 5, 1864, to July 17, 1866. Speed wrote a letter to the new president, Andrew Johnson (1808–1875) informing him of Lincoln's death on April 15, 1865, and, together with Navy Secretary Gideon Welles (1802–1878), personally delivered the letter to Johnson. In Johnson's cabinet, Speed frequently sided with Secretary of War Stanton and the Radical Republicans in Congress, who favored a harsh policy for the postwar South.

Speed hesitated over issuing an opinion supporting the military trial of the assassination conspirators, but gave way under pressure from Stanton and Holt. When Speed's support of the trial by a military court became known, former Attorney General Edward Bates (1793–1869) wrote in his diary, "I am pained to be led to believe that my successor, Atty. Gen. Speed, has been wheedled out of an opinion to the effect that the trial is lawful. If he be, in the lowest degree, qualified for his office, he must know better." In his published opinion, written after the trial was over and the sentences carried out, Speed justified a military trial by noting that Washington was under martial law when the assassination occurred. He argued that the "Law and Usage of War" governed the military in wartime, and that these "Laws of War" provide exception to the normal guarantees, even those described in the Constitution. He likened the conspirators to "bandits," and called John Wilkes Booth a "public enemy" of the sort who had to be dealt with, in wartime, by the military.

Speed's opinion contains problems. He declared that Washington, D.C., was under martial law at the time of the assassination, though he admitted that the civilian courts were open and functioning. He described the "Law of Nations," an unwritten body of laws or agreements, which include the "Laws of War." Those "laws" were not created by the U.S. Congress, but are defined by Congress. Speed said that "banditti that spring up in time of war … must be apprehended and dealt with by the military."

3. Military Justice

In a passage which must have been recognized at the time as highly ironic, in light of the harsh sentences meted out, Speed urged that military courts were necessary to "soften by mercy" the harshness of war.[2] Former attorney general Edward Bates denounced the military trial, and newspaperman Horace Greeley's (1811–1872) criticism was so harsh that Stanton considered bringing suit against him for inciting assassins to murder the Secretary of War.[3]

Military commissions were first used against civilians during the Mexican War, although prosecutor John A. Bingham (1815–1900) cited an even earlier use of martial law, as far back as the American Revolution. Confusion existed at the time, and still does to this day, between martial law and military law. The two are not exactly the same, as was explained in an 1866 article:

> Military law is a portion of the law of the land, by which the army is governed as a distinct organization. It has its own distinct laws and rules. Martial law, on the other hand, is that system of law which is enforced by a conquering army in territory of the enemy occupied by it, and in place of civil, or is declared by the sovereign power of the state in time of rebellion. Military law exists by force of statute; martial law by the custom of war alone.[4]

By this definition, the Lincoln conspiracy trial was entirely under martial law, for none of the defendants were members of the armed forces of either side. Furthermore, a proclamation of President Abraham Lincoln issued on September 4, 1862, was cited as authority for holding a military trial. That proclamation stated:

> All Rebels and Insurgents, their aiders and abettors within the United States, and all persons ... guilty of any disloyal practice, affording aid and comfort to Rebels against the authority of the United States, shall be subject to martial law and liable to trial and punishment by Courts Martial or Military Commission.[5]

The attorneys for the defense made a spirited attack on the application of martial law in this case, and even questioned its validity in any case. Reverdy Johnson (1796–1876), representing Mrs. Mary E. Surratt, argued that the Constitution was always the supreme law of the land and that the president's powers derived only and entirely from it, even in wartime. Citing various authorities, Johnson declared that the military had no power to try civilians. He reminded the court that the Constitution established the war powers in the legislative branch, not the executive. Though the president is the commander-in-chief of the armed forces, he does not have the authority to declare war or carry it on without the approval of Congress. This is a principle which has been abused numerous times in recent American history, as we shall see in Chapter 9.

Reverdy Johnson pointed out that military commissions are not mentioned in the laws of the United States before 1862, and even then are not defined. The Act of April 10, 1806, which established the articles of war, specified various courts and the types of cases to be tried by each, with no mention of military commissions or the trial of civilians by the military. Although Johnson recognized the power to suspend habeas corpus was in the Constitution, he noted that the other rights of defendants were not suspended by the same power. He also reminded the court that the defendants were not residents of any rebellious state. He called upon the members of the commission to understand that they, the judges, and their actions might face condemnation in the future.[6]

There was precedent involved, for a military commission in February of 1864, ruling in a case involving blockade runners, stated,

> that no persons except such as are in the military or naval service of the United States are subject to trial by military courts, spies only excepted; and that except in districts under martial law, a military commission cannot try any person whatsoever not in the U.S. military or naval service for any offense whatever.

Here the exception "in districts under martial law" must be noted, though it can be argued that, although Washington, D.C., was under military guard at the time of the assassination, it was not entirely under martial law, as the civilian courts were open and functioning.

The use of military commissions in the New Mexico Territory during the Civil War to try cases not normally coming under military law brought the following order from Major General Henry Wager Halleck (1815–1872), Army Chief of Staff:

> Military commissions in your department have taken cognizance of and adjudicated upon actions of debt, trespass, etc., between persons not in the military service. I am directed by the Secretary of War [Stanton] to say that military commissions and military courts in your department have no jurisdiction of such cases, and that their decisions are entirely null and void. Moreover, the individual members may thus render themselves liable to punishment and damages. The practice, if it exists, should be immediately discontinued.

These official statements reinforce the idea that military laws administered through military courts and military commissions are intended for use by the military and naval forces in dealing with crimes committed by members of the armed forces.[7]

Another defense attorney also issuing a powerful challenge to the jurisdiction of the Military Commission was General Thomas Ewing, Jr. (1829–1896). Citing Article V of the Constitution, Ewing told the commissioners, "None but courts ordained or established by Congress can exercise judicial power, and those courts must be composed by judges who hold their offices during good behavior. They must be independent judges, free from the influence of Executive power.... You are, therefore, no court under the Constitution, and have no jurisdiction in these cases." Moving on to the Fifth Amendment of the Constitution, Ewing quoted, "No person shall be held to answer for a capital or otherwise infamous crime, unless on a presentment or indictment of a grand jury," which Ewing described as "a thing unknown and inconsistent with your commission." Reading from Article III, Ewing noted that the Constitution requires that "the trial of all crimes, except in cases of impeachment, shall be by jury," and he emphasized the word "impartial" in describing that jury. The Act of February 26, 1853, Section 117, required that "if two or more crimes of a like nature be charged, they must be set forth in separate counts," something which the charges and specifications at the conspiracy trial failed to do. As attorney for defendants Samuel A. Mudd, Edman Spangler, Samuel B. Arnold, and Michael O'Laughlen, Ewing challenged the prosecution to prove them guilty of murder, when they were not "present, aiding in or actually committing the overt act." He further challenged them on the basis that the charges were not specific, and the laws violated were not named. Ewing also argued that the judge advocate, as legal advisor to the commission, cannot fulfill that function impartially, since he is also the chief prosecutor.[8]

In recognition of the power of these arguments against the jurisdiction of the commission, John A. Bingham devoted the greater part of his lengthy summation to this question, in some cases taking on specific points raised by Johnson and Ewing. Bingham declared, "This court has no power, as a Court, to declare the authority by which it was constituted null and void, and the act of the president a mere nullity, a usurpation." Thus, Bingham denied the question of whether the Commission was legal simply by stating that the Commission had no authority to consider that question. Moving from there to the heart of his argument, Bingham noted, "The power to establish such a court ... is *implied* from the provisions of the 8th section, 1st Article, that 'Congress shall have power to ... make rules for the government of the land and naval forces.' ... It is necessarily implied that in time of war the Congress may authorize military commissions, to try all crimes committed in aid of the public enemy, as such tribunals are *necessary* to give effect to the power to make war and suppress insurrection." One could wonder if Bingham meant to suggest that the existence of a state of war can be used as justification for the suspension of any or all of the nation's laws or liberties. Citing the assassination itself as proof that the rebellion was not over, Bingham drew upon the words of Founding Fathers Alexander Hamilton (1755–1804) and James Madison (1751–1836), who both argued on behalf of the national government's right to defend itself in wartime. Hamilton and Madison did not specifically deal with military commissions, though, but only with the broad generalities of not shackling the government at a time when it is endangered. Bingham also cited a 1795 statute allowing the president to call forth the state militia to enforce the laws if the normal means are inadequate to the task. Lincoln's proclamation, mentioned earlier, and reinforced by act of Congress in 1863, also mentions military commissions for the trial of "all rebels, their aiders and abettors." As members of a conspiracy, Bingham charged, all those conspiring together are guilty even if only one member actually commits the act.[9]

The 56th Article of War covers the trial of persons who aid the enemy without wearing his uniform. Included were "guerrillas, blockade runners, persons trading with the enemy, those violating their oath of allegiance, assassins, poisoners, spies, bush whackers, and other criminals by stealth and in disguise." "Many offenses," said General Halleck, in taking command of the Department of Missouri in 1862, "which in time of peace are civil offenses, become in time of war military offenses, and are to be tried by a military tribunal, even in places where civil tribunals exist." This statement is from Halleck's General Order No. 1, dated January 1, 1862. This statement was, of course, contradicted in Halleck's later order on the New Mexico cases, quoted earlier.[10]

Military commissions existed throughout the Civil War, and they had been used against civilians previous to the assassination conspiracy trial. The military commission was, therefore, not something new and unique, and its use in a loyal state or territory where civilian courts were functioning had already been done.

The government's own laws and regulations, however, became a sword which cut both ways. The "Instructions for the Government of Armies of the United States in the Field" must have been considered an important corroborating document, for portions were appended to the official transcript of the trial. But these instructions contain many curious passages which might suggest that Stanton, Holt, or Bingham had not read them too carefully. Martial law, according to the instructions, can be

3. *Military Justice* 49

Military Commission and Prosecutors. From left to right, standing: T.M. Harris, L. Wallace, A.V. Kautz, H.L. Burnett. Seated: D.R. Clendenin, C. Tomkins, A.P. Howe, J.A. Ekin, D. Hunter, R.S. Foster, J.A. Bingham, J. Holt.

substituted for civil law "in a hostile country," when "face to face with the enemy." Jurisdiction of the military is described as referring to "military offenses." War is described as taking place between "sovereign nations or governments," a status which, during the Civil War, the North denied ever applied to the South. Punishments refer only to crimes committed by U.S. soldiers against inhabitants of a hostile country. Contrary to the statement of President Lincoln or General Halleck, the instructions state that "no belligerent has the right to declare that he will treat every captured man in arms ... as a brigand or bandit." Soldiers armed by a sovereign government commit no crime when acting in their official capacities. Spies are declared as those seeking information for the enemy. The above statements and definitions might fairly be said to raise questions about the government's own rules as they relate to the case of the Lincoln assassination conspiracy defendants. The instructions do, however, also contain statements which bolster the prosecution's case. They define enemies not uniformed or organized as members of a military force as "highway robbers or pirates." Those conducting secret communications with the enemy are guilty of treason. Capital punishment is proscribed for those engaging in "clandestine or treacherous attempts to injure an enemy." No allowance is made for leniency for an offender because of her sex. A forthright statement about assassination is made: "The law of war does not allow proclaiming either an individual belonging to the hostile army, or a citizen, or a subject of the hostile government, an outlaw, who may be slain without trial.... The sternest retaliation should follow the murder committed in consequence of such proclamation, made by whatever authority."[11]

It is obvious that there were arguments to be made by both sides, among the contemporary authorities as well as in the historic record. In British law, the preponderance of history argued against the trying of civilians under military law, going back to the Magna Charta in the 13th century. In America prior to the Civil War, the trial of civilians by the military had been virtually unknown. General Winfield Scott (1786–1866) had established military commissions during the Mexican War, but they were for the trial of U.S. forces committing crimes on foreign soil. Under President Lincoln's order of 1862, arrests could be made, civilians could be held indefinitely without trial, and they could be tried by military courts with no process of appeal except to the president. By one estimate, the number of trials by army military commissions during the Civil War exceeded 4,000.

The heart of the case, as far as jurisdiction is concerned, is that the defendants claimed that, as civilians residing in the loyal states, they should be tried in civilian courts with a civilian jury and have all the rights enumerated in the Constitution applied to them. The government argued that they had acted in aid of the rebellion, while the rebellion was still in effect, and that the crime committed against a military officer (the president, in his capacity as commander-in-chief of the armed forces) in an area subject to martial law (Washington, D.C.), and therefore trial by a military commission was appropriate and even necessary.[12]

A transcript of the trial of the conspiracy suspects was made by hand at the time, and has since been reprinted. False or misleading information has been published over the years about the transcript, and the various versions of it.

The official court reporter for the trial was Benn Pitman (1822–1910). Born in England, he had worked with his brother Isaac Newton Pitman (1813–1897) in developing one of the early systems of phonography, or shorthand. The transcript was taken down by Pitman's assistants, Dennis F. Murphy, James J. Murphy, Edward V. Murphy, Robert Roberts Hitt (1834–1906), and Richard Sutton. After writing down the testimony in phonetic symbols, they had to transcribe it into plain language, by hand. The exhausting work required them to labor as many as twenty hours a day. The record of the previous day's testimony was read to the court each day before new testimony was taken. Copies were made by letterpress, pressing the original onto treated paper, which transferred some of the ink. The official record of the trial was carefully guarded to prevent tampering.

3. Military Justice

At first, the conspiracy trial was declared to be secret, its proceedings unknown to the public, as reported by the press at the time.

> To the surprise of everybody, the assassination trials were commenced today with closed doors. No one will be permitted to be present during the hearing except those who are officially engaged in the trials, and all those are sworn to secrecy as to what may transpire in the court-room. It was expected that the Associated Press reporters, who had been engaged to give verbatim reports of the testimony, would be permitted to be present, but the order positively prohibits the presence of any save those above mentioned. The testimony, when written out in full, is to be placed in the hands of Judge Advocate Holt, who will designate such portions of it as may be proper for publication. This action of secrecy is based upon the fact that the developments of the trial will implicate many parties not under arrest, who may escape should publicity be given to the proceedings.

Beginning May 13, 1865, after vigorous protests by the press, the secrecy requirement was lifted and each day's transcript was given to the press. The Washington *Daily National Intelligencer* and the Philadelphia *Daily Inquirer* both published the transcripts in full at the time.

At the conclusion of the trial, three versions of the transcript were published in book form. Pitman's has the advantage of being the official version, sanctioned by the government. The other two were the Peterson Brothers version, and Benjamin Perley Poore's (1820–1887). Each of the three versions had drawbacks, as well as strengths. Pitman, in addition to being the "official" version, had an index (actually a table of contents, and not as full a listing of information as we might prefer), making it easier to use than the others. The principal drawback of Pitman is that it is a summary of the testimony, not always quoting verbatim. Also, it was edited by Henry L. Burnett (1838–1916), a member of the prosecution team. Poore is a verbatim record, but is incomplete, abruptly stopping with the June 13 testimony and not including the final arguments, which are included in Pitman. The Peterson Brothers version contains many errors in spelling, especially the spelling of names, caused by mistakes in transmitting the transcript by telegraph.

Author Otto Eisenschiml (1880–1963) and others have suggested that Pitman mischaracterized the transcript, perhaps as part of a conspiracy to cover up the real truth of the assassination. Comparison of the three versions does reveal occasional variations, sometimes influencing the meaning of what was said, but it would be impossible to prove this was deliberately done for sinister purposes. At one point during the trial, comments were made about the transcript, and defense council Thomas Ewing, Jr., described the record as "quite accurate." This is probably the strongest refutation possible of the idea that the transcript was being tampered with or misrepresented.[13]

The great majority of trials held before military commissions took place in the border states of Missouri, Kentucky, and Maryland, as well as in the District of Columbia. Most of these were for "civil disorder," presumably actions in support of the Confederate rebels. Military commissions were also used in the rebel states occupied by the Union forces. It was not always clear that the defendants in these cases were civilians or members of the Confederate forces. Rebel soldiers did not always wear uniforms or act as part of organized forces. Thorough investigations which might have established the facts were not always possible amid the fast-moving circumstances of war. Another factor complicating these cases was the use of conscription to fill the ranks on both sides. Being forced to serve, whether or not one believes in or supports the cause of the army involved, does not negate a soldier's individual responsibility for his actions, but could be seen as a mitigating factor.[14]

The use of a military commission to try the Lincoln assassination conspiracy defendants is thus confused, arguments and precedents existing on both sides. Even the victim, President Lincoln himself, had something to add to the question:

> You claim that men may, if they choose, embarrass those whose duty it is, to combat a giant rebellion, and then be dealt with in turn, only as if there was no rebellion. The Constitution itself rejects this view. The military arrests and detentions, which have been made, ... are not different in principle from the others, have been for *prevention,* and not for *punishment*—as injunctions to stay injury, as proceedings to keep the peace—and hence, like proceedings in such cases, and for like reasons, they have not been accompanied with indictments, or trials by juries, nor, in a single case by any punishment whatever, beyond what is purely incidental to the prevention.... You omit to state, or intimate, that in your opinion, an army is a Constitutional means of saving the Union against a rebellion.

While this statement seems to legitimize military commissions used against civilians, it does modify this idea by emphasizing that the commissions are preventative, and not instruments of punishment. We cannot be sure what Lincoln's attitude on this might have been. On the one hand he was determined to save the Union, but on the other he was a lawyer who was always concerned to abide by the law, and restrained some of his actions, such as the abolition of slavery, to insure that whatever he did fell within the framework of the laws of the land.

The Congress passed the Habeas Corpus Act in 1863, which recognized the president's ability to suspend the writ of habeas corpus. The act also required that lists of prisoners should be furnished to civilian circuit and district courts, so that grand juries could investigate to see if any indictments had been issued against those listed. If not, they could be ordered to be discharged from custody by courts, responding to writs of habeas corpus. So, while the writ of habeas corpus had been suspended for the purpose of arrest of suspects, it could still be brought to civilian courts to obtain a suspect's release if no grand jury had indicted them. A limit of twenty days detention was set, with a suspect to be released if no charges were brought against him during that time. These provisions of the act restored the functions of the legislative branches, as balances to the power of the executive.

Laws can be passed; however, their enforcement comes under the duties of the executive branch. Although Stanton ordered that lists of prisoners should be furnished to the courts, Judge Advocate General Holt, considering the act to be "extremely difficult of construction," decided that it did not apply to military tribunals, their decisions or sentences. This was not clarified until the *Milligan* decision by the U.S. Supreme Court in 1866, which ruled that the military could not try civilians in areas where civilian courts were functioning.[15]

To summarize, the Constitution of the United States, in Article III, section 1, states:

> The Judicial power of the United States, shall be vested in one Supreme Court, and in such inferior courts as the Congress may from time to time ordain and establish.

Article III, section 2, includes the following:

> The trial of all crimes, except in cases of impeachment, shall be by jury, and such trial shall be held in the state where the said crimes shall have been committed.

Amendment V states:

> No person shall be held to answer for a capital, or otherwise infamous crime, unless on a presentment or indictment of a Grand Jury, except in cases arising in the land or naval forces, or in the militia, when in actual service in time of war or public danger ... nor be deprived of life, liberty, or property, without due process of law.

Amendment VI states:

> In all criminal prosecutions, the accused shall enjoy the right to a speedy and public trial, by an impartial jury of the state and district wherein the crime shall have been committed, which district shall have been previously ascertained by law, and to be informed of the nature and cause of the accusation; to be confronted with the witnesses against him; to have compulsory process

for obtaining witnesses in his favor, and to have the assistance of counsel for his defense.

Amendment VIII states:

Excessive bail shall not be required, nor excessive fines imposed, nor cruel and unusual punishments inflicted.

Article I, section 9, states:

The privilege of the writ of habeas corpus shall not be suspended unless when in cases of rebellion or invasion the public safety may require it.[16]

All of these provisions of the Constitution were violated, in one way or another, during the Civil War, and especially in the trial of the Lincoln assassination conspiracy defendants.

While it was accepted that the military had a right to maintain a system of laws to deal with transgressions committed by members of the military services, especially illegal acts committed by military personnel on foreign soil, the use of military law to try and punish the conspiracy suspects was challenged because (1) the defendants were not members of any military service, either Union or Confederate, and (2) the crimes committed took place on American soil. The question of proper jurisdiction, of who shall try those charged, was never debated. Secretary of War Stanton decreed that the investigation, trial, and punishment be solely carried out by the military under military law. As we have seen, when defense lawyers Reverdy Johnson and Thomas Ewing, Jr., questioned the authority of the military commission to try the defendants, the commission resorted to a technicality, the assertion that as officers of the army, they did not have the right to nullify their orders, which had been given to them by the president of the United States. As we shall see, the authority of the military to try civilians under military law was questioned in a later case, when the United States Supreme Court denied that the military had jurisdiction under those circumstances.

4.

Prosecution

Appointed to assist Judge Advocate General Joseph Holt (1807–1894) in prosecuting the accused at the trial of the conspiracy suspects, John Armor Bingham (1815–1900) provided the principal intellectual foundation for the government's case. His very lengthy summation was full of legal interpretations and citations, and contained just the right combination of eloquence, righteousness, and fervor. Possibly more than any other individual, Bingham made the government's case against the defendants.

Born January 21, 1815, in Mercer, Pennsylvania, Bingham worked for a printer for two years, then entered Franklin College, in Ohio, but health problems prevented his graduation. After studying law in Mercer, Bingham moved to Cadiz, OH, finishing his law studies there. Bingham first met Edwin M. Stanton in 1836, getting to know him well during the campaign of 1840, when they debated each other, Bingham for the Whig Party and Stanton for the Democrats. Admitted to the bar in 1840, Bingham was Tuscarawas County, Ohio, district attorney from 1846 to 1849. In 1848 he was a delegate to the state Whig Party convention in Columbus. He married his first cousin, Amanda Bingham (1825–1891), and they had a daughter, Emma, born in 1849. The Binghams moved to Cincinnati in 1850, but returned to Cadiz the following year. Active in politics, Bingham supported the Whigs in 1848 and 1852, then helped to found the Republican Party and became its candidate for Congress in 1854. Elected, Bingham served in the House of Representatives from 1855 to 1863. Although he had not supported Abraham Lincoln for the 1860 Republican nomination, by 1864, having lost his House seat, Bingham accepted Lincoln's appointment as judge advocate of the army, with the rank of major. Stanton, now secretary of war, recommended Bingham for the post. Later in 1864, Bingham was appointed solicitor of the court of claims, and then

56   The Lincoln Assassination Conspiracy Trial and Its Legacy

Left: John A. Bingham was an assistant to the chief prosecutor, Judge Advocate General Holt. He provided much of the intellectual foundation for the prosecution and wrote the lengthy summary. *Right:* Judge Advocate General Joseph Holt was the head of the Army Bureau of Military Justice and leader of the prosecution.

elected to the House of Representatives, where he served from 1865 to 1873.[1]

Bingham was working on the Lincoln assassination case well before the trial began. Although already a member of Congress, he also conducted interviews with some of the suspects and witnesses, and assisted Holt and Colonel Henry L. Burnett in preparing the government's case. He also served on a commission, along with Holt and Brigadier General Lafayette C. Baker (1826–1868), and others, charged with identifying the remains of John Wilkes Booth. Because of threats received by government officials, including the prosecutors, guards were assigned, Bingham having the protection of four soldiers. Although the majority of the questioning during the trial was conducted by Holt, Bingham occasionally handled such duties, and he frequently voiced the prosecution's objections during the defense presentations. The lengthy and effective summation for the prosecution was entirely Bingham's work. He also composed the petition for mercy for Mrs. Mary E. Surratt (1823–1865), on behalf of five members of the Military Commission. He was present, with Holt and Burnett, as "legal advisors" during the Commission's deliberations. Stanton asked for and received Bingham's promise of silence regarding Mrs. Surratt's case.

Bingham supported Holt in the controversy concerning whether or not the petition for mercy for Mrs. Surratt was shown to the president.[2]

The assistant judge advocate at the trial, Henry Lawrence Burnett (1838–1916), did much of the actual preparation of the government's case against the defendants. Burnett wrote dozens of letters soliciting information, and received and evaluated hundreds of responses, collecting and arranging them for use as evidence. Attending the trial as part of the prosecution team, Burnett occasionally interrogated witnesses or voiced objections. He was well qualified for the role he played.[3]

Burnett was born in Youngstown, Ohio, on December 26, 1838. Running away from home in 1854, he walked a hundred miles to Chester Academy, where he was admitted as a student. After three years he was ready for the Ohio State National Law School, and by 1859 he graduated with an L.L.B. degree. Admitted to the bar, he began the practice of law at Warren, Ohio. Enlisting in Co. C, 2nd Ohio Cavalry, he was elected captain on August 23, 1861. He served in Missouri in the battles of Carthage and Fort Wayne, and Gibson, and in southern Kentucky. Promoted to major in 1863, he became judge advocate of the Department of the Ohio. In 1864, Burnett was requested by Indiana governor Oliver Hazard Perry Throck Morton (1823–1877) to prosecute at the trial of members of the Knights of the Golden Circle, a pro–Confederate organization. Following this case, Burnett prosecuted several defendants, including Confederate colonel George St. Leger Grenfell (1808–1868), convicted of aiding the scheme to cause rebellion in Chicago and other areas, a plan known as the Northwest Conspiracy. In this trial by military commission, Burnett presented an elaborate refutation of the defense's argument that a military trial was unjustified. As at the Lincoln assassination conspiracy suspects' trial, the military judges almost always sustained Burnett's objections but overruled the defense's. Also, as in the later trial, the military judges almost always sustained Burnett's objections but overruled the defense's. Also, as in the later trial, there were claims of perjured testimony and discrepancies in the record of the testimony. Grenfell was sentenced to death, his sentence was commuted to life, and he was sent to Fort Jefferson, where he met the Lincoln conspiracy defendants. Burnett also prosecuted Lambdin P. Milligan (1812–1899), a similar case, whose conviction was overturned by the U.S. Supreme Court in 1866.[4]

Burnett received an order, dated April 17, 1865, from Secretary of War Stanton to report for duty "to aid in the examination respecting the murder of the president." Arriving in Washington on the 19th, Burnett set about the work of gathering evidence. "Many nights I worked with him

John A. Bingham, Joseph Holt and Henry L. Burnett made up the prosecution. All three questioned witnesses, but Holt asked the majority of the questions.

[Stanton] until the morning dawn began to steal in at the windows," Burnett later wrote. Once, when Louis J. Weichmann (1842–1902) had been released from custody on Burnett's order, Stanton vehemently denounced Burnett, who threatened to resign. Changing his tone, Stanton implored Burnett to stay, telling him how important he was to the case. On May 6, Burnett was officially appointed assistant to Holt for the trial. He was present throughout the trial, from May 10 to June 30, 1865. When the trial ended, Burnett became custodian of the official trial records, including the sentences, which were kept secret for a short time. Burnett was also responsible for the transcript of the trial, and for assuring its accuracy.[5]

    The prosecution was attempting to prove more than the guilt of those in the defendant's dock. It wanted to show that the plot to kidnap or kill the Union leaders was planned and supported by the Confederacy at the highest levels, and was, therefore, part of the Southern rebellion. Several witnesses relating to this idea testified to the involvement of the Confederate leaders, especially the group of Confederate agents operating in

Canada. One of the most important witnesses was Richard Montgomery (c.1841–?), who described the Confederate organization in Canada. Montgomery testified that Jacob Thompson (1810–1885), the leader of the Confederate agents in Canada, told him "he could at any time have the tyrant Lincoln, and any other of his advisors that he chose, put out of the way ... that they would not consider it a crime when done for the cause of the Confederacy." Montgomery also stated that he had seen Lewis Powell (1844–1865) in Canada with the Confederates there.[6]

Another major witness against the Confederate connection was Sanford Conover, whose real name was Charles A. Dunham (c.1832–1900). Dunham testified that he had known the Confederate agents in Canada and had heard them discussing the assassination of Lincoln and other Union leaders, naming Jacob Thompson, William Walter Cleary (1831–1897), and George Nicholas Sanders (1812–1873). Dunham also said he saw John Wilkes Booth (1838–1865) and John H. Surratt (1844–1916) in Canada. He testified that Thompson indicated to him that a plot to assassinate Lincoln had been approved in Richmond. Dunham also testified to the existence of Confederate plots to destroy the Croton Dam, New York City's main water supply, and to attempt to spread yellow fever in the North. Dunham was exposed as a perjurer and eventually went to prison.

A native of Croton, New York, Dunham studied law in New York City around 1852, but never completed his studies. Instead, he became a swindler, supposedly looking for the heir to an English fortune. When the war began, Dunham tried to recruit men for the army. Unsuccessful at that, he turned to writing, using various aliases. Heading south in 1863, he claimed to have been a clerk in the rebel war department, but instead seems to have spent most of his time confined to the Confederate prison, Castle Thunder, in Richmond. Traveling across the North to Canada, he was arrested by the Canadians as a suspect in the Confederate raid on St. Albans, Vermont. In a Canadian prison Dunham met George N. Sanders, one of the Confederate agents in Canada. Dunham testified for the defense in the trial of the St. Albans raiders, using the alias James Watson Wallace.[7]

Henry Von Steinacker (1835–?), another prosecution witness of doubtful quality, described speaking with Confederate soldiers in Virginia shortly after the battle of Gettysburg, traveling in company with John Wilkes Booth, who told Von Steinacker, "Old Abe must go up the spout." He described a secret meeting of Confederate officers, which he said included Booth, and was told that plans were being made to free Confederate prisoners of war, set fire to Northern cities, "and finally to get after the members of the cabinet, and kill the president." The defense made little effort to cross-examine these witnesses, for they maintained that it did not specifically relate to their clients. The prosecution introduced testimony relating to Confederate plots to destroy ships, burn New York City, introduce infectious disease into Union cities and the army, starve and otherwise abuse Union prisoners of war, and to strike at the heart of the Union's ability to wage war.[8]

The government had strong cases against David Edgar Herold (1842–1865), who had been captured with Booth, and Powell, who was positively identified as the man who had attacked Secretary Seward and others simultaneously with the assassination of Lincoln. The case against the other defendants was largely circumstantial. Atzerodt, Arnold, and O'Laughlen admitted being involved with Booth in a conspiracy to kidnap the president, but denied having anything to do with murder. Mrs. Surratt, Dr. Mudd, and Edman Spangler all maintained their innocence.[9]

The most important witnesses against David Herold were John Minchin Lloyd (1824–1892), William Storke Jett (1847–1885), and the soldiers who captured Herold at the Garrett farm. Lloyd, a tavern keeper at Surrattsville, testified that Herold joined John Surratt and Atzerodt at the Surratt tavern five or six weeks before the assassination. On that occasion, Surratt gave Lloyd two carbines, a rope, ammunition, and a monkey wrench to hide at the tavern. Lloyd described how Herold and Booth arrived together at the tavern on the night of the assassination, and Herold came inside while Booth remained on his horse. This showed Herold's willing involvement with the conspirators. Jett was one of the three Confederate soldiers who said they met Booth and Herold at the Rappahannock River crossing at Port Conway, Virginia. Jett quoted Herold as telling him, "We are the assassinators of the president." Although using aliases at first, Herold finally gave Jett his true name, and Booth's as well. Everton J. Conger (1834–1918) and Edward P. Doherty (1840–1897), officers among the soldiers who captured Booth and Herold, testified to their being together in the Garrett barn.[10]

The best witness against Powell was William H. Bell (1846–?), houseboy at the Seward home, who stood face to face with Seward's assailant and spoke with him before the attack. He positively identified Powell as that man. Two of the men who fought Powell also identified him, though less positively than had Bell. George Robinson (1832–1907), on duty as Seward's nurse, stated "He looks like him, to me," and Augustus H. Seward (1826–1876), one of secretary's sons, said, "I saw this large man ... that night (pointing to Lewis Payne)."[11]

Damning testimony against both Atzerodt and O'Laughlen came from Marcus P. Norton, who described seeing Booth meeting with them early in 1865 at the National Hotel in Washington. Norton claimed to have overheard part of Booth's conversation with Atzerodt, a discussion which involved "Mr. Johnson." Atzerodt was accused of being the conspirator who was to kill Vice President Andrew Johnson. The same Norton also told how a man came to his room at the National Hotel about March 3, 1865, asking if that was Booth's room. Norton identified Dr. Mudd as that man. Detective John Lee, who searched Atzerodt's hotel room on April 15, said he found "a white handkerchief with 'Mary R.E. Booth' on it," and a bankbook, in which was written, "Mr. J. Wilkes Booth, in account with the Ontario Bank, Canada."[12]

One of the strongest pieces of evidence against Samuel Arnold was his letter to Booth of March 27, 1865, found in Booth's trunk. The importance of this letter, known as the "Sam" letter, is obvious for the government's case. In the letter, Arnold acknowledged his membership in the conspiracy with Booth, and also mentioned "Mike," Michael O'Laughlen (1840–1867) by name, likewise implicating him. Discussing his reluctance to continue in the conspiracy with Booth, Arnold wrote, "None, no, not one, were more in for the enterprise than myself," and "I was one with you." Testimony was given by an officer who took a statement from Arnold that the handwriting of the letter was by the same man.[13] Arnold's statement, taken at Baltimore on April 18, 1865, described his meeting with Booth and the other conspirators. Mary Van Tine rented rooms to Arnold and O'Laughlen, and testified that they were visited there "frequently" by Booth. David Stanton testified that he saw O'Laughlen at the Stanton home on the night of April 13: "He asked me where the Secretary was."[14]

The prosecution established Dr. Samuel A. Mudd's pro–Southern sentiments through the testimony of his former slaves. Melvina Washington said she heard Mudd say Lincoln "would not keep his seat long," and described Mudd entertaining visitors who posted a watch and hid in the trees whenever anyone came by. Another ex-slave, Mary Simms (1818–1867), provided more details about the mysterious visitors at the Mudd house, stating that they came from the South, and identifying one as John Surratt. Simms said Surratt "was there from almost every Saturday night to Monday night. When he would go to Virginia, or come back from there, he would stop." She stated that when Mudd and Surratt spoke together, "they always went off by themselves to talk." Daniel J. Thomas testified that in late March 1865, Dr. Mudd "said that the president ... was an abolitionist; that the whole cabinet were such; ... and that [they] would be killed in six or seven weeks."[15]

The most damaging witness for the prosecution, especially against Dr. Mudd and Mrs. Surratt, was Louis J. Weichmann. As a boarder at Mrs. Surratt's, he met most of the defendants. Particularly harmful to Dr. Mudd was Weichmann's testimony of their first meeting. "Mr. Surratt introduced Dr. Mudd to me; and Dr. Mudd introduced Mr. Booth, who was in company with him, to both of us." Weichmann described how the four of them went to Booth's hotel, where Booth, Mudd, and Surratt held conversations in the hallway, which Weichmann said was just out of his hearing. "Booth at one time took out the back of an envelope, and made marks on it with a pencil. I should not consider it writing, but more in the direction of roads or lines. Surratt and Booth and Dr. Mudd were at that time seated round the table."

Weichmann's testimony probably did more than any other's to hang Mrs. Surratt. He stated that Booth visited the Surratt house "frequently.... He generally called for ... John H. Surratt; and, in the absence of John H. Surratt, he would call for Mrs. Surratt." Often these conversations, Weichmann reported, were held apart from others. He placed Atzerodt, Herold, and Powell at Mrs. Surratt's house. On one occasion, Weichmann said he walked in on Powell and John Surratt, finding them surrounded with pistols and knives. They instinctively tried to hide them.[16]

Ironically, another lodger at Mary Surratt's house in Washington, Honora Fitzpatrick (1846–1896), may have contributed to the case against her landlady and friend.

Honora's father, James Fitzpatrick, employed as a bank collector in Washington, sent Honora to board with Mrs. Surratt on October 6, 1864. Described as plain and shy, she was known by her nickname, Nora. Sharing a room with Mrs. Surratt's daughter, Anna (1843–1904), Nora was characterized by fellow resident Weichmann as "in every respect a very good and excellent woman."

She was introduced to John Wilkes Booth on January 1, 1865, by John Surratt, at the Surratt house. As a resident at Mrs. Surratt's, Nora was a witness to the comings and goings of those who would later be charged with conspiring to assassinate the president, though she was an innocent witness, a young girl whose head was turned by the handsome and famous actor who became a frequent visitor. She was unable to recognize Lewis Powell as the same man she had seen at the Surratt house several times, until his clothing was arranged more the way it had been then. Unknowingly drawing herself and her landlady into the conspiracy, Nora had herself photographed, and when she and Anna Surratt went to the photographers to pick up the photos they also bought portraits of John Wilkes Booth and some of the war leaders, both North and South. The presence of these photos in her house was used against Mrs. Surratt at the trial. The conspirators also used Nora for their own purposes, as when she went to Ford's Theatre in company with John Surratt, Lewis Powell, and Mary Apollonia Dean (1855–1894). While attending the performance on March 15, 1865, the girls were thrilled when Booth called on them in their box, the same one in which Abraham Lincoln would be shot a month later. The two girls paid no attention to the men's conversation.

On Monday, April 17, detectives arrived at Mrs. Surratt's house and took all those present to General Christopher C. Augur's (1821–1898) headquarters, including Nora. Held at Carroll Prison, adjacent to the Old Capitol Prison, Nora and the other women were questioned extensively. Nora was finally released on May 11, along with Anna Surratt, but was required to testify at the trial. She had no revelations for the court, but her confirmation of the comings and goings of the conspirators at Mrs. Surratt's house may have aided the prosecution's case, especially against Mrs. Surratt. Testifying again at John Surratt's trial in 1867, Nora described how Mrs. Surratt had visited the Herndon House, but didn't know what her business there had been. Other witnesses revealed that Lewis Powell was registered there at the time.[17]

The case against Edman Spangler was the weakest one against any of the defendants. Jacob Ritterspaugh (1840–1926), a fellow stagehand at Ford's Theatre with Spangler on the night of the assassination, ran out after Booth but could not catch him. He testified that when he came back inside, Spangler "hit me on the face with the back of his hand, and he said, 'Don't say which way he went.' I asked him what he meant by slapping me in the mouth; and he said, 'For God's sake, shut up!'" Another theatre employee, Joe Simms, said he saw Spangler leave the theatre with Booth on the afternoon of the 14th, Booth having "invited him to take a drink." Simms added, "they were quite intimate together." Theatre stagehand Joseph Burroughs, describing an incident from the afternoon of the day of the assassination, testified, "He [Spangler] said, 'Damn the president and General Grant!' ... I said to him, 'what are you damning the man for,—a man that has never done any harm to you?' He said he ought to be cursed when he got so many men killed."[18]

Although hundreds of suspects had been arrested, why were only eight brought to trial? Two who might have been included, John Lloyd and Louis Weichmann, were needed as witnesses. Since those charged could not testify at that time, prosecuting Lloyd and Weichmann would have prevented their giving testimony, and without their testimony, most of the case against Mrs. Surratt and much of the case against Dr. Mudd would not have existed. But there were others, whose testimony was far less central to the cases of the eight defendants, than Lloyd and Weichmann. Samuel Knapp Chester (c.1836–1921), a fellow actor and friend of Booth, had been strongly urged to join the conspiracy by Booth himself. Though not at first specifying what he wanted Chester to do, in December 1864, Booth finally explained to his friend that

> he was in a large conspiracy to capture the heads of the government, including the President, and to take them to Richmond.... He urged the matter, and talked with me, I suppose, half an hour; but I still refused to give my assent. Then he said to me, "You will at least not betray me"; and added, "you dare not." ... He told me that the affair was to take place at Ford's Theatre in Washington, and the part he wished me to play, in carrying out this conspiracy, was to open the back door of the theatre at a signal.... He said everything was in readiness, and that there were parties on the other side ready to cooperate with them. By these parties I understood him to mean the rebel authorities and others opposed to our government. He said there were from fifty to one hundred persons engaged in the conspiracy.

Chester thus had advance warning of Booth's kidnap plot against Lincoln. He also was told of others involved. He testified that Booth named another actor, known to Chester, John Mathews (c.1836–1905), whom Booth had also tried to enlist in the conspiracy, unsuccessfully. He also testified that he met Booth in New York, only a week before the assassination, and Booth told him on that occasion, "What an excellent chance I had to kill the president, if I had wished, on inauguration day!" Booth threatened Chester if he told anyone about this, which accounts for his not warning the authorities ahead of time, but it does not explain why the government made no charge against Chester. His testimony formed part of the evidence in the government's attempt to link the Confederate government with the assassination, but, in spite of the government initially charging several Confederate officials, including President Jefferson Davis (1808–1889), none of these men was ever brought to trial.[19]

In reporting on the trial, the political orientation of the papers made all the difference, as pro-administration papers generally supported the prosecution, while anti-administration papers took the part of the defendants. The Baltimore *American* (July 10, 1865) wrote:

> Any one who attentively reads the evidence will be convinced that they [the defendants] are guilty of the crimes laid to their charge.... The people will feel that detection, condemnation and punishment have not followed too

swiftly, and they will experience relief from the thought that retributive justice has so completely overtaken and so sternly avenged the culprits who so terribly outraged humanity.

The New York *Evening Post* (May 11, 1865) said:

For the first time within our recollection all the newspapers of this city are agreed upon an important question of law and propriety. *The Evening Post, The Commercial Advertiser, The Journal of Commerce, The Times, The Tribune, The World,* and *The Daily News* unite in exposing the blunder of the authorities in ordering the conspiracy trials to be before a military court, and in declaring this purpose to be in violation of the Constitution, unnecessary, injudicious, and without justification.

The London *Times* (June 27, 1865) fumed:

The court has become such a monument of injustice that it has sickened even the most ardent supporter of the administration with the "Bureau of Military Justice." The day of military trials is over.

And for its part, the Detroit *Free Press* (May 10, 1865) said:

This change of venue in the case of the assassins from the cognizance of the regular tribunals, amounts, in fact, to a condemnation of all British and American common laws for, the courts of the District of Columbia would most assuredly have meted out full justice under judges of Mr. Lincoln's own appointment. Why Mr. Stanton, and upon what authority under the Constitution, should have superceded [sic] such able jurists ... is certainly worthy of more particular enquiry, and the country should insist upon an explanation of this high-handed measure.

5

Defense

On trial for their lives, the eight defendants presented contrasting appearances to onlookers.

Samuel Arnold ... had a rather intelligent face, with curly brown hair and restless dark eyes.... Samuel A. Mudd, M.D., was the most inoffensive and decent in appearance of all the prisoners ... rather tall, and quite thin, with sharp features, a high bald forehead, astute blue eyes, compressed pale lips, and sandy hair, whiskers, and mustache. He took a deep interest in the testimony, often prompting his counsel during the cross examinations. Edward Spangler* was a middle-aged man, with a large, unintelligent-looking face, evidently swollen by an intemperate use of ardent spirits, a low forehead, anxious-looking gray eyes and brown hair.... Doleful as Spangler looked when in court, the guards declared that he was the most loquacious and jovial of the prisoners when in his cell. Michael O'Laughlin* ... was a rather small, delicate-looking man, with rather pleasing features, uneasy black eyes, bushy black hair, a heavy black mustache and imperial, and a most anxious expression of countenance, shaded by a sad, remorseful look. George B. Atzerodt* ... was a short, thick-set round shouldered, brawny-armed man, with a stupid expression, high cheek bones, a sallow complexion, small grayish-blue eyes, tangled light-brown hair, and straggling sandy whiskers and mustache. He apparently manifested a stoical indifference to what was going on in the court, although an occasional cat-like glance would reveal his anxiety concerning himself. Lewis Payne* ... sat motionless and imperturbed, defiantly returning each gaze at his remarkable face and person. He was very tall, with an athletic, gladiatorial frame; the tight knit shirt which was his only upper garment disclosing the massive robustness of animal manhood in its most stalwart type. Neither intellect nor intelligence was discernible in his unflinching dark gray eyes, low forehead, massive jaws, compressed full lips, small nose with large nostrils, and stolid, remorseless expression. His dark hair hung over his forehead, his face was beardless, and his hands were not those of a man who had been accustomed to labor.... David E. Herold was a doltish, insignificant looking young man, not much over one and twenty years of age [Herold was twenty-three], with a slender frame, and irresolute, cowardly appearance. He had a narrow forehead, a somewhat Israelitish nose, small dark hazel eyes, thick black hair, and an incipient mustache which

5. Defense

occupied much of his attention.... Mrs. Mary E. Surratt, who was a belle in her youth, has borne her five and forty years or more [Mrs. Surratt was forty-two] bravely; and, when she raised her veil in court that some witness might identify her, she exposed rather pleasing features, with dark gray eyes and brown hair.... Whether she was guilty or innocent, it was easy to perceive that she desired to make a favorable impression upon the court, and to inspire feelings of pity.[1] *[*Published accounts often had variations in spelling of names. Edward Spangler was Edman Spangler; Michael O'Laughlin was Michael O'Laughlen; George B. Atzerodt was George A. Atzerodt; Lewis Payne was Lewis T. Powell. Comments such as the "Israelitish nose" portrays an age when the American population was not so diverse as it is today, and such descriptions commonly appeared in the press.]*

Although the prisoners were seated at one end of the room behind a railing and with guards separating them, Mrs. Surratt was at first allowed to sit near the defense lawyers until it was ordered that she sit behind the rail with the others.[2] Uncertainty has often been expressed as to whether Mrs. Surratt wore chains or handcuffs. The men had "stiff shackles," handcuffs connected by a rigid bar, on their wrists, and chains on their ankles. Atzerodt and Powell each had an iron ball attached to their ankle chains. According to at least one newspaper account, Mrs. Surratt "wears steel anklets connected by a steel bar about ten inches or a foot in length." General John F. Hartranft (1830–1889), the officer directly in charge of the prisoners, denied that Mrs. Surratt was ever chained, and Henry Kyd Douglas (1838–1903), a Confederate officer appearing as a witness, also confirmed that she "was not ironed during the trial."[3] A member of the military commission, August V. Kautz (1828–1895), stated that at least the first time the defendants were brought before the court, "they were masked and chained, and clad in black dominos so that we could not identify the prisoners."[4] Most of the male defendants did wear hoods and chains, but had Mrs. Surratt been wearing such devices—called "lilly irons"—she would have had great difficulty walking, which would have been obvious to everyone who saw her.

The defendants were represented, on the whole, by competent legal counsel. Reverdy Johnson, U.S. senator and former attorney general of the U.S., agreed to represent Mrs. Surratt without accepting compensation. Johnson's fitness to appear before the commission was questioned by General T.M. Harris, one of the commissioners, on the grounds that Johnson had protested against a loyalty oath. Summoning all of his considerable dignity, Johnson demanded to know "who gives to the Court the jurisdiction to decide upon the moral character of the counsel who may appear before them? ... I have taken the oath in the Senate of the United States ... and it would be a little singular if one who has a right to appear before the supreme judicial tribunal of the land [the U.S. Supreme Court], and who has a right to appear before one of the legislative departments of the government, whose law creates armies, and creates judges and courts-martial, should not have a right to appear before a court-martial." After a denial of intimidation, the court withdrew the objection.[5] Although having so ably defended himself, Johnson took very little direct part in the trial. His summation, dealing mainly with the court's jurisdiction, was read by co-counsel John W. Clampitt.[6]

Born in Annapolis, Maryland, May 21, 1796, Reverdy Johnson attended St. John's College, Annapolis, before being admitted to the bar in 1816. His career in law and politics made him one of the foremost public figures of his time. He served as deputy attorney general of Maryland from 1816 to 1817, state senator from 1821 to 1829, United States senator from 1845 to 1849, and attorney general of the U.S. from 1849 to 1850.

When the Whig Party broke up, Johnson became a supporter of Democratic senator Stephen Arnold Douglas (1813–1861). Although he originally referred to Abraham Lincoln as "reeking with the greatest heresies of political abolitionism," Johnson was nevertheless a strong advocate of the Union, describing the Confederates as "traitors, rebels or insurrectionists." He represented Maryland at the Peace Conference in Washington in 1861. Johnson blamed the Confederate leaders, not the Southern people, for the war.

A state senator again from 1860 to 1861, Johnson was elected U.S. senator in 1862. By this time opposed to slavery, he voted for the 13th Amendment, considering the extinction of slavery to be the one great good accomplished by the war.

Reverdy Johnson, as well as being a U.S. senator and diplomat, was one of the most respected lawyers of his time. He supervised the defense of Mrs. Surratt, but left most of the details to his younger associates.

When Lincoln died, Reverdy Johnson served as one of the pallbearers, representing the Senate. Soon, though, he

5. Defense

accepted the defense of Mary E. Surratt. Did Johnson believe Mrs. Surratt to be innocent? At one point he stated he would not protect anyone, "even her," whom the evidence showed to be guilty. Was this a possible hint explaining Johnson's seeming lack of enthusiasm for Mrs. Surratt's case?

General Thomas Ewing, Jr., represented Dr. Samuel Mudd, Edman Spangler, Samuel Arnold and Michael O'Laughlen. Son and namesake of Thomas Ewing (1789–1871), a powerful and influential cabinet member and U.S. Senator from Ohio, Thomas Ewing, Jr., was born in Lancaster, Ohio, on August 7, 1829. His foster brother was General William Tecumseh Sherman (1820–1891). The senior Ewing's appointment to be secretary of the interior in the administration

After a distinguished record as a general in the Union army, Thomas Ewing, Jr., a member of a famous and influential family, defended Dr. Mudd and other prisoners.

of President Zachary Taylor (1784–1850) brought young Thomas a position as one of the president's private secretaries. Graduating from Brown University in 1854, Thomas, Jr., attended the Cincinnati Law School, was admitted to the bar and began his practice in Cincinnati in 1855. Moving to Leavenworth, Kansas, in 1856, he practiced law and managed his father's extensive properties. He became a delegate to the Constitutional Convention of 1858, then served as a member of the peace convention of 1861 in Washington. Strongly opposed to slavery, Ewing campaigned for the admission of Kansas as a free state. When Kansas became a free state in 1861, Thomas Ewing, Jr., was elected its first chief justice.

Resigning from the State Supreme Court in September 1862, Ewing raised the 11th Kansas Volunteer Cavalry, becoming its colonel. Seeing service in Arkansas, Kansas and Missouri, Ewing was promoted to brigadier general on March 13, 1863. After commanding the District of the Border in Kansas and Missouri, he distinguished himself at the battle of Pilot Knob, defending St. Louis in 1864. He resigned his commission on February 23, 1865, after unsuccessfully seeking election to the U.S. Senate. Practicing law, he was a partner of Lincoln's friend Orville Hickman Browning (1806–1881).

Thomas Ewing, Jr., was brought into the Lincoln conspirators' defense by Sarah Frances Mudd (1835–1911), who employed him to defend her husband. Although his friends tried to talk him out of it, fearing that his career would be hurt by an association with the defendants, Ewing took Dr. Samuel A. Mudd's case, as well as Spangler's, Arnold's, and O'Laughlen's. His interrogation of the witnesses was hard hitting, and he clashed frequently with the prosecution over points of procedure, especially over the question of whether the court had jurisdiction over the defendants. Ewing was aided in the defense of his clients by his father, and by Orville Browning. Although all of the defendants were convicted, none of Ewing's clients were executed.[7]

Although a willing member of the conspiracy to kidnap the president, Samuel Arnold always denied any involvement in a plot to assassinate Lincoln. Engraving from *Harper's Weekly*, July 1, 1865.

Frederick Stone, a respected lawyer from Maryland, represented Dr. Mudd and David Herold. Stone was born in Charles County, Maryland, on February 7, 1820, into a distinguished family which included Thomas Stone (1743–1787), a signer of the Declaration of Independence. Graduating from St. John's College in Annapolis, Maryland, in 1839, Frederick Stone studied law and was admitted to the bar in 1841. He settled in the Potomac River town of Port Tobacco, Maryland, and practiced law there. In 1852, Stone was appointed to the Maryland legislature to be one of the commissioners revising the state's legal rules of pleading and practice. In 1864 Stone was elected a delegate to the state constitutional convention, but declined the office.

5. Defense

David Herold requested to be represented by Frederick Stone. Dr. Mudd had previously made use of Stone's services for minor legal matters. Stone's reputation in Washington was as yet rather modest, and Dr. Mudd's wife secured the services of General Thomas Ewing, Jr., to head the doctor's defense, with Stone playing a lesser role. Ewing and Stone shared the duties of examining witnesses, but since Stone was also representing Herold, and Ewing also represented Samuel Arnold, Michael O'Laughlen, and Edman Spangler, the attorneys had to be vigilant in helping one client without hurting another. As the evidence built up against her, Mrs. Surratt requested Stone to join her other attorneys, and he accepted, though he contributed little to her defense.

Dr. Samuel A. Mudd treated Booth's broken leg, and while he denied any involvement in the assassination, he was sentenced to life at hard labor.

Stone's defense of Herold was hampered by the overwhelming evidence against the defendant. Stone pictured Herold as weak-willed, susceptible to influence by stronger personalities, and mentally deficient, though he did not attempt an insanity defense for Herold. It also did not help that Stone was not present in the courtroom to give the defense argument for Herold; it was read by one of the court stenographers, James J. Murphy. In a later interview, Stone said the defense of Dr. Mudd was hampered by the doctor "not trusting even his counsel or neighbors or kinfolks," and by Mudd having denied knowing John Wilkes Booth before the assassination. The judgment that Stone and the other defense attorneys failed to properly represent their clients is unfounded. The nature of the trial and the weight of evidence against the accused probably would have defeated any lawyer, however shrewd. After the trial, Stone pronounced the military commission, "a fair court and one of ability." Mudd's family were dissatisfied with Ewing's and Stone's lack of action to release the doctor during his imprisonment, but the attorneys replied that there was little that could be done and the best course was to wait upon events.[8]

William Emile Doster (1837–1919), a former Washington provost marshal, appeared for George Atzerodt and Lewis Powell. Doster was born in Bethlehem, Pennsylvania, on January 8, 1837. He was educated at Yale University, graduating in 1857, and graduated from Harvard Law School in 1859, later attending the University of Heidelberg, Germany. During the Civil War he served with the 4th Pennsylvania Cavalry, rising to the rank of lieutenant colonel. Appointed provost (pronounced *pro vo*) marshal for the District of Columbia, he was brevetted brigadier general on March 13, 1865.

Doster was hired by John C. Atzerodt, brother of George, and Colonel Henry L. Burnett prevailed upon Doster to also represent Lewis Powell, who had not found a lawyer. Doster was a realist when it came to his chances for a successful defense, writing in his memoir,

> He [Powell] had about as much of a chance to get off as the other [Atzerodt], that is—none at all. This [agreeing to defend Powell] I, at first, refused to do, on the ground that I had my hands full with one, considering the excited state of public feeling, and that, in fact, this was a contest in which a few lawyers were on one side, and the whole United States on the other—a case in which, of course, the verdict was known beforehand. I finally allowed my name to go down for Payne [Powell] temporarily, but with the understanding that as soon as he could secure counsel for himself, I might and would withdraw. He never secured other counsel and I had to do the best I could for both clients.

Doster's further comments on the nature of military justice further elaborate on this point.

> Before military courts prisoners are practically situated in a direction directly opposite from what they are in civil courts. They are presumed to be guilty and are called on to prove their innocence. In this case most of the evidence taken at the Bureau of Military Justice had been daily published as it was taken. The court had doubtless read it. The members could not help feeling that the country expected them, on the evidence already known, to find the prisoners guilty. Their business was chiefly to discover the degrees of guilt and impose the sentences in regular form. They knew that one of their party [Booth] had been shot without any trial, and the country applauded. Was it likely they apprehended trouble for or during the execution of the rest, with all the paraphernalia of a military trial and after six weeks' hearing? The brutal nature of a military court appears in this.[9]

Doster's defense of Powell was focused upon saving his life by reducing the charge against him. Powell had been positively identified by the

Sewards' houseboy as the man who viciously attacked Secretary Seward and four others who had tried to stop him. Pointing out that none of Powell's victims had died, Doster said that at most his client could be charged with assault and battery with intent to kill, not a capital offense. The defense of Atzerodt was similar, since Atzerodt had not attempted to kill Vice President Johnson, the task which Booth had assigned to him. Atzerodt's willingness to cooperate with the authorities—he made four separate confessions—was brushed aside by the military commission.[10]

John Wesley Clampitt (1839–1906) and his partner, Frederick Augustus Aiken (1832–1878), were young lawyers without a lot of experience, though in representing Mrs. Surratt they had the advice of Reverdy Johnson, and they made a truly heroic effort to save their client's life.

Frederick Augustus Aiken was born to a distinguished family in Boston, Massachusetts, in 1832. He graduated second in his class from Middlebury College in Vermont, then studied law at Harvard University. Dividing his interests between law and journalism, he was editor of the Burlington, Vermont, *Sentinel*, and was a correspondent in Washington from 1858–1859. While residing in Washington, D.C., he became secretary of the National Democratic Committee. Serving in the Union army, he became a captain on the staff of General Winfield Scott Hancock (1824–1886), seeing action and being wounded. His strong identification with the Democratic Party moved him to oppose the accumulation of power by the Lincoln administration, especially Seward and Stanton. A protégé of Reverdy Johnson, Aiken joined the defense effort for Mrs. Mary Surratt.

John Wesley Clampitt was born in the District of Columbia in 1839 and graduated from Columbian College (now George Washington University) in 1864. He served in the Washington Light Infantry, Company C, of the Union army. Active in Democratic politics, he became associated with Senator Reverdy Johnson, one of the leading lawyers of the day. When Johnson accepted the defense of Mrs. Surratt, it fell to Clampitt and Aiken to handle most of the work of the case. It was the first important legal case for either of the young lawyers. Although Johnson advised his two assistants, he made few appearances in court, and confined most of his active participation in the case to questioning the legal jurisdiction of the military commission. That left most of the weight of the defense of Mrs. Surratt on the shoulders of the two relatively inexperienced young lawyers.[11]

Walter Smith Cox (1826–1902), a prominent attorney in Washington, also represented O'Laughlen. Born in Georgetown, D.C, on October 25,

1826, Cox graduated from Georgetown College (now Georgetown University) in 1843, from Harvard Law School in 1847, and was admitted to the DC bar in 1847. He practiced law in Washington until 1879, also serving as alderman, recorder and auditor of the District of Columbia Supreme Court.

At the trial of the conspiracy suspects in 1865, Cox was presented not only with the challenge of the trial being before a military court under military law, but also with eight defendants all being tried together. Cox and the other attorneys tried to avoid testimony about one defendant implicating others. This happened during the questioning of Provost Marshal James L. McPhail (1816–1874), who was called upon to identify the handwriting of Samuel Arnold. When Cox asked McPhail how he happened to know what Arnold's handwriting looked like, McPhail replied that Arnold had given him a written confession. When fellow defense attorney Thomas Ewing tried to explore this matter, Cox argued with him, concerned that Arnold's confession would implicate O'Laughlen. The court ruled against Cox, and the confession named O'Laughlen as a co-conspirator. Cox was not afraid to question the prosecution's evidence as well as to cast doubt on how that evidence had been obtained, as when he stated that an incriminating letter, which the prosecution claimed had been found floating in a river in North Carolina, showed no blurring or other signs of having been in water.

O'Laughlen was supposed to have visited the home of Secretary of War Edwin M. Stanton on the night of April 13, possibly to identify Stanton and general Ulysses S. Grant (1822–1885) as potential victims of the assassination plot. Cox showed that his

Michael O'Laughlin, a boyhood friend of Booth, also refused to be a party to murder. Imprisoned at Fort Jefferson, he died in the yellow fever epidemic of 1867. Engraving from *Harper's Weekly*, July 1, 1865.

client had been drinking that night and making the rounds of the homes of prominent individuals in the company of friends, in the same way as crowds of other tourists celebrating the end of the war. In summation, Cox, while admitting that O'Laughlen had been a part of the kidnap conspiracy, argued that he had had nothing to do with the assassination.[12]

The defense of the several accused differed according to their different personalities, the different specifications of the charges against them, and their different circumstances. Francis S. Walsh, who had employed David Herold at his drugstore, described him as "light, trifling in a great many things," and agreed with attorney Stone that Herold was "more of a boy than a man," and was "easily persuaded or influenced by any one around him." James Nokes, a neighbor of the Herold family, agreed that David was "a light and trifling boy" who could easily be influenced. Dr. Samuel A.H. McKim (1826–1900), another longtime family friend, described Herold as "a very light, trivial, unreliable boy,—in mind about eleven years of age," adding that Dr. McKim would not allow Herold to deliver a drug prescription, for fear he might tamper with it as a joke.[13]

Edman Spangler was a stagehand at Ford's Theatre; it is uncertain how much, if anything, he know about Booth's plot. The evidence against him was weak and his sentence reflects that: six years at Fort Jefferson. Engraving from *Harper's Weekly*, July 1, 1865.

Edman Spangler was described by his employer, John Thompson Ford (1829–1894), as "a very good-natured, kind, willing man.... I never knew him to be but in one quarrel since he has been in my employ; and that was through drink." When Ewing asked if Spangler could be "trusted with the confidence of others," Ford replied, "I should think not to any extent. He had no self-respect. He was not one who had many associates ... very harmless." Asked about Spangler's politics, Ford said, "I never heard an expression of political sentiment from him." The long rope found in Spangler's possession after the assassination was explained by James

Lamb (?–1906), a theatre employee, to be identical to the ropes used in the theatre for shifting scenery. Ewing's questioning of Louis J. Carland, another theatre employee, cast doubt upon the testimony of Jacob Ritterspaugh (1840–1926), who said Spangler had slapped him and cautioned him not to say which way Booth fled on the night of the assassination. Carland said that Ritterspaugh told him that Spangler had actually said, "You don't know who it is: it may be Mr. Booth, or it may be somebody else." Likewise, James J. Gifford (1814–1894), the theatre carpenter, denied that Ritterspaugh had said anything to him about the slapping incident. "He [Ritterspaugh] asked me if he could amend the statement he had made. He said he had not told all he knew."[14]

Atzerodt was particularly difficult to defend, since he had admitted to being a member of Booth's conspiracy. The main focus of the defense was an attempt to minimize Atzerodt's involvement through uncomplimentary references to his cowardly character, and emphasizing his failure to seek to escape. His cousin, Ernest Hartman Richter (1834–1920) described Atzerodt's behavior in the days following the assassination, when he was staying at Richter's house in Montgomery County, Maryland. He stated that Atzerodt did not appear at all unusual, worked in the garden and visited the neighbors. He made no attempt to hide himself. When officers arrived, "he was willing to go with them when they asked him." On the question of Atzerodt's lack of courage, Samuel McAlister and Washington Briscoe, acquaintances of Atzerodt's, agreed that the defendant was known to be a coward.[15] The defense was seeking to show that Atzerodt was too cowardly to kill Vice President Johnson, and he made no effort to escape because he did not consider himself in serious trouble.

As weak as the defense of Atzerodt was, it appeared strong when compared with the case of Powell, who had been positively identified as the man who had attacked Seward, viciously wounding five men. Doster attempted to set up an insanity defense, calling Dr. Charles H. Nichols (1820–1889), superintendent of the government Hospital for the Insane. Nichols was very careful to qualify his answers, seeking to avoid saying anything which would strongly bolster Powell's defense. The following exchange was typical.

> DOSTER: If one should try to murder a sick man in his bed, without ever having seen him before, would it not be presumptive proof of insanity?
> NICHOLS: It would give rise in my mind to the suspicion that a man was insane. I would not regard it as proof.

In spite of this, the prosecution objected to the testimony, stating that it was too long, that the questions referred to a hypothetical person rather than a specific defendant, and that Dr. Nichols was being asked to make conclusions about the law, something which he was not competent to do. Nichols himself agreed, saying, "Every case of insanity is a case of itself, and has to be studied with all the light that can be thrown upon it; and it is impossible for me to give an opinion upon a hypothetical case."[16] The prosecution had clearly derailed Doster's only hope of saving the life of Powell.

The primary witnesses for Michael O'Laughlen were three friends who rode the train from Baltimore to Washington with him on April 13, 1865, James B. Henderson, Edward Murphy, and Bernard J. Early. These men testified that they were with O'Laughlen continuously on Thursday the 13th and Friday the 14th until late. As the prosecution had alleged that O'Laughlen had been seen on the evening of the 13th at the home of Secretary Stanton, the purpose of this testimony was to show that O'Laughlen was having a good time with his friends and did not visit the Stanton home. Attorney Cox also sought to show that O'Laughlen's demeanor was not that of a man planning murder.

> Cox: During this trip, what was O'Laughlin's manner? Was he in good spirits, or did he betray any nervousness or anxiety, or any knowledge of anything desperate going on?
> Murphy: I never saw him in better spirits in my life than he was then.

However, Murphy made a damaging admission that O'Laughlen had briefly visited the National Hotel on Thursday evening. The National was John Wilkes Booth's hotel.[17]

Samuel Arnold's defense was similar to O'Laughlen's in that it sought to show him going about his business during the period just before the assassination rather than plotting with Booth. George Craig, a salesman at Wharton's store at Old Point, Virginia, where Arnold worked, testified that he saw Arnold at the store every day until his arrest. Charles B. Hall, another of Wharton's employees, corroborated that Arnold worked there at least two weeks before the assassination, and that he slept nights in the store. John W. Wharton, the store owner, also testified that Arnold worked for him beginning on April 2, and that Arnold had applied for the job by letter, stating that he had "abandoned the business in which he had formerly been engaged." Assistant Judge Advocate Bingham objected, saying that Arnold's own statement in the letter was proof of nothing and was therefore inadmissible. The letter in question had been seized by the government, and by the time of the trial they "had been unable to find it."[18]

The prosecution suggested that Samuel Arnold's service in the Confederate army could be used against him, as an indication of disloyalty.

I think the testimony in this case has proved, what I believe history sufficiently attests, how kindred to each other are crimes of treason against a nation and the assassination of its chief magistrate. I think of those crimes as one seems to be, if not the necessary consequence, certainly a logical sequence from the other. The murder of the president of the United States, as alleged and shown, was preeminently a political assassination. Disloyalty to the government was its sole inspiration.

General Ewing attacked this idea in his objection.

Before any jury, or almost any body of men, proof that a person charged with one crime, and on trial, had before that committed some other crime, would prejudice his case materially.... The prisoners who are here on trial, are to be tried on evidence admissible under the rules of law, and the accused was not called upon to show here whether or not, a year of eighteen months before this alleged conspiracy was begun, he committed the crime of having taken up arms against the government. He is not on trial for that, and I think it is unjust to prejudice his case by hearing and recording evidence of it, if such evidence can, in fact, be produced.

After lengthy arguing back and forth, Bingham boiled it down to this:

He entered into it [the Booth conspiracy] to assassinate the president; and everybody else that entered into the rebellion, entered it to assassinate everybody that represented this Government, that either followed the standard in the field, or represented its standard in the councils.

According to this argument, everyone who served the Southern rebellion in any capacity, whether as soldiers in uniform, or as diplomats or agents of any sort, were guilty not only of treason, but were accessories to the assassination of Lincoln. No sooner had this absurdity been spoken by Bingham, then the court overruled Ewing's objection, allowing this impossible proposition to stand. The U.S. government never attempted to follow up upon this idea, which would have been impossible to implement, involving mass trials of thousands, even millions, of people. Even leaders of the Confederate cause, such as Jefferson Davis (1808–1889) and Robert E. Lee (1807–1870) were never put on trial for treason, or anything else. A general amnesty for nearly all who took part in the rebellion was issued on December 25, 1868, by President Andrew Johnson.

The defense of Dr. Samuel Mudd was the longest and most complicated of any of the defendants. Numerous character witnesses described Mudd as a gentleman of good reputation. As one of the principle witnesses against Mudd was Daniel J. Thomas, who had told the court that Mudd had predicted Lincoln's death, several witnesses described Thomas as unreliable. Dr. John C. Thomas, brother of Daniel, who had treated him as his physician, described his brother as having suffered from "a very serious paralytic attack.... He was mentally affected from it. His mind was not exactly right for a long time." On the previous testimony of Mudd's having met with Confederates and helped them to hide, including John Surratt, Julia Ann Bloyce, one of Mudd's house servants, stated she never heard of such an incident, and, when shown a photograph of John Surratt, said,

BLOYCE: I have never seen it before.
EWING: You never saw that man before?
BLOYCE: No, Sir.

To refute the testimony of Marcus Norton, who said he saw Dr. Mudd in Washington on March 3, 1865, asking after Booth, Mary Clare Mudd (1838–1882), the doctor's sister, stated that she was taken ill on the first of March, and her brother attended her, including coming for dinner on the third, "between eleven and twelve o'clock to see me, and he dined with us.... He left at two o'clock and returned again at four." She also testified that Mudd attended one of the slaves: "She was ill of typhoid pneumonia, and he saw her every day until the 23rd of March."

A crucial witness for Dr. Mudd was his cousin, Dr. George D. Mudd (1826–1899). Seeing his cousin at church on Sunday morning, April 16, the defendant told George Mudd about the two suspicious men at his house and asked George to tell the military authorities in Bryantown. The prosecution sought to block this testimony as hearsay, and under the restriction which prevented prisoners from testifying. Although the objection was sustained, General Ewing was able to get it into the record simply by rephrasing the question. George Mudd stated that he told Samuel Mudd that detectives had come to his house to question him, and that Samuel Mudd went inside and spoke with them after being told the purpose of their visit, and that George Mudd heard no denial that Booth and Herold had visited Samuel Mudd's house. Along with several witnesses, George Mudd also testified about the unreliable nature of Daniel Thomas.[19]

Ewing had put on a thorough defense in depth, with multiple witnesses corroborating each other, sometimes as many as five or six. All of the prosecution's most damaging testimony had been answered, whether in cross-examination or through presenting witnesses who would refute it or offer innocent explanations for what had seemed suspicious behavior. Dr. Mudd unquestioningly had the best defense of any of the accused, and even the press, which had originally characterized the doctor as highly questionable, was reporting by the end of May that Mudd's guilt was certainly in doubt.[20]

Probably the most controversial of the defendants was Mary Surratt

(1823–1865). We must remind ourselves that by the standards of the Victorian era, women were treated differently throughout society, so the prosecution of a respectable widow for such an infamous crime was sensational and unprecedented. Just as some were prepared to be more lenient with her because she was a woman, others were inclined to be even more harsh with her for the same reason. It has been said that Mrs. Surratt was tried in order to cause her son John to give himself up, and had he done so her life would have been spared.[21] This is a highly questionable assumption. John Surratt, had he surrendered in order to save his mother, would certainly have gone to the scaffold, and judging by the things that were said about her, Mrs. Surratt probably would have shared her son's fate.

To defend Mrs. Surratt, her lawyer, Frederick Aiken, called witnesses to counter the damaging testimony of John M. Lloyd, who had leased the Surrattsville tavern, and had testified that Mrs. Surratt had told him on the day of the assassination to have the "shooting irons" ready that night. Lloyd's drunkenness on April 14 was confirmed by two witnesses, Joseph T. Knott and James Lusby. Burnett's cross-examination of Lusby tried to suggest that the witness was drunk, as well, which he denied, then switched to the tactic of emphasizing how long it had been since Lloyd had had a drink—about two and a half hours, by Lusby's estimate.

Mrs. Surratt's eyesight was called into question, as she denied recognizing Powell when he came to her house while detectives were questioning her. Honora Fitzpatrick, one of her boarders, testified that she "often threaded a needle for her [Mrs. Surratt] when she was sewing during the day.... I have never seen her read or sew by gaslight." Burnett's cross-examination brought the admission from Fitzpatrick that she was in the parlor when Powell arrived and did not accompany Mrs. Surratt into the hallway to make the identification.

The most crucial witness against Mrs. Surratt was Louis J. Weichmann (1842–1902). Aiken called Augustus Howell (1837–1869), who told of meeting Weichmann at Mrs. Surratt's house. According to Howell, Weichmann must have been aware that Howell was a Confederate spy. Howell showed Weichmann how to make a cipher for encoding messages, and Weichmann inquired "if I thought he could get a situation [job] there [Richmond].... He said that he [Weichmann] intended going South." Howell also said Weichmann expected the Southern rebellion to succeed and he told Howell how many prisoners of war were being held by the North.

Several character witnesses testified for Mrs. Surratt, including clergymen, the Reverend Bernardin Francis Wiget (1821–1883) being an especially strong witness. He stated that he had known Mrs. Surratt "ten or

5. Defense

eleven years," that he "knew her well," and "I have always heard every one speak very highly of her character as a lady and as a Christian." When Aiken and Clampitt attempted to have Wiget describe whatever theological school might exist in Richmond, in order to attack Weichmann's statement that he wanted to go to Richmond to study, the prosecution strongly objected, which the court sustained. Holt's cross-examination managed to cast doubt on how well Father Wiget really knew Mrs. Surratt, and sought to cast suspicion upon her loyalty by going through the back door:

> HOLT: Have you ever heard her, in all of your conversations since the beginning of the Rebellion to this time, utter one loyal sentiment?
> WIGET: I do not remember.[22]

In 1977 a document was discovered which was another confession by George Atzerodt. It was found by historical researcher Joan Chaconas among the papers of William E. Doster, attorney for Atzerodt. Atzerodt stated in this confession, "Booth told me that Mrs. Surratt went to Surrattsville to get out the guns which had been taken to that place by Herold. This was Friday [April 14, 1865, the day of the assassination]."

> "I saw a man named Weightman [Louis J. Weichmann] who boarded at Surratt's at Post Office. He told me he had to go to Country with Mrs. Surratt. This was on Friday, also. I am certain Dr. Mudd knew all about it, as Booth sent (as he told me) liquors & provisions for the trip with the president to Richmond [the kidnap plot], about two weeks before the murder to Dr. Mudd's."
>
> "Booth never said until last night [Friday, April 14] that he intended to kill the president."

Although this document contains much interesting information, including the highly incriminating passages quoted above, we must approach such "confessions" cautiously. This is one of several confessions Atzerodt made. He was very cooperative, and the confessions were taken down by others, not written out by Atzerodt. A comparison of the confessions shows contradictions. In the confession made to Colonel Henry H. Wells (1823–1900), on April 25, 1865, Atzerodt does not mention being told that the purpose of Mrs. Surratt's trip to Surrattsville was "to get out the guns," nor does he say that Booth "sent ... liquors and provisions ... to Dr. Mudd's." Comparison of his descriptions of the events of April 14 are confusing and do not compare favorably. Atzerodt was scared and wanted to be cooperative in hopes that would be in his favor at the trial. It is possible that at least some elements of his "confessions" were suggested by Wells and other interrogators. It is also possible that Atzerodt was telling the truth about what Booth said to him. Historian Michael W. Kauffman believes that Booth was deliberately seeking to incriminate others and to confuse those who would attempt to follow his trail, both the original investigators and later historians.

The confusions and contradictions in Atzerodt's confessions, Booth's deceptions, and the fact that a witness's statements about what another person told him about yet another party would be hearsay evidence, and thus inadmissible in a genuine legal proceeding, combine to require us to consider anything Atzerodt said to be unreliable.[23]

The defense lawyers, especially General Ewing, made one last effort to question the legitimacy of the court, to determine what precisely the charges were, and to ascertain where these laws and crimes were published. It was in vain, as they knew it would be. Holt repeated "the common law of war" as covering all.

6

WITNESS OR DEFENDANT?

The part played by John Minchin Lloyd (1824–1892) in the Lincoln assassination story came into focus on March 18, 1865, when three of John Wilkes Booth's fellow conspirators, John Harrison Surratt, Jr. (1844–1916), George Andrew Atzerodt (1835–1865), and David Edgar Herold (1842–1865) arrived at the tavern in Surrattsville, Maryland, and brought objects with them for Lloyd to hide: two carbines, a box of ammunition, a length of rope, and a monkey wrench. Lloyd reluctantly agreed to hide these things in a space between the floors upstairs. In his testimony at the conspiracy trial, Lloyd was asked about his meeting with Mrs. Surratt on April 10 in Uniontown, D.C. "I am quite positive she asked me about the 'shooting irons.' I am quite positive about that, but not altogether positive. I think she named 'shooting irons' or something to call my attention to those things; for I had almost forgotten about their being there. I told her that they were hid away far back; that I was afraid the house would be searched, and they were shoved far back. She told me to get them out ready: they would be wanted soon."

On April 14, 1865, John Lloyd went to Upper Marlboro, in Prince George's County, Maryland, to testify in court against a man accused of assaulting him the previous February. The case was postponed, so Lloyd spent part of the day "drinking and playing cards." Upon returning late that afternoon to Surrattsville, Lloyd again met Mrs. Surratt, who had come down from Washington with her boarder, Louis J. Weichmann (1842–1902). Lloyd told the court that on April 14 Mrs. Surratt again told him "to have those shooting irons ready that night,—there would be some parties call for them." He also said that she gave him a field glass wrapped in paper. Weichmann corroborated that these meetings had taken place, and that Mrs. Surratt referred to the package as belonging to Booth. This testimony was more damaging to Mrs. Surratt than any other, and perhaps furnishes the answer to why Lloyd became a witness instead of a defendant. In 1865 defendants in most trials were not allowed to testify. Had Lloyd or Weichmann been charged and put on trial instead of serving as witnesses, there would have been little evidence against Mrs. Surratt; certainly not enough to hang her.

Questioned by detectives after the assassination, Lloyd at first denied knowing anything, then admitted to having supplied Booth and Herold on the night of the assassination with rifles and whiskey, only to deny that they had told him they had assassinated the president. In addition, Lloyd at first misled the assassins' pursuers about the direction Booth and Herold had taken after leaving the tavern at Surrattsville. It is possible to say that Lloyd had more to hide and was more involved in the crime than either Mrs. Surratt or Dr. Samuel A. Mudd (1833–1883). If Lloyd eventually told the truth (and we do not know to this day that he did), it was only after much pressure and duress.[1]

Louis J. Weichmann was born on September 29, 1842, in Baltimore. His family moved to Washington in 1843, where his father worked as a tailor. Moving to Philadelphia in 1853, Weichmann attended Philadelphia Central High School until February 1859. Although he wanted to enter the pharmacy business, his mother, a devout Catholic, insisted that he study for the priesthood. By the time he entered St. Charles College in Howard County, Maryland, on March 1, 1859, he knew seven languages and had studied the Pitman system of shorthand. He left college in July 1862, and became a teacher at St. Matthew's College in Washington. At this time, Weichmann renewed his friendship with John Surratt, with whom he had attended St. Charles College. Visiting with the Surratt family in 1863, Weichmann soon became a close friend. Taking a clerical position with the War Department's Commissary General of Prisoners, Weichmann learned that Mrs. Surratt planned to open a boarding house in Washington.

Weichmann become a boarder at Mrs. Surratt's house at 541 H Street (now 604 H Street) in Washington, on November 1, 1864, and continued to live there until the time of the assassination. His testimony established that John Wilkes Booth knew the Surratts well, as this exchange, early in the trial of the assassination conspiracy suspects, established:

> Q. Will you state whether Booth called frequently at Mrs. Surratt's?
> A. He called there frequently.
> Q. Whom did he call to see?

A. He generally called for Mr. Surratt—John H. Surratt; and, in the absence of John H. Surratt he would call for Mrs. Surratt.

Q. Were their interviews always apart from other persons...?

A. They were always apart. I have been in the company of Booth in the parlor; but Booth has taken Surratt out of the room and taken him upstairs, and engaged in private conversations in rooms upstairs ... which would sometimes last two or three hours.

Q. Did the same thing ever occur with Mrs. Surratt?

A. Yes, Sir.

Union major general Winfield S. Hancock commanded the Washington area during the trial. He later ran for president and nearly won.

Weichmann further established that Mrs. Surratt knew other conspirators, including George Atzerodt and Lewis Powell (1844–1865), who used the aliases "Wood" and "Payne."

Q. Have you ever seen the prisoner Atzerodt?
A. I have.
Q. Have you seen him at Mrs. Surratt's?
A. He came to Mrs. Surratt's house...
Q. For whom did he inquire?
A. He inquired for John H. Surratt or Mrs. Surratt....
Q. Will you state whether you remember some time in the month of March, of a man calling at Mrs. Surratt's ... giving the name of Wood?
A. Yes, Sir; I myself went to open the door, and he inquired for Mr. Surratt. I told him Mr. Surratt was not at home, but I would introduce him to the family if he desired it. He thereupon expressed a desire to see Mrs. Surratt.
Q. Do you recognize him among these prisoners?
A. That is the man (pointing to Lewis Payne, one of the accused).[2]

Lloyd's testimony against Mrs. Surratt at the trial would also prove to be devastating. Asked if he knew John Surratt, David Herold, and George Atzerodt, Lloyd said he did.

> Q. Will you state whether or not, some five or six weeks before the assassination of the president, any or all of these men ... came to your house?
> A. Yes: John H. Surratt, Herold, and Atzerodt were there together.... John Surratt called me into the front parlor, and on the sofa were two carbines with ammunition.... There was a rope, and also a monkey wrench....
> Q. Were those articles left at your house?
> A. Yes, Sir. Surratt asked me to take care of them, to conceal the carbines....
> Q. For what purpose, and for how long, did he ask you to keep those articles?
> A. He said he would call for them in a few days....
> Q. Will you state whether or not, on the Monday or Tuesday preceding the assassination of the president, Mrs. Surratt came to your house?
> A. I was coming to Washington, and I met Mrs. Surratt at Uniontown on the Monday previous [Tuesday, April 11, 1865].
> Q. Did she say anything to you in regard to those carbines?
> A. When she first broached the subject to me, I did not know what she had reference to: then she came out plainer; and I am quite positive she asked me about the "shooting irons." ... She told me to get them out ready; they would be wanted soon.
> Q. Will you state now whether or not, on the evening of the night on which the president was assassinated [April 14, 1865], Mrs. Surratt came to your house with Mr. Weichmann?
> A. I went to Marlboro on that day to attend a trial there in court; and in the evening it was probably late when I got home, I found Mrs. Surratt there when I got home....
> Q. What did she say to you?
> A. ... she told me to have those shooting irons ready that night,—there would be some parties call for them....
> Q. State now whether they were called for that night by Booth and Herold.
> A. The carbines and ammunition were called for that night.... [Booth] called for the carbines in such terms that I understood what he wanted. He told me, "Lloyd, for God's sake, make haste and get those things!" ... From the way that he spoke, he must have been apprised that I already knew what I was to give him.

[Here Lloyd admits that in having knowledge of the weapons left at the tavern, Lloyd was an accessory to the crime.]

> Q. Did they say anything in regard to the assassination as they rode away?
> A. Just as they were about leaving, ... [Booth] said ... "I am pretty certain that we have assassinated the president and Secretary Seward." I think that was his language as well as I can recollect: "we have assassinated" or "killed the president and Secretary Seward."[3]

If he had been innocent, Lloyd would have reported this encounter to the authorities at the earliest possible time. He did not do so.

Later, Weichmann was recalled, and corroborated that the meetings between Lloyd and Mrs. Surratt had taken place.

6. Witness or Defendant?

Q. Do you recollect seeing him by the buggy at any time on your way between Washington and Surrattsville on that Tuesday?
A. Yes, Sir; we met his carriage. His carriage drove past ours; and Mrs. Surratt called after Mr. Lloyd; and Mr. Lloyd got out and approached the buggy; and Mrs. Surratt put her head out, and had a conversation with him.
Q. From the buggy?
A. Yes, sir.
Q. Did you hear it?
A. No, sir.... I leaned back in my buggy; and Mrs. Surratt leaned sideways in the buggy, and whispered, as it were, in Mr. Lloyd's ear.[4]

Weichmann was a key witness, the only source for some of the evidence against Mrs. Surratt and others. His testimony was highly praised. Joseph Holt, chief prosecutor at the trial of the conspiracy suspects, said:

> In giving his testimony ... which I verily believe he did with entire truthfulness, he performed a public duty imposed on him with a conscientious faithfulness which entitles him to support of the government and to the commendation of all loyal and honorable men.[5]

General James A. Ekin, member of the military commission, said:

> During the memorable trial of the conspirators, your testimony was considered by the court as conclusive and clear, and your evidence was regarded as truthful in every particular. It stood the test of cross-examination and remained unshaken on the record.[6]

General Thomas M. Harris, another member of the military commission, noted:

> After every effort was made that could be devised by the ingenuity of man, Weichmann stood before the court ... as an honest, conscientious, truthful man. He was also a man of superior talent, education and intelligence. In short, he established a character that must challenge the admiration of every candid man.[7]

General Lew Wallace, also a member of the military commission, remarked:

> I have never seen anything like his steadfastness. There he stood, a young man only twenty-three years of age, strikingly handsome, self-possessed, under the most searching cross-examination I have ever heard.... Although the Surratts were his personal friends, he was forced to appear and testify when subpoenaed. He realized deeply the sanctity of the oath he had taken to tell the truth, the whole truth, and nothing but the truth, and his testimony could not be confused or shaken in the slightest detail.[8]

At least one member of the military commission at the trial thought Lloyd's testimony was even more damaging to Mrs. Surratt than Weichmann's. General Thomas M. Harris later wrote that if her fate had depended on Weichmann alone, "not a hair of her head would have been harmed. The man who did the mischief was John M. Lloyd."[9]

All of the evidence against Mrs. Surratt was circumstantial. The strongest evidence we have of her outright involvement in the Booth conspiracy is Lloyd's statements about the "shooting irons." Louis Weichmann said he was present on both occasions when Mrs. Surratt allegedly made this statement to Lloyd, but both times Weichmann said he didn't hear what was said, even though Weichmann was sitting beside Mrs. Surratt in a "buggy," which is, by definition, a small carriage. Sitting next to Mrs. Surratt, perhaps even close enough to touch her, the naturally curious Weichmann says he could not hear what she said. In his testimony against Dr. Samuel A. Mudd, Weichmann described their meeting:

> Mr. Surratt introduced Dr. Mudd to me; and Dr. Mudd introduced Mr. Booth, who was in company with him, to both of us.... Booth then invited us to his room at the National Hotel.... Dr. Mudd ... went out into the passage, and called Booth out, and had a private conversation with him. Booth and Dr. Mudd came in, and they then called [John] Surratt out.... Booth went out with Surratt; and then they came in, and all three went out together, and had a private conversation in the passage, leaving me alone.... I do not know the nature of the conversation.... Booth at one time took out the back of an envelope, and made marks on it with a pencil. I should not consider it writing, but more in the direction of roads or lines. Surratt and Booth and Dr. Mudd were at that time seated round the table,—a centre table—in the centre of the room.
>
> Q. But you did not hear a word spoken yourself ... in their conference?
> A. No, Sir; I do not know the nature of the conversation they had at all.

Although he was in the same hotel room with Booth, John Surratt, and Dr. Mudd, who Weichmann tells us were in the center of the room, he couldn't hear what they were saying.[10] We do not know the exact dimensions of the hotel room, but it is hard to believe that the room was so big that a conversation, taking place in the middle of the room, even with lowered voices, would have been totally inaudible to Weichmann. We might have cause to wonder whether Weichmann suffered from selective hearing loss. He never claimed to have any such condition. A curious case, for a twenty-three-year-old to have such a loss of his hearing, and only on certain crucial occasions.

In his statement dated April 23, 1865, taken by Old Capitol Prison Superintendent William P. Wood (1820–1903), Lloyd contradicted Weichmann, saying, "Weichmann was in the buggy with Mrs. Surratt and heard the conversation" on April 11. Lloyd stated that on Friday, April 14, "Weichmann was with Mrs. Surratt, but did not hear the conversation." On both occasions, Mrs. Surratt spoke of the "shooting irons."[11] Weichmann claimed he did not hear the conversation on either occasion. He never said that there were any distractions of any sort which could have accounted for his failure to hear these conversations at such close quarters.

An examination of statements by Weichmann and by those who knew him may shed light upon his role. An old friend of both Weichmann and John Surratt, Henri B. Ste. Marie, had this to say on May 23, 1865:

Lincoln's first attorney general, Edward Bates, disagreed with James Speed's opinion about the government's right to try the suspects by a military commission.

> I have known Weichmann at Ellen Gowan, a small village fifteen miles from Baltimore.... He and Surratt visited me there in the Spring of 1863.... By their conversation understood they were strong secessionists and more particularly Weichmann.... Surratt then told me that his house [the tavern in Surrattsville] was the rendezvous of all the land blockade-runners to Richmond—that he often went to Richmond and was in communication with prominent men there. Weichmann, a base low-minded and presumptuous man, often acknowledged his sympathy for the South and his intention to go there. Weichmann and Surratt were intimate friends, and I do not understand how blind the [military] commission is not to arrest him at once.[12]

An official report on Weichmann by William P. Wood, superintendent of Old Capitol Prison, echoed this information:

> Up to his arrest Sunday, April 30, 1865, [Weichmann] was in the employ of the government in the office of the Commissary General of Prisoners. From that office I am satisfied he has frequently purloined important papers which have been forwarded to Richmond by or through John Surratt.[13]

One of Weichmann's colleagues at work, Gilbert J. Raynor, sat in front of Weichmann in the office. Weichmann told him how he could make money, "twenty or thirty thousand dollars."[14]

Weichmann had a more explicit conversation with another co-worker, Daniel H.L. Gleason, who said:

His desk is next to mine.... He came and said, "I want your advice about some things." He had been acquainted, he said, since the war began more or less with blockade-runners.... He said there was a party who were getting up some enterprise.... Although they had not asked him to join them he thought he could.... I told him I thought he should if for a good purpose. I said, "You better go to the provost marshal's office here, lay open this plot and then get the sanction of that officer and then join them to expose the whole." He said he thought it would be too much risk. He is a man that I put very little confidence in in regard to what he said.... He never gave me to understand what the nature of the plot was.... At one time he thought it was the assassination of all the officials.... He spoke to me about this plot before the inauguration.... He ... dropped the name of Booth as one of this party.[15]

A letter from one of Weichmann's lady acquaintances, "Clara," provides interesting implications:

I have often thought of you lately, and sincerely hope your prospects are fair for gaining the heart you seem to covet. You see I understand your affectionate remarks about Mr. Surratt, and the conclusion: "I love him, indeed I do, and his sister too."[16]

Did Weichmann have a romantic interest in Mrs. Surratt's daughter Anna? If this letter is genuine it seems to suggest this possibility. Under questioning by Secretary Stanton, Weichmann described a dispute he had had with Anna Surratt (1843–1904) before the assassination. Weichmann said they argued about politics, about his pro–Union attitude, an argument strong enough to cause Anna to slap Weichmann's face.[17] Once again, we have only Weichmann's account of what happened. The important thing is that Weichmann's interest in Anna was obviously not returned. Might that have embittered him toward the Surratts? On the other hand, could such a rejection have injured him so much that he wanted to see Mrs. Surratt and her son hanged? This possible rejection is not an explanation all by itself for Weichmann's testimony, but it might have made it less difficult for him to say what he did about his former friends.

Weichmann himself told about his association with a known Confederate spy named Augustus Spencer Howell (1837–1869):

I did not know what his business was, but I soon found out that he was in the habit of running the blockade from Maryland into Virginia.... He taught me a cipher which he said he learned from a magician's book, and had been familiar with for six or seven years.

At the conspiracy trial, when he was shown the cipher found among the effects of Booth, he said it was the same as he had taught me, and Booth's cipher, by the testimony of Mr. Charles A. Dana, was the same as that used by the Confederates. But I never made any use of it except to translate a few poems into it.[18]

John Surratt himself, who had good reason to denounce his former friend, described his sending a telegram to Booth, using only the initials "JWB"; he said:

> During our whole conversation we rarely wrote or telegraphed under our proper names, but always in such a manner that no one could understand but ourselves. One way of Booth's was to send letters to me under cover of my quondam friend, Louis J. Weichmann.... They were sent to him because he knew of the plot to abduct President Lincoln.... He had been told all about it, and was constantly importuning one to let him become an active member. I refused for the simple reason that I told him he could neither ride a horse nor shoot a pistol, which was a fact.... My refusal nettled him some; so he went off, ... and told some government clerk that he had a vague idea that there was a plan of some kind to abduct President Lincoln.... Booth sometimes was rather suspicious of him, and asked me if I thought he could be trusted. Said I, "certainly he can. Weichmann is a Southern man.... He had furnished information for the Confederate government, besides allowing me access to the government records after office hours.

Edman Spangler said he was told by Atzerodt, Powell and Herold that Weichmann had given the conspirators information from the Commissary General of Prisoners office.[19]

John P. Brophy (1842–1914) was a friend of the Surratts but was not a party to any conspiracy. He also knew Weichmann. Years later he related events for a newspaper:

> When the trial was near its end, Mr. Brophy said, Louis J. Weichmann ... came to Mr. Brophy and wanted to know what the effect of his testimony had been. Mr. Brophy accused him of attempting to have an innocent woman killed, and Weichmann acknowledged to Mr. Brophy that he believed Mrs. Surratt to be innocent.... Mr. Brophy quotes the man [Weichmann] as saying: "Stanton gave me the choice between turning state's evidence and hanging. Terrified, I told what I had heard, and, although I believed Mrs. Surratt to be innocent, Mr. Stanton appeared to believe her guilty. I did not want to be hanged.[20]

Author R.Z. Chamlee tells us that

> Joseph Clark informed the War Department that "Louis Weichmann ... is in all probability an accomplice of Booth." ... When Stanton heard that Weichmann had been sent out of the country, he was furious and ordered him returned under guard immediately. Convinced that Weichmann was in on the conspiracy, Stanton was particularly irate with [A.C.] Richards [Metropolitan Police Superintendent] for having allowed him to go to Canada [in search of John Surratt] where he was free of United States jurisdiction.... The Secretary of War was so fearful that Weichmann might escape that he sent [Colonel John] Foster to question suspects imprisoned on the ironclads, hoping to get a clue as to Weichmann's involvement.

Chamlee quotes General Robert Foster (1834–1903), a member of the military commission, as saying, "It seems extremely improbable that Weichmann was ignorant of the entire plot, if he was not an accomplice."[21]

Colonel John A. Foster, of the War Department's Bureau of Military Justice, wrote of Weichmann, "He had frequent conversations with fellow clerks about the blockade-running business and the money that could be made out of it. About time of Inauguration, spoke of a plot to assassinate all the government officers."[22]

Weichmann himself made reference to his questioning in a letter to Judge Advocate Colonel Henry L. Burnett:

> You confused and terrified me so much yesterday that I was almost unable to say anything.... For God's sake do not confound the innocent with the guilty.[23]

Lewis J. Carland, an employee of Ford's Theatre, went walking with Weichmann after Weichmann had testified. At the trial of John Surratt, Carland testified that Weichmann had interrupted their walk, stopping at a church to make confession.

> Q. Did he say to you that he was going to confession to relieve his conscience?
> A. Yes, Sir; he did.
> Q. Did you say to him, "That is not the right way, Mr. Weichmann, you had better go to a magistrate and make a statement under oath."
> A. I did.
> Q. Do you remember his replying to you, "I would take that course if I were not afraid of being indicted for perjury."?
> A. He did make that remark to me, and I then asked him the particulars. He said if he had been let alone, and had been allowed to give his statement as he had wanted to, it would have been quite a different affair with Mrs. Surratt than what it was....
> Q. Did he say to you that he had been obliged to swear to the statement that had been prepared for him, and that he was threatened with prosecution for perjury—threatened with being charged as one of the conspirators unless he did?
> A. Yes, Sir; he did; that it was written out for him, and that he was threatened with prosecution as one of the conspirators if he did not swear to it.[24]

John Thompson Ford (1829–1894), the theatre owner, was arrested after the assassination and held at Carroll Prison for thirty-nine days. While he was there he met and talked with both Weichmann and Lloyd.

> [I] was, by what I heard from them, convinced of [Mrs. Surratt's] innocence of any knowledge of or complicity in the assassination of President Lincoln.... Weichmann sought advice from [me], saying that Secretary

Stanton had, in a threatening manner, expressed the opinion "that [Weichmann's] hands had as much of the president's blood on them as Booth's." ... Of Lloyd, several there said that ... he had been threatened with torture, and intimidated that he had to say what he did to secure relief.

[Lloyd] was quite drunk the evening of the 14th of April ... before he started for home, where he met Mrs. Surratt.[25]

We have already heard Lloyd say that he was "quite positive she asked me about the 'shooting irons,'" but the next line of his testimony is revealing. "I am quite positive about that, but not altogether positive." A few pages later, Lloyd is again asked about the weapons, and again qualifies his answer in a very ambiguous way:

Q. The word "carbine" was not mentioned?
A. No. She finally came out, and, I am quite positive, *but cannot be determined about it* that she said "shooting irons" [italics added by author].

Later, Lloyd announces again that he is "very positive that she named 'shooting irons' on both occasions," but then qualifies his statement yet again, saying "not so positive as to the first [occasion] as I am about the last."[26]

Was he positive or not?

In his testimony at the trial of John Surratt in 1867, Lloyd's account became even more shaky.

Q. I believe you were a witness before the conspiracy trial, were you not?
A. Yes, Sir; unfortunately.

Twice, when asked if he knew John Surratt and his mother, Lloyd said, "My acquaintance with them was very short the whole time." When asked to relate again about the meetings with Mrs. Surratt, including the "shooting irons" remark, Lloyd said: "I do not wish to state one solitary word more than I am compelled to." Finally, after some prodding by the attorneys and the judge, Lloyd stated: "As well as I recollect, in speaking of the shooting irons, she told me to have them ready; that they would be called for, or wanted soon, I forget now which."

When Lloyd said he told Mrs. Surratt he was uneasy about having the weapons at the tavern and was tempted to take them out and bury them, he said she changed the subject and "laughed very heartily" at the idea of John Surratt going to Richmond. This might seem to be an odd response by someone whose mission allegedly was to instruct Lloyd to have the weapons ready, weapons which would be very important to the fleeing assassins.

Lloyd was asked about the events of April 14, 1865. His replies compare unfavorably with what he said two years before at the trial of the conspiracy suspects.

> Q. What time did you return home?
> A. I staid in Marlboro' for some time ... drinking and playing cards.... I suppose it was five or six o'clock, maybe later, when I got home. I do not remember distinctly, but it appears to me *in the confused memory I have of it,* that the sun was not more than half an hour high when I got home.... When I drove up in my buggy to the back yard, Mrs. Surratt came out to meet me.... [She] told me, as well as I remember, to get the guns, or those things—I really forget now which, though my impression is that "guns" was the expression she made use of ... ["guns," not "shooting irons"?]
> Q. What did you say to her?
> A. I do not know that I made any reply to her at all. *I was in liquor at the time,* and being so, I did not want to have any conversation with her [italics added by the author].
> Q. How long did she stay there after this?
> A. I do not remember. I went into my back room and threw myself on the lounge, when I immediately turned sick from the effect of the liquor.

A little later, Lloyd again refers to his poor memory.

> Q. Have you testified to-day to the same facts you testified to before the military commission?
> A. I may have been mistaken in some of them. My memory is not sufficient to go back over the whole that has transpired here.

The following exchange is on the record of the trial of John Surratt; Lloyd's extraordinary admission which, for a telling moment, draws back the curtain to reveal the truth:

> Q. Will you state whether or not, at the time of, or prior to, your examination before Colonel Wells, or at the time of or before your examination before Colonel Foster, any offer of reward was held out to you in regard to your evidence, or any threats used in reference to your testimony?
> A. While I was in Carroll Prison, this military officer came there and told me he wanted me to make a statement, as near as I remember.... He said that [my previous statement] was not full enough....
> Q. Did he say anything to you in the way of offering a reward, or use any threat toward you, for the purpose of getting you to make it fuller?
> A. When I told him what I had repeated before, that I did not remember any person saying thus and so, he jumps up very quick off his seat, as if very mad, and asking me if I knew what I was guilty of. I told him, under the circumstances I did not. *He said you are guilty as an accessory to a crime the punishment of which is death* [italics added by the author].

Here is an admission by the prosecution that they believed Lloyd was guilty and could be prosecuted.

We can infer that the reason for, or at least a contributing factor to

Lloyd's poor memory, was alcohol. The following exchange brings this out, and in Lloyd's own words. They are speaking of the evening of April 14, 1865.

> Q. Had you not been drinking during the day?
> A. I do not think I drank anything until the court adjourned. I knew what effect liquor had on me.
> Q. What effect has it?
> A. A very singular effect, upon my mind chiefly. *It makes me forget a great many things.*
> Q. How much did you drink after the court adjourned?
> A. I drank enough to make me drunk.
> Q. Were you very drunk?
> A. *I was so drunk that when I lay down I felt sick.* I could not lie down....
> Q. How long after Mrs. Surratt went away did you lie down?
> A. *I lay down before she left* [italics added by the author].
> Q. Did you not take something to drink after she went away that night?
> A. I have no doubt I did.
> Q. Don't you recollect it?
> A. I am not positive about it. I may have done so. I was drinking very freely....
> Q. Did you keep liquors at the bar?
> A. I did.... Unfortunately for me, I was the best customer.[27]

Another witness, Joseph T. Knott, a bartender at the Surratt Tavern while Lloyd was managing it, shed additional light on Lloyd's drunkenness. This testimony is from the 1865 trial of the conspiracy suspects.

> Q. Did you see Mr. Lloyd on the 14th of last April?
> A. Yes, sir.
> Q. At what time in the day?
> A. I saw him in the morning, and I saw him again just before sundown.
> Q. What was Mr. Lloyd's condition at that time?
> A. He was pretty tight....
> Q. Has Mr. Lloyd been in the habit, for weeks past, of drinking a great deal?
> A. Yes, sir; Mr. Lloyd drank a great deal.
> Q. Has he been drunk for almost every day for some time past?
> A. Yes, sir.
> Q. State how that was.
> A. *He was pretty tight nearly every day, and night too* [italics added by author].
> Q. Did he or not really have the appearance of an insane man from drink?
> A. He had at times.[28]

We saw from Lloyd's testimony at the trial of John Surratt that he had been threatened. The government knew Lloyd had not told everything he knew. When soldiers first questioned him shortly after Booth and Herold stopped at the tavern, Lloyd said no one had been there that night. It was a few days before he admitted he knew anything about the assassination.²⁹ Once he began talking, there was no longer any doubt that he was involved in the conspiracy, as in this excerpt from a telegram sent by Samuel H. Beckwith (1839–1916), General Grant's telegrapher, to Thomas T. Eckert (1825–1910), head of the War Department Telegraph Office:

> Port Tobacco, MD, April 24, 1865—10 a.m.
> John M. Lloyd has been arrested, and virtually acknowledged complicity.³⁰

Detective George Cottingham, who had interviewed Lloyd, wrote,

> John M. Lloyd is accessory to the murder of President Lincoln before and after the deed. He concealed firearms in his house brought by [John] Surratt. He has also given aid and comfort to Booth and Herreld [sic] and furnished them with additional firearms after Booth had told him that he had murdered the president. He ... denied everything until they had affected [sic] their escape and knew where they had gone. He had remained two days in the guardhouse before he made his confession.... He told me if he made his confession that they would murder him.... Lloyd afterwards admitted to me that he concealed the carbine in the place where it was found [at the Surratt Tavern] through fear of being implicated in the affair.

Another detective, J.W. Ridenour, asked Cottingham about Lloyd's confession. "Lloyd [was] charged with aiding and abetting with others in the assassination of the president. I was informed by the said Cottingham that the said Lloyd had made a confession of his guilt. I inquired of the said Cottingham how it was obtained. His answer was, 'I dragged it out of Lloyd.'"

Together, these statements indicate that Lloyd was as guilty as anyone in aiding the assassins. A case could have been made against him which could be considered to have been stronger than that against either Mrs. Surratt or Dr. Mudd. Ridenour's statement also suggests that Lloyd's confession may have been obtained under duress.³¹

We have already seen where William P. Wood referred to Weichmann's arrest and John Ford described how he met and conversed with both Weichmann and Lloyd in prison before the trial. Why did the government not prosecute either Weichmann or Lloyd? At the time, a prisoner charged with a crime could not also be a witness. If Weichmann and Lloyd had been charged and placed in the prisoner's dock along with the others at the trial of the conspiracy suspects, they could not have told their stories about Mrs. Surratt. Without Weichmann's testimony of Mrs. Surratt meeting with the conspirators, including Booth himself, without his statements about her vague remarks which seemed to be hints that she knew all about the conspiracy, without Lloyd's "shooting irons," there would have been very little else to support charges against Mrs. Surratt, certainly not enough to hang her. Weichmann's testimony had also been a powerful part of the case against Dr. Mudd. The government needed Weichmann and Lloyd to seal the fate of Mrs. Surratt, and it was not above threatening them with the noose if they didn't cooperate.

After the John Surratt trial, Lloyd returned to his former trade of bricklaying, which he continued to practice until he was injured falling from a scaffold, the bricks coming down on top of him, causing head and internal injuries. He died about two weeks after the accident, on his birthday, December 18, 1892. After a funeral mass at St. Dominic's church at 6th and E Streets, John M. Lloyd was buried at Mt. Olivet Cemetery in Washington. His grave is about fifty yards from that of Mrs. Surratt.[32]

After the trial of the conspiracy suspects, Weichmann found himself out of work and without money. On August 4, 1865, he wrote to Secretary of War Edwin M. Stanton for help in "procuring a situation for a few months, at least, in the Custom House or post office of this city [Philadelphia] or of Boston." His plea was filed on August 16 and went without an answer.[33] On December 27 Weichmann wrote to the commission deciding the distribution of rewards, saying:

> It was my intention on leaving Washington not to ask for any reward for I desire everyone to understand that I acted solely from principle; but when I reflect how shamefully my father's family and I have been treated, how my brother was banished from a religious institution, how I have been vilified by a disloyal press, how I was abused when in October last I exercised the right of sufferage; all this because I sustained the government in its darkest hour.... The Government has indeed been very kind to me for through the indefatigable exertion of Judge Holt I was lately appointed to a position in the Custom House of this city [Philadelphia]. This kindness can never be repaid.[34]

Of course, it can be said that Weichmann had already been paid in advance.

Weichmann's sisters, Mrs. Philomena O'Crowley and Tillie Weichmann, told author Lloyd Lewis (1891–1949) that their brother received "letters attacking him" and people made "ugly remarks" to the sisters about their brother and the rest of the family. The sisters maintained that there were attempts made on Lou Weichmann's life.[35]

Dismissed from the Custom House late in 1866, Weichmann worked part-time for a newspaper, the *Globe,* and also received money from the War Department, thanks to Judge Holt. When John Surratt was captured in Egypt, Weichmann volunteered to go there to help identify his former friend. His offer was declined as unnecessary, but Weichmann did testify at the trial of John Surratt in 1867.[36] His testimony was so similar to what he had said at the original trial that he could state where it appeared in the published record of the trial, leading to the following exchange:

Q. Then you have examined carefully the testimony that you gave down there?
A. I have studied it over the last two years. You do not suppose that such an incident as that is an every-day incident in my life, and that I have not been thinking of it....
Q. Have you not written out a very full statement within the last few months?
A. Yes, sir; I thought it was my duty.
Q. Have you not read it over more than once?
A. Yes, sir; I have read it over several times.[37]

If Weichmann had been coached, or provided with a statement to memorize, his rereading it "over several times," would have been a natural thing to do in preparing for the second trial.

When Republicans returned to the White House in 1869, Weichmann returned to his position at the Philadelphia Custom House, where he was employed until 1886. Moving to Anderson, Indiana, Weichmann opened the Anderson Business School, where he taught shorthand, bookkeeping, and languages. His income was supplemented by his obtaining a position as stenographer for the Indiana Republican State Committee, from March to December of 1888. General Lew Wallace (1827–1905), a former member of the military commission at the trial of the conspiracy suspects, and by this time the acclaimed author of *Ben-Hur*, obtained the appointment for Weichmann. Although he might have gotten a position in the Harrison administration in 1889, Weichmann did not want to return to Washington.[38]

In his later years, Weichmann kept up a correspondence with several people who had been involved in the assassination investigation and trials. Weichmann began writing a history of the assassination, with emphasis on his part in the story. Again and again he asserts his honesty and truthfulness, and he included letters and comments tending to support his assertions from Joseph Holt, John F. Hartranft, Henry L. Burnett, Lew Wallace, James A. Ekin, August V. Kautz, George P. Fisher, A.C. Richards, James McPhail, William D. Kelley, and others. Although he considered publishing his book, he had not done so by the time of his death, and the manuscript remained with his family until its publication in 1975.[39]

Corresponding with Osborn H. Oldroyd (1842–1930) about the latter's book, which Oldroyd published in 1901, Weichmann wrote Oldroyd, "Your book ... will have an immense sale and hence I am anxious for you to have the exact truth in every respect. There have been so many lies told about the thing that it is time there should be a little volume before the public telling the truth and representing the government."[40] "I am pleased to read that your book will place me all right in the minds of the public. This is what I desire above all else."[41] "I would like to have the privilege of correcting the proof of my own article.... There is only one side for you to present, and that is the side of the government, of truth and decency."[42]

From this correspondence we learn that the chapter in Oldroyd's book which deals with Weichmann was entirely written by Weichmann himself, including proofing. Note, also, that he maintains that his version represents "truth and decency." Throughout his writings, Weichmann was especially eager to assure the reader that he was always telling the truth, an eagerness which at times almost amounts to near desperation.

Commander of the Arsenal John F. Hartranft was the chief jailer of the conspiracy suspects. He tried to provide humane treatment, especially for Mrs. Surratt.

He continued to operate his business school until the last weeks of his life. He became ill on June 5, 1902, and seeming to sense that his end was near, he sent for his brother, Father Frederick C. Weichmann, to give him the last rights of the church. He died at 7:45 that evening, at the home of his sister, Mrs. Philomena O'Crowley, with his brother and other sister, Matilda, also present. On his death bed, he told a friend, H.J. Creighton, that "he wished the people of this country to understand that in the great trial, and while on the witness stand, he told the truth and nothing but the truth."[43]

It is not possible now to say whether or not Mary Surratt was guilty of being one of the key figures of the conspiracy against Lincoln, or was a totally innocent woman whose denunciation and execution was a brutal injustice. As we have seen, in the testimony by and about both Weichmann and Lloyd, doubt cannot be banished. We have evidence that the government knew all about this doubt, knew about the possibility of involvement in the crime by both men, and yet chose to proceed with its case against

Mrs. Surratt, vigorously fighting all the efforts of her defenders. Truth is famously elusive, and it is unlikely that anyone will ever be able to discover exactly what was the truth about Mary Surratt, but we should remember that, in our legal system, and in history, too, one must be proven to be guilty, beyond a reasonable doubt.

Louis Weichmann may have felt that he was speaking to future generations when he wrote, "I submit everything to your judgment and will be content with your decision for I am aware that you will do what is just."[44]

7

VERDICT

The military commission met on June 29, 1865, in closed session to deliberate and reach their verdicts, and continued the following day. Holt, Bingham and Burnett deliberated with them, a practice provided for under military law, in which the prosecutors became "legal advisors" to the commission, most of whose members were not lawyers. The defense lawyers were not allowed to be present at these deliberations.

On June 30, 1865, the decisions on the fate of the defendants were announced. All eight were found guilty. David E. Herold, George A. Atzerodt, Lewis Powell, and Mary E. Surratt were sentenced "to be hanged by the neck until he/she be dead." Michael O'Laughlen, Samuel B. Arnold, and Dr. Samuel A. Mudd were "to be imprisoned at hard labor for life." Edman Spangler was "to be imprisoned at hard labor for six years." President Andrew Johnson was shown the record of the trial and approved both the record and the sentences on July 5, 1865, ordering that the executions be held on July 7.[1]

The deliberations of the military commission were held in secret. No official record was made of what was said, but one member of the commission, Brigadier General August V. Kautz, left notes which help to illuminate for us the thinking of the members, who were serving as both judges and jurors.

> The court met as a rule in the morning, and sat until after six p.m., usually taking a recess about noon for lunch which the Secretary of War had served for us in an adjoining room to save time and the necessity of our going back to the city. Ambulances were supplied by the Q.M. [Quartermaster] Dept. to take us to and from the court room to our rooms. This was the daily program. The weather soon became very warm and the confinement was very trying on account of the number of visitors that were permitted by pass to visit the courtroom, preventing the free circulation of the air.
> ... We worked very faithfully and there was very little leisure, often sitting until near seven o'clock in the evening, and rarely adjourning before six.

> ... The evidence was very clear as to the conspiracy and that all the parties arraigned were connected with it in various ways. The original and avowed object was a conspiracy to kidnap the president and it was so understood by nearly all concerned. The testimony showed J. Wilkes Booth and John Surratt to be the heads of the conspiracy. The order to kill did not go forth until about eight o'clock p.m. on the 14th of April. There was evidence produced that tended to show that the heads of the Confederate government knew of the conspiracy and also that the agents of the same in Canada were cognizant of it.
>
> ... An attempt was made at the close to prove insanity on the part of Payne [Powell], who finally defeated the attempt of his counsel by maintaining his sanity, that he knew what he was doing when he tried to kill Mr. Seward. The interest of the case centered mostly about Mrs. Surratt and Payne. Dr. Mudd attracted much interest and his guilt as an active conspirator was not clearly made out. His main guilt was the fact that he failed to deliver them, that is, Booth and Herold, to their pursuers.
>
> Mrs. Surratt was shown to have been active in the conspiracy to kidnap, prior to the capture of Richmond. That she was a willing participant in his [Lincoln's] death was not clearly made out. My own impression was that she was involved in the final result against her will by her previous connection with the conspiracy.... [Booth] no doubt, held most of his confederates in the conspiracy under the impression that it was organized for the purpose of kidnapping, who would have been deterred if they had known that they might be required to kill.

Kautz wrote his impressions of the accused, seemingly based as much upon their physical appearance as upon the evidence presented against them. Powell "was a sullen character whose expression rarely changed ... how much moral character there was in his makeup was not apparent on the surface." Atzerodt "looked the hired assassin and the testimony went to show that he failed to perform his part of the compact ... either from want of courage or want of sufficient intelligence. He excited no sympathy from anyone." In saying this, it almost seems that Kautz is holding it against Atzerodt that he did not attempt assassination. "Dr. Mudd was the most intelligent looking and attracted the most attention of all the prisoners." "Spangler does not seem to have been a conspirator knowingly. He was simply a tool of Booth's.... His greatest crime was his ignorance and that he did not see the ends to which he was being used." If Spangler was not a conscious conspirator, would that not argue for his innocence? "Arnold ... was a good looking, amiable young man, who seemed to have gotten into bad company. The same degree and character of guilt applied to O'Laughlen." Again, does this sound as if Arnold and O'Laughlen deserved a sentence of life imprisonment at hard labor?

Kautz also confirmed that the prosecution were tools of Stanton. "The Judge Advocates, under the influence of the Secretary of War,

Lewis Powell, known by the alias "Payne," attacked Secretary Seward and others at the Seward home, seriously wounding three of them. Powell seemed the most composed of all the defendants during the trial. Engraving from *Harper's Weekly* April 27, 1865, from a photograph by Alexander Gardner.

evidently, were very persevering and wanted evidently to have the seven [eight] prisoners all hung. They were very much put out when a paper was signed by a majority of the commission recommending Mrs. Surratt to executive clemency on account of her sex. We, who signed it, did not deem it wise or expedient to hang her." This raises the question of whether the members of the commission were sincere in voting to convict all the defendants, and really wanted the harsh penalties imposed to be carried out. General Kautz further states, "It was apparent to me ... that there would be a reaction and that those who were instrumental in causing [Mrs. Surratt's] execution would regret that they had permitted Mrs. Surratt to be hung."

The idea that military trials would be faster and provide a surer chance of success for convictions, an issue which we will confront again in Chapter 9, is suggested by Kautz in his account of the Lincoln conspiracy trial: "It [a military trial] was the only way for [a] speedy result which the loyal spirit of the country seemed to demand at the time. The result of the trial of John Surratt by the civil courts a few years later [1867], go to show that the civil courts could not have been depended upon for a speedy result in this remarkable case."[2] The trial of John H. Surratt, Jr., was convened on June 10, 1867, and ended on August 10, ninety-four days later. By comparison, the 1865 trial convened on June 9, 1865, and ended June 30, twenty-two days later. While the first trial was certainly shorter, it must be noted that the second trial involved more testimony by a larger number of witnesses. The important thing about the contrasting trials is not their length, but the fact that the John Surratt trial, held in a federal court with a jury, and consisting of much of the same evidence as had been presented at the first trial, resulted in the jury being unable to reach a verdict.

General Kautz called the military trial a "remarkable case," and we can certainly agree with him that it was remarkable, as was his admission of this fact, since he suggested that the trial of the conspiracy suspects was basically a show trial, the verdict and sentences decided in advance.

Although Mrs. Surratt's lawyers, Clampitt and Aiken, had been congratulated for their defense by some of their legal colleagues, some of whom stated their belief that their client, Mrs. Surratt, would be acquitted, the verdict not only went against them, but Mrs. Surratt was condemned to hang. Clampitt and Aiken only heard about this in the late afternoon of July 6, 1865. The execution was scheduled for the following day. The two attorneys immediately sought an audience with President Johnson, but were denied. They sought the intercession of Judge Advocate General Joseph Holt, who told them the president was unyielding.[3]

7. Verdict

A petition had been prepared by the military commission requesting that the president of the United States commute the sentence of Mrs. Surratt. The petition read:

> To the President: The undersigned, members of the military commission appointed to try the persons charged with the murder of Abraham Lincoln, etc., respectfully represent that the commission have been constrained to find Mary E. Surratt guilty, upon the testimony, of the assassination of Abraham Lincoln, late President of the United States, and to pronounce upon her, as required by law, the sentence of death; but, in consideration of her age and sex, the undersigned pray your Excellency, if it is consistent with your sense of duty, to commute her sentence to imprisonment for life in the penitentiary.

The petition was signed by commission members Major General David Hunter, Brevet Major General August V. Kautz, Brigadier General Robert S. Foster, Brevet Brigadier General James A. Ekin, and Brevet Colonel Charles H. Tomkins. Who actually wrote the petition is uncertain, some saying General Ekin, other sources naming Special Judge Advocate John A. Bingham. Copies exist in the handwriting of both men. The petition was attached to the official record of the trial, in the keeping of the Judge Advocate General, Joseph Holt, who had headed the prosecution team.

Holt met with President Andrew Johnson at the White House on July 5, 1865, bringing a summary of the record of the trial for the president to study. Guards were posted to prevent any interruption as Holt went immediately to the War Department, where he announced to Secretary of War Edwin M. Stanton that the president "has approved the findings and sentences of the court." President Johnson ordered that all four prisoners sentenced to hang would be executed, with the date set for July 7. Pleas for mercy for Mrs. Surratt were directed to Johnson, but all but one were turned aside, and the president remained steadfast in his desire to punish the woman.

It was two years later, at the trial of John Surratt, that the controversy over the military commission's plea for mercy for Mrs. Surratt really began. Joseph H. Bradley, Sr. (1803–1887), John Surratt's lawyer, mentioned it prominently in his summation, and strongly suggested that the truth about it was being suppressed. "President Johnson, President of the United States, when that record was presented to him, laid it before his cabinet, and every single member voted to confirm the sentence, and that the president, with his own hand, wrote his confirmation of it, and with his own hand signed the warrant ... and when it was suggested by some of the members of the commission that in consequence of the age and sex of

Mrs. Surratt it might possibly be well to change her sentence to imprisonment for life, he signed the warrant for her death with the paper right before his eyes." The prosecutor, Edwards Pierrepont (1817–1892), confirmed Bradley's account. "I sent ... to the Judge Advocate General, in whose possession these records are. He brought it to me with his own hand, and told me with his own voice, in the presence of three other gentlemen, that the identical paper, then a part of the record, was before the president when he signed the warrant of execution, and that he had a conversation with the president at that time on the subject."

President Johnson ordered that the trial records be sent to him on August 5, 1867. Included was the petition of the military commission for mercy for Mrs. Surratt. Upon examining that document, Johnson told his secretary, "He was positive that it had never before been brought to his knowledge or notice.... He felt satisfied that it had been designedly withheld from his ... knowledge."

Holt then began a long campaign to discredit the suggestion that he had failed to show the petition to the president. He defended himself in the Washington *Daily Morning Chronicle* of August 26, 1873, and issued his argument as a pamphlet, *Vindication of Hon. Joseph Holt Judge Advocate General of the United States Army.* Holt secured letters from several witnesses which he presented as proof that he had shown Johnson the petition. James Harlan (1820–1899) and James Speed (1812–1887), former members of Johnson's cabinet, offered some corroboration, though they did not make unequivocal claims in support of Holt. Johnson formally replied on November 12, 1873, producing his own witnesses. Holt had mentioned that Secretaries William H. Seward (1801–1872) and Edwin M. Stanton (1814–1869) had told Bingham that the petition had been discussed by the cabinet. Johnson pointed out that by 1873 both of these men were dead and thus unable to speak for themselves. Johnson noted that he had been very ill at the time and had not met with his cabinet between June 30 and July 7, 1865. Former Navy Secretary Gideon Welles (1802–1878) confirmed that no cabinet meeting had taken place at that time. Johnson further made much of the fact that the petition had not been included in Benn Pitman's (1822–1910) official record of the trial, stating that either the Pitman transcript or Holt must be untrue.

The debate over who was telling the truth, Johnson or Holt, went on for years and was never definitely resolved. John W. Clampitt, one of Mrs. Surratt's attorneys, wrote, "It is doubtless true that the recommendation for mercy was not placed before the president with the findings of the commission at the time they were presented for his approval, but was retained by those in authority, who sought the blood of this innocent woman."

Holt turned to former Attorney General Speed, stating his case firmly against Speed's reluctance to discuss what may or may not have been said in a cabinet meeting. "The relations between a President and his cabinet are relations of honor, and that, therefore, they cannot be held to oblige any member in it—any criminal or wrongful act into which the president may be drawn, by a guilty ambition or by any other unworthy passion or purpose.... No custom or usage can possibly impose upon you as a duty an obligation to stand guard over and shield, by your silence, from exposure, a base falsehood ... destroying the reputation of an officer of the government performing a public service in his presence." After much delay and excuse making, Speed finally replied, "Certain it is, that I never saw such a document [the petition] in the president's hands or at any other place." Holt, unwilling to give up on his best witness, sought to remind Speed of the circumstances of the occasion, that Speed had seen Holt meeting with the president and showing him the petition. He again appealed to Speed, in the strongest language, to respond as requested. In reply, Speed stated that President Johnson had told him not to disclose anything, and had never released him from that promise. When Holt published this correspondence in 1888, Speed's family published an excerpt from a speech delivered by Speed only two months before his death in 1887, in which he said, "Judge Holt performed his duty kindly and considerately. In every particular he was just and fair. This I know. But Judge Holt needs no vindication from me nor any one else. I only speak because I know reflections have been made, and because my position enabled me to know the facts, and because I know the perfect purity and uprightness of his conduct."

John T. Ford, the theatre owner, in commenting on the Holt-Speed exchange, kept the pressure on, saying, "It is far more important to history that Mrs. Surratt should be vindicated before the world than that Judge Holt should be exculpated from his share in her hanging, for which exculpation he begged so piteously from Attorney-General Speed. The living can write and talk, but the dead must depend on the supreme right of legal justice either to justify or condemn their fate."

The argument continues to this day over whether Holt or Johnson told the truth. The preponderance of evidence, as well as logic, would seem to lean in the direction of Holt. Newspapers referred to the petition at the time, and shortly after the execution. General Winfield S. Hancock attempted to get Johnson to commute the sentence, as did John T. Ford.

Johnson must have known that he had the authority to commute the sentence; if he did not know that, he could have asked Holt, Speed, or Stanton. Johnson did not need the petition to commute the sentence if he had wanted to, and the fact that he did not is consistent with his statements, both at the time of the trial and later, that he believed Mrs. Surratt to be guilty and deserving of punishment. The public was angry and shocked at the death of Lincoln, as well as over the long and bloody war, and was not in a mood to be merciful or forgiving. Johnson the politician was well aware of that. Why he did not say so instead of insisting that he had not seen the petition, we will probably never know. Either way, the petition alone would not have saved Mrs. Surratt from her fate.[4]

Little sympathy was shown for the three men, Herold, Atzerodt, and Powell, public attention centering on Mrs. Surratt. The United States government had never before executed a woman, and she was the only one of those four whose guilt could be called into question.

Around noon on July 6, the military commanders having authority over the prisoners visited them in their cells at the Washington Arsenal. General Hancock, commander of the army's Department of the East, and General Hartranft, provost marshal general in charge of the prison, made their rounds.

Winfield Scott Hancock (1824–1886), Union major general, commander of the Washington, D.C., area, was the senior military officer overseeing the execution of the conspirators. Born in Montgomery Square, Pennsylvania, on February 14, 1824, Hancock grew up in nearby Norristown. Appointed to West Point in 1840, he graduated eighteenth in his class of twenty-five in 1844. His early military career included the Mexican War, fighting the Seminole Indians, and quartermaster duties in Utah and California.

He was promoted to brigadier general late in 1861, and his brigade took part in the Peninsular Campaign. A division commander at Sharpsburg, he became a major general at the end of 1862. After playing important roles at the battles of Fredericksburg and Chancellorsville, Hancock took command at Gettysburg until the arrival of Major General George G. Meade (1815–1872), providing crucial leadership in that battle that helped the Federal line to hold. Seriously wounded at Gettysburg, Hancock was out of action for some time and never fully recovered. After participation in the battles of the Wilderness and Petersburg, his wound required him to accept less strenuous duties.

As commander of the Middle Division, which included Washington, Hancock became the officer with ultimate responsibility for the military activities associated with the trial and punishment of the assassination conspirators. His "calmness and equipoise in the midst of excitement," which he had earlier shown on the battlefield, helped calm others. It was Hancock who had to receive the tearful Anna Surratt, seeking any source of hope for her mother, Mary Surratt. The general advised her to see President Andrew Johnson. Hancock's wife later reported that he had personally sought to change the president's mind and spare Mrs. Surratt. Because of his position, Hancock was required to appear in the Supreme Court of DC and refuse the writ of habeas corpus for Mrs. Surratt. Hoping up to the last moment for a reprieve, Hancock had horsemen posted to bring orders from the White House, but no word came.[5]

Major General John Frederick Hartranft (1830–1889) received an order saying "that Brevet Major General Hartranft be assigned to duty as Special Provost Marshal General for the purposes of said trial, and attendance upon said commission, and the execution of its mandates." His unenviable task was to serve as the Lincoln assassination conspirators' jailer and preside over the hanging of four of them.

Born near Pottstown, Pennsylvania, on December 16, 1830, Hartranft graduated from Union College in 1853 as a civil engineer. He then studied law, and he was admitted to the Montgomery County bar in 1860. Serving as a colonel of a regiment of Pennsylvania militia, he went on active duty on April 20, 1861. As part of General Ambrose Everett Burnside's (1824–1881) occupation of the North Carolina coast in 1862, Hartranft was promoted to brigadier general on May 12, 1864, after his service at the battle of Spottsylvania Court House. Commanding a division at Petersburg, Virginia, he repulsed the attack of the Confederate Second Corps on Fort Stedman, for which he was brevetted a major general.

As special provost marshal, the accused conspirators were placed directly in Hartranft's care, and it became Hartranft's duty to supervise the often severe treatment of them during their imprisonment and trial. As restrained and humane as he could be with the prisoners, he visited them and talked with them regularly. Especially solicitous of Mary Surratt, he denied the charges that he had permitted her to be chained. It was later reported that the general sent Mrs. Surratt the same food he was served, rather than have her eat the prison food. His consideration was also extended to Anna Surratt, daughter of the accused, when she became faint during the trial and had to be helped from the courtroom. His letter passing on the statement made to him by Lewis Powell, that Mrs. Surratt was innocent, was ignored by the court, and Hartranft was required to read the death sentences to the prisoners, including the woman he believed to be innocent.[6]

The first prisoner Generals Hancock and Hartranft visited was Powell, in cell 195, on the north side of the second tier. Powell was calm, and told the generals that he had been well treated as a prisoner, and that although he had originally believed in the rightness of what he had done, he now regretted his action. Atzerodt, in cell 161, south side of the second tier, turned pale upon being told his fate. His hands shook as he requested that a minister be allowed to see him. The reaction of Herold, in a cell in the third tier, was similar to that of Atzerodt. Denying his involvement in the assassination, he did express his allegiance to the South. When the generals told Mrs. Surratt, in cell 200, north side of the third tier, she sobbed uncontrollably at first, then, regaining some of her composure, requested that the following individuals be sent for: Father Jacob Ambrose Walter (1827–1894), of St. Patrick's church in Washington, Father Bernadin F. Wiget (1821–1883), president of Gonzaga College, and John P. Brophy (1842–1914), who taught at St. Aloysius School. She also wanted to see her daughter, Anna. Later that afternoon the four condemned prisoners were moved to ground tier cells on the south side.

It fell to a member of Hartranft's staff, Captain Christian Rath, to head the detail of soldiers who would carry out the execution. Rath went on duty at the Arsenal prison just before the trial began, and had been one of the officers involved with security during the trial. Although Rath had been ordered by General Hartranft to remain in the room when Anna Surratt visited her mother, Rath was moved by the stress the women displayed and allowed them privacy for about two hours. Mrs. Surratt kept up a brave front for her daughter, but collapsed in tears afterwards. Rath was surprised when told by Hartranft on July 6 that he needed to prepare to hang all four prisoners. He had expected that Mrs. Surratt would be spared. He also had to arrange for graves to be dug, near to the gallows in the prison yard. Rath personally tested the gallows to insure that all was in working order. Obtaining rope from the Navy Yard, Rath tied the knots in the 31-strand, ¾ inch Boston hemp, winding the knot seven times for the first three, but only five times for the fourth, saving himself the trouble, since he still could not believe that Mrs. Surratt would actually hang.[7]

All through the final hours, efforts were being made to save Mrs. Surratt's life. Several people tried to obtain an interview with the president to ask for mercy. Anna Surratt, refused at the White House, went to General Hancock, who did everything he could. John Brophy, likewise refused by the president, managed to obtain a visit with Lewis Powell, who expressed his belief that Mrs. Surratt was innocent. Brophy beseeched

The execution took place in the yard of the Washington Arsenal prison, beside the building where the trial had been held.

General Hartranft to hear Powell's statement. The general, believing Powell, wrote to the president and arranged for Brophy to deliver the note personally. He even promised Brophy he would try to delay the execution until he received word from the president. Anna Surratt, waiting at the White House after having been refused admittance to the president, met Brophy upon his arrival, allowing her hopes to be raised upon hearing of Powell's statement and Hartranft's note. But not only was Brophy refused admittance to see Johnson, he was even refused when he begged that anyone else show the note to the president. Adele Cutts Douglas (1835–1899), widow of Senator Stephen Arnold Douglas (1813–1861), arrived at the White House about this time and pushed her way past the guards. Johnson spoke with her, but would not change his mind. Mrs. Douglas again forced her way into the president's office to deliver Brophy's note from Hartranft, but again Johnson sent her away.

Mrs. Surratt's lawyers, Frederick Aiken and John W. Clampitt, were also pursuing last-minute legal efforts to save her. At the advice of their senior colleague on the defense team, Reverdy Johnson, they applied to Judge Andrew B. Wylie (1814–1905) of the Supreme Court of the District of Columbia, to issue a writ of habeas corpus, requiring the government to produce Mrs. Surratt before the Judge at 10 o'clock in the morning of July 7. Alluding to the political implications of this act, Judge Wylie told the young lawyers, "I am about to perform an act which, before tomorrow's sun goes down, may consign me to the Old Capitol Prison." In spite of that dangerous possibility, Judge Wylie signed the writ. At ten o'clock the next morning, General Hancock, accompanied by Attorney General James Speed, appeared before Judge Wylie with an Executive Order from the president suspending the writ. The execution would go on. Every plea, every legal remedy, all influence from the powerful and humble alike, had failed.

Abram Dunn Gillette (1807–1882), minister of the First Baptist Church in Washington, was sent to the Arsenal Prison by Secretary of War Stanton, to provide whatever spiritual comfort might be possible to the conspiracy prisoners before their execution. Gillette attended all of the condemned except Mary Surratt, who already had Catholic priests. He spoke for some time with Lewis Powell, who told him much about his life and about the conspiracy. Puzzled as to why Powell had asked for him, Gillette was told by Powell that he had heard Gillette preach and had been impressed. Staying with the prisoners throughout the night of July 6–7, 1865, Gillette was with them through the execution, offering a fervent prayer in behalf of Powell.

Gillette was born in Cambridge, Washington County, New York, on September 8, 1807. Largely self-educated before he attended Granville Academy, he furthered his education attending lectures at Union College. Making his living at first as a teacher, he became a Baptist minister in 1832, serving in churches in Schenectady, Philadelphia, New York City, and Washington. He also served as a manager of the American Baptist Publication Society from 1836 to 1848.

After visiting Atzerodt and Herold, Gillette returned to see Powell again and remained with him throughout much of that last night. Powell's stoical reserve and silence, maintained throughout his captivity, finally gave way, and Gillette learned many details about the prisoner's life. Powell had little new to say about the conspiracy, though he did admit to a realization of the terrible nature of the crime for which he had been condemned. Gillette observed that Powell, heretofore believed to be dull-witted, was actually intelligent and had had some education. Gillette's efforts to console Powell apparently were successful, for the prisoner appeared calm and dignified throughout his execution. Gillette wrote to Powell's father, offering information and what consolation he could to the elder Powell.[8]

Each of the condemned had clergymen with them in their final hours. Atzerodt was attended by the Reverend John George Butler (1826–1909) of the Lutheran Church, who spent the whole night with him. Herold received the services of the Reverend Olds of Christ Episcopal Church, and Powell was ministered to by the Reverend Gillette. Mrs. Surratt continued to have the services of Fathers J.A. Walter and B.F. Wiget. Atzerodt received visits from his brother and mother, and Herold was visited by five sisters the night before the execution, and by all seven sisters the following morning. Mrs. Surratt spent many hours with Anna and the faithful Brophy. Only Powell had no family or friends to visit with him. Curiously, Powell seemed the calmest of the four, even to the point of eating breakfast on his final morning, the only one of the four to do so.

July 7, 1865 was oppressively hot. On the high wall overlooking the prison yard soldiers were spaced closely together, all armed. In the yard itself were more soldiers, around 3,000 in all. Although many people had applied to witness the execution, very few had been allowed, beside the soldiers, and numerous officers and reporters were there with paper and pencils at the ready.

The scaffold was ready. It measured twenty feet long and twenty feet high from ground to the top of the beam, from which were suspended four ropes. The floor was ten feet above the ground and fifteen feet from front to back. Two drops, each four feet by six feet, were held up by supporting beams underneath. When the support beams were knocked loose, the hinged traps would fall. The bodies would drop six feet. Captain Rath had selected his men from the thousands available.

Although he denied knowing Booth, David E. Herold was captured with the assassin, tried and executed. Engraving from *Harper's Weekly*, July 1, 1865.

I chose two husky fellows to knock the posts from the platform under the drop. I instructed them in the signals, and everything went off without a hitch. Four others were chosen to place the nooses around the necks of the condemned, and I had three to lead the condemned men from their cells and bind them securely before they were executed. I had Lieutenant Colonel [William Henry Harrison] McCall [1841–1883] lead Mrs. Surratt from her cell to the gallows, as I didn't want an ordinary soldier to lay his hands on her. I told these men that they must volunteer their services, as I could not command them to take part in the gruesome work. I was simply overrun with volunteers; seemingly they regarded it as an honor to serve in any capacity in avenging the death of Lincoln. I told my men I would relieve them from all other duties for the day, and would, in addition, give them each a drink when the thing was over.

The four soldiers chosen by Rath were stationed beneath the scaffold. They were Corporal William E. Coxshall (1843–1922), Private Daniel F. Shoup (1839–1913), Private George F. Taylor (1835–1915), and Corporal Joseph B. Haslett (1841–1916), all of Company F, 14th Veteran Reserve Corps. Although they had volunteered for duty, it had been to relieve the boredom of hot days at the prison, for, as Coxshall later wrote, "had we known what it was we were to do that day we volunteered, none of us would have stepped forward." At 11:30 a.m., Rath ordered the drops tested, using 140-pound cannon shells as stand-ins for the condemned. The drop on one side worked flawlessly, but the other one stuck. Carpenters went to work and it was soon adjusted and Rath was satisfied.[9]

Around noon, General Hancock arrived at the arsenal. He had come from the White House, where he had made a last personal appeal to the president to spare the life of Mrs. Surratt. Those who saw him knew what the answer had been. Hancock spoke bluntly to General Hartranft: "Get ready, General, no time must be lost now." Mrs. Surratt's lawyer, Frederick Aiken, spoke briefly with General Hancock, and exclaimed as he turned away, "My God! Mrs. Surratt must be hung today!" The cells of the prisoners were cleared of all visitors except clergy, and the screams of the anguished Anna Surratt could be heard everywhere.

Time passed, and when the procession of the condemned did not emerge, rumors began to circulate that there had been a last-minute reprieve, or that General Hancock had refused to hang Mrs. Surratt and had been arrested. Finally, at a quarter past one, Hancock was seen again, ordering the troops to dress parade. Then General Hartranft came out, followed by members of his staff, Brevet Brigadier General Levi Axtell Dodd (1833–1901), Lieutenant Colonel McCall, and others. The first prisoner was Mrs. Surratt, wearing a full black dress and a heavy veil, her step very unsteady. She was supported by Fathers Walter and Wiget, on either

In this engraving of the execution from an engraving in *Frank Leslie's Illustrated Newspaper*, July 22, 1865, the prisoners have been prepared for hanging by binding their arms and legs, and the ropes and hoods are in place.

side, one holding a crucifix and with an open breviary hung from his sash. Four soldiers and an officer followed. Next came Atzerodt, with the Reverend Butler beside him, and more soldiers. Herold came third, with the Reverend Olds, four more soldiers, and finally Powell, with the Reverend Gillette and the Reverend Augustus P. Stryker, an Episcopalian minister from St. Barnabas Church, Baltimore, and another four soldiers.

On the scaffold, clergymen can be seen praying for the souls of the condemned. Left to right: Mrs. Surratt (under the umbrella), Lewis Powell, David Herold, George Atzerodt. Beneath the scaffold can be seen the props, to be dislodged by the soldiers, allowing the platforms to fall. Engraving from *Harper's Weekly* April 27, 1865, from a photograph by Alexander Gardner.

Mrs. Surratt, Atzerodt and Herold were clearly distraught, particularly when they saw the waiting coffins and open graves close by the gallows. Of the four prisoners, only Powell seemed composed. They were arranged, as one faced the scaffold, with Mrs. Surratt and then Powell on the left drop, Herold and Atzerodt on the right. They were allowed to sit in chairs as the final preparations were made, and umbrellas shielded condemned and executioners alike from the hot sun. As he observed the proceedings, one spectator loudly protested to those around him, "Gentlemen, I tell you this is murder; can you stand and see it done?"

The prisoners were told to stand and step forward. Powell did so boldly, the others shrinking back, having to be prodded forward. As her hands were tied, Mrs. Surratt said, "It hurts." She was told, "Well, it won't hurt long." Bands of cloth were tied around them, securing their arms and legs. Hoods were fitted and pulled down over their heads. Rath whispered to Powell, "I want you to die quick." The big man answered, "You know best, Captain." Atzerodt began a rambling speech, saying, "Good-bye gentlemen before me now. May we all meet in the other world." The clergymen continued to say their prayers. Rath stepped down the stairs and took up his place in front of the scaffold, where the soldiers underneath could see him. He brought his hands together in a prearranged signal, with the third time being the signal for action. At 1:26 p.m. the soldiers knocked out the supporting beams and the drops fell. Mrs. Surratt, still standing back, barely on the drop, fell forward and swung back and forth. The others dropped straight down. Powell's strong neck did not break immediately, and he was seen to struggle before losing consciousness.

Assigned by Booth to shoot Vice President Andrew Johnson, George A. Atzerodt lost his nerve and made no attempt on Johnson's life. In spite of this, he was among those executed. Engraving from *Harper's Weekly*, July 1, 1865.

After twenty minutes the bodies were cut down, that of Mrs. Surratt being lowered gently, with Rath personally taking her in his arms. The prison doctor, Major George Loring Porter (1838–1919) pronounced each one to be dead. The remains were placed in the waiting coffins, along with a bottle containing the name of each one. They were lowered into the ground and covered over. Eventually their families would be permitted to claim the remains and they would be reburied, but for now, it was over.[10]

The four men who escaped the scaffold found themselves facing an ordeal beyond imagining. They were to endure not only the prospect of years of confinement, but to again have to confront the issue of their survival. They were sent to Fort Jefferson.

Built in the early 19th century as part of a system of coastal defenses intended to protect America, Fort Jefferson was the largest of the forts designed and built at that time. It is located on Garden Key, one of a group of seven islands called the Dry Tortugas, so named by their discoverer, Juan Ponce de Leon (1460–1521), who claimed them for Spain in 1513. Las Tortugas, the turtles, were named for the many sea turtles which abounded in those waters. When Florida was acquired by the United States in 1819, the strategic location of the Dry Tortugas was appreciated. First a lighthouse was built there in 1825, then in 1847 work began on the fort.

The building of Fort Jefferson, designed by Lieutenant Montgomery Cunningham Meigs (1816–1892), progressed slowly, using slaves and immigrant laborers. The need to keep the fort out of Confederate hands prompted the government to increase the garrison to more than 1,000 men by 1862, and to equip the fort with the first of its large guns. The walls reached their height of fifty feet by late 1862, being ten feet thick at the base and eight feet at the top. Even before the war was over it was realized that the island could not properly support such a massive structure, and the development of rifled cannons which could penetrate the fort's walls made the whole concept of stone forts obsolete.

The first prisoners arrived in September 1861, and their numbers grew throughout the war, climbing into the hundreds. When the slaves were freed, construction work was carried on entirely by prisoners. Four convicted of involvement in the Lincoln assassination, Dr. Samuel A. Mudd, Samuel B. Arnold, Michael O'Laughlen, and Edman Spangler, arrived at Fort Jefferson on July 24, 1865. They later described the difficult conditions all who lived there, prisoners and guards alike, had to endure. The tropical heat and dampness combined with poor quality food and harsh treatment by the officers, earned Fort Jefferson the nickname of "America's Devil's Island."

Although epidemics had been known there before, the bout of yellow fever which began on August 18, 1867, was particularly severe. Major Joseph Sim Smith, the post doctor, was an early fatality, and Dr. Mudd was for a time the only doctor available.

When Dr. Daniel Winchester Whitehurst (1807–1872) arrived from Key West, Dr. Mudd continued to work with him in the treatment of the sick, as did other prisoners, including Arnold and Spangler. O'Laughlen was another fatality. In all, thirty-eight died and another 232 were stricken, out of a total of about 300 guards and prisoners. By mid–November the epidemic had run its course.

George St. Leger Grenfell (1808–1868) was a British soldier of fortune. His involvement with the Confederate Secret Service led to his arrest and imprisonment at Fort Jefferson, where he met and befriended the Lincoln conspirators. Born in London on May 30, 1808, of a prosperous family, Grenfell fled the banking business for a life of adventure. He was involved in the street fighting of the July 1830 uprising in Paris, then spent five years in the French National Guard. Abandoning his wife and two daughters, he became an arms dealer and military advisor to the Moroccans resisting French conquest. When the Crimean War began in 1854, Grenfell managed to get a commission in the "Anglo-Turkish Contingent," Turkish troops with British officers. His hopes of seeing combat in Russia were dashed by poor planning and logistics.

Grenfell arrived at Charleston, South Carolina, in April of 1862, with letters of introduction, and offered his services to the Confederacy. He joined the staff of John Hunt Morgan (1825–1864) and quickly earned the respect of the officers for his military knowledge and of the men for his camaraderie. He received a formal commission as a Lieutenant Colonel in May 1863. After serving under Generals Joseph Wheeler (1836–1906) and James Ewell Brown Stuart (1833–1864), he became a Confederate undercover agent, sailing for Canada in the spring of 1864. On the way, he brazenly secured an interview with Secretary of War Edwin M. Stanton and plied him with phony information, later claiming that this act earned him Stanton's particular hatred. In Canada, Grenfell became involved in the Northwest Conspiracy, a Confederate scheme to free prisoners of war.

Arrested late in 1864, Grenfell was prosecuted by Henry L. Burnett (1838–1916), who was soon after involved in the trial of the Lincoln assassination conspiracy suspects. Grenfell was the only defendant at the earlier trial who was sentenced to death. Thanks to the entreaties of the British minister, President Andrew Johnson commuted Grenfell's sentence to life at hard labor. Harsh treatment by the guards was added to the heat and humidity at Fort Jefferson. Grenfell soon befriended Dr. Mudd, Spangler, O'Laughlen and Arnold, who admired his fierce spirit of resistance. When Grenfell managed to smuggle out an article critical of the treatment the prisoners were receiving, he was singled out for especially harsh retaliation. Too ill to work, he was bound hand and foot and exposed to the full force of the sun. When that failed to break him, he was repeatedly dunked in water, while bound, and with his feet weighted, until he passed out.

With little hope of being released, Grenfell characteristically took matters in hand and conspired with a guard to secure a boat. On the night of March 6, 1868, Grenfell and four others escaped in an open boat, sailing out into the storm-tossed Gulf of Mexico. Though rumors of Grenfell in Cuba were heard, such stories could not be substantiated. He no doubt drowned, but he died a free man.

The Lincoln conspiracy convicts were pardoned and left Fort Jefferson in 1869. Another epidemic and a hurricane in 1873 led to the final abandonment of the fort in 1874. Buildings, piers and gun platforms rotted and fell apart. For a time the fort was used to quarantine those with infectious diseases. By the mid–1890s, the navy was using Fort Jefferson as an anchorage. The battleship USS *Maine* sailed from there to Cuba for her ill-fated rendezvous with history in 1898. After the Spanish-American War, work got under way to build a coaling station, completed in 1904. Storm damage and problems with dredging caused it to be abandoned by 1907. During World War I, Fort Jefferson was used as a wireless station and seaplane base. Efforts to preserve Fort Jefferson for its historic value as well as for the importance of the plant and animal life of the islands and surrounding waters led to the designation of the area as a national monument in 1935, with its status further elevated to national park in 1993.[11]

8

JUSTICE?

The dictionary defines the word justice as that which is "right and fair."[1] Presumably, this applies to both sides in a legal case. The state has a right to demand justice in prosecuting those accused of wrongdoing, and the defendants also are entitled to every protection which our laws and traditions allow. In the Anglo-American system of law, the burden of proof lies upon the prosecution. No one, no matter who he is or what is the nature of the crime of which he is accused, can ever be required to prove he is innocent. This is why, in reporting on criminal cases, the media must describe someone as a "suspect," or of having "allegedly" committed an offense. They cannot call someone "the assassin of——" unless that person has been convicted by a duly authorized court.

Beyond the actual innocence or guilt of the accused, it is necessary that the forms and procedures required by law are properly followed. A person may be obviously guilty according to the evidence against him, but if that evidence was not properly obtained, or if the court which tried him did not follow the necessary procedure required by law, or if suspects were illegally treated or witnesses pressured, then a person convicted under such circumstances can be said to have been denied his rights and the full protection of the laws intended to protect those rights. Regardless of the strength of the case against anyone in such circumstances, a conviction thus obtained cannot be considered lawful, and consequent punishment administered must be described as being unjust.

It is not always easy to determine whether flaws in a legal case are severe enough to effect the outcome of the case. Lawyers do not know all the answers to these questions, nor do judges. Legal decisions considered acceptable and proper under certain circumstances, or in certain times and places, can be seen to be inadequate, or even in error, upon later examination. This is also true in history. Those who write history must try their best to present the truth of the case as they see it, always aware that others may disagree with them, and the passage of time, with changing ideas and attitudes, may bring about a change of opinion.

In the case of the Lincoln assassination suspects, we must decide whether justice was done. This is not a matter of revisionism, for many of the questions we must consider were raised at the time, both in the courtroom and among the public at large.

We have already dealt with the question of whether the trial was legal. Did the federal government have jurisdiction over the case? Did the military have jurisdiction, rather than a civilian court? Were the defendants denied their basic rights and protection of the laws? Was the testimony given tainted by improper conduct, both by witnesses and by the prosecution?

A landmark decision by the United States Supreme Court was handed down on April 3, 1866. The case is titled *Ex parte Milligan*. Lambdin P. Milligan (1812–1899), a resident of Huntington County, Indiana, was a Democrat who believed strongly in states' rights. With the coming of the Civil War, Milligan found himself in complete agreement with the South. The Lincoln administration's suspension of the writ of habeas corpus cleared the way for severe violations of basic rights. *The New York Daily News* of July 1, 1861, put it this way:

> The sacred privilege of habeas corpus had been thrust aside; homes were illegally entered and searched; the private papers of citizens were seized without warrant; men were arrested without legal process, and held behind bars without a hearing. Almost every right which American citizens have been taught to consider sacred and inalienable, has been trampled upon.

Prominent leaders echoed these sentiments, such as this from Senator Lyman Trumbull (1813–1896) of Illinois: "I think that the idea that the rights of the citizen are to be trampled upon, and that he is to be arrested by military authority, without any regulation by law whatsoever, is monstrous in a free government."

Agreeing with such statements, as did many throughout the Northern states, Milligan denounced the Lincoln administration and tried to persuade his fellow citizens not to answer Lincoln's call for more enlistments for the Union army. Lincoln issued a proclamation on September 24, 1862, which stated that "all Rebels and insurgents, their aiders and abettors within the United States, and all persons discouraging volunteer enlistments, resisting militia drafts, or guilty of any disloyal practice … shall be subject to martial law and liable to trial and punishment by Courts Martial or Military Commission." Pro-Union agents were watching Milligan and gathering evidence of disloyalty against him, and others. It was alleged that a plot existed to bring about an uprising in the states of Illinois, Indiana, Michigan, and Wisconsin, known as the "Old Northwest," as this area had been the northwestern part of the United States prior to the Louisiana Purchase. Milligan, it was said, together with William A. Bowles, Andrew Humphreys, Stephen Horsey, and others, were organizing a group called the "Order of American Knights." It was said that they were supplying arms for draft resisters, and were seeking help from the Southern Confederates for the Old Northwest Conspiracy.

Milligan was arrested on October 5, 1864, and tried by a military commission in Indianapolis. Pronounced guilty of inciting insurrection and giving aid and comfort to the Southern rebels, he was sentenced to be hanged on May 19, 1865. Fighting for his life, Milligan claimed he had been unlawfully tried and imprisoned. Instead of contesting his guilt, he based his legal challenge on the idea that the military commission which had tried him lacked legal jurisdiction, since he was not serving in the military, the state—Indiana—where his alleged crimes took place was not in rebellion, and the civilian courts were open and functioning.

Milligan was represented by four well-known and respected lawyers, James A. Garfield (1831–1881)—a future president of the United States; Jeremiah S. Black (1810–1883)—a former U.S. attorney general; Joseph Ewing McDonald (1819–1891)—former representative and future U.S. senator; and David Dudley Field (1805–1894)—who later would also serve in Congress.

The case for the defense concentrated on the legality of the trial, rather than the guilt or innocence of the accused. Arguing for the prosecution were James Speed (1812–1887)—an attorney general who also wrote an opinion justifying the military trial of the Lincoln conspiracy suspects; Henry Stanberry (1803–1881)—who succeeded Speed as attorney general in 1866; and Benjamin F. Butler (1818–1893)—a Union general and future congressman and governor of Massachusetts.

The defense showed that not only was Indiana a loyal state, but that there were no invading rebel forces in the state at the time of the alleged crimes. Military necessity could not justify the execution of Milligan and the others, because the rebellion had ceased by May of 1865. It was also pointed out that President Washington, who called for troops to put down the Whiskey Rebellion in 1794, did not suspend the writ of habeas corpus or any other constitutional guarantees. Also cited were cases from British law in which military authority had been overturned in civil courts.[2]

The Supreme Court was convinced, *unanimously* declaring,

The act of Congress "relating to habeas corpus," approved March 3, 1863, conferred jurisdiction on the circuit court of Indiana to hear such a case.

A military commission has no jurisdiction, legally, to try and sentence one not a resident of one of the rebellious states, nor a prisoner of war, but a citizen of Indiana who never was in the military or naval service, but was while at his home, arrested by the military power of the United States, imprisoned, and on certain criminal charges preferred against him, convicted, and sentenced to be hanged by a military commission organized under the military commander of the military district of Indiana....

In a state where Federal authority was always unopposed, and its courts always open to hear criminal accusations and redress grievances, no usage of war could sanction a military trial for any offense whatever, of a citizen in civil life, in no wise connected with the military service. Congress could grant no such power....

The right of trial by jury is preserved to every one accused of crime, who is not attached to the Army, or Navy, or Militia in actual service....

Martial law cannot arise from a threatened invasion. The necessity must be actual and present; the invasion real, such as effectually closes the courts and deposes the civil administration....

If, in foreign invasion or civil war, the courts are actually closed, then, on the theater of active military operations, where war really prevails, as no power is left but the military, it is allowed to govern by martial rule until the laws can have their free course....

Martial rule can never exist where the courts are open, and in the proper and unobstructed exercise of their jurisdiction. It is also confined to the locality of actual war....

The suspension of the privilege of the writ of habeas corpus does not suspend the writ itself.

The writ issues as a matter of course; and on the return made to it the court decides whether the party applying is denied the right of proceeding any further with it....

If the trial of Milligan was contrary to law, then he was entitled, on the facts stated in

Attorney General James Speed was pressured into writing an official opinion upholding the right of the military to try the defendants under military law.

his petition, to be discharged from custody by the terms of the act of Congress of March 3, 1863.

He could not be treated as a prisoner of war, when he had lived in Indiana for the past twenty years, was arrested there, and had not been, during the late troubles, a resident of any of the states in rebellion.[3]

The Supreme Court's decision in the Milligan case was denounced at the time by Congressman Thaddeus Stevens (1792–1868), who said, "That decision, although in terms not as infamous as the Dred Scott decision, is yet far more dangerous in its operation upon the lives and liberties of the loyal men of this country." Historian Allan Nevins (1890–1971), however, said, "The Milligan decision represented a great triumph for the civil liberties of Americans in time of war or internal dissention.... The Supreme Court established the rule that, no matter how grave the emergency, and no matter how high the public excitement, the civil authority is supreme over military authority; that whenever such civil authority is established and its ordinary judicial procedures are operating, its protections of the citizen shall remain absolute and unquestionable. The heart of this decision is the heart of the difference between the United States of America and Nazi Germany or the Soviet Union."[4]

When the Milligan decision was made public, attorneys for Dr. Samuel A. Mudd sought to draw a parallel with their client's case. Milligan was tried before a military commission, even though the civil courts in his state were open and functioning. The same had been true of Dr. Mudd and the other Lincoln assassination defendants. Milligan was not serving in the military forces and had not served in the military of either North or South. The same applied to Dr. Mudd. Therefore, it seemed that the Milligan decision, which came less than a year after the Lincoln assassination, vindicated the arguments of Reverdy Johnson and Thomas Ewing, Jr., at the trial of the conspiracy suspects, that the military commission lacked jurisdiction to try the case.

It was hoped that President Andrew Johnson would, in light of the Milligan decision, order Dr. Mudd released from prison. At first, the president indicated he would do so, "at the earliest moment that he could consistently do so." However, by 1866, Johnson had parted company from the congressional "Radical Republicans," who sought a harsh occupation of the South under military law. In light of this political friction—which ultimately led to the impeachment and trial of the president—Johnson chose not to further antagonize such powerful congressmen as Thaddeus Stevens and others. Attorney Richard T. Merrick (1826–1885), who had assisted Dr. Mudd's lawyers during the assassination suspects trial, presented a writ of habeas corpus to the Supreme Court. By this time, the wartime suspension of habeas corpus had been lifted. Chief Justice Salmon P. Chase (1808–1873) denied the writ, and said that the Milligan decision did not apply to Mudd. No explanation was given, and Chase apparently consulted no one in making this decision. War Secretary Stanton ordered the release of those convicted in military courts, "except those under sentence in the Dry Tortugas." These included the Lincoln assassination defendants, Mudd, Arnold, O'Laughlen, and Spangler.[5]

The Milligan decision was not publicized until December 1866, so Dr. Mudd made no mention of it until then. Upon hearing of Chase's refusal of his writ, Dr. Mudd wrote, "It is vexatious to see how partial the laws are made applicable and administered. Milligan was tried during the existence of active war. His case is declared illegal. We are tried after the war, and peace declared. If the trial of Milligan was wrong, certainly ours was more so, and no necessity can be pleaded in palliation."[6]

Vice President Andrew Johnson succeeded Lincoln as president and refused to modify the sentences of any of the accused, although he later pardoned the surviving prisoners.

An editorial in the New York *Herald* suggested that, in light of the Milligan decision, the Supreme Court should be "reconstructed": "By increasing or diminishing the number of judges, the Court may be reconstructed in conformity with the supreme decisions of the war." *Harper's Weekly* added, "Like the Dred Scott decision [the Milligan decision was] not a judicial opinion; it [was] a political act." The opposition press, of course, took a different view. The New York *World* called the Milligan decision "a triumphant vindication of the Democratic Party and a happy augury of the future." The Washington *National Intelligencer* stated, "the laws are no longer silenced by the clash of arms. The supreme tribunal of the country has vindicated their assaulted majesty." The Washington *Evening Star* added, "This decision is a very important one, and will doubtless lead to a great deal of litigation in the civil courts, by persons who have suffered in person or property through the actions of military tribunals…. The rebellion having been suppressed it is the duty of the judiciary, as it is of other branches of the government, to demand and enforce a strict conformity to the laws; to right the wrongs committed while the nation was struggling for existence, and to efface, so far as can be done, all trace of the disorders which were the natural result of a fierce and desolating civil war."[7]

Dr. Mudd's lawyers applied to the District Court of the United States for the Southern District of Florida for a writ of habeas corpus on August 28, 1868. Judge Thomas Jefferson Boynton (1838–1871) stated, in his opinion denying the writ,

> The facts here are a part of the history of the country … I do not think that Ex parte Milligan is a case in point here…. The President was assassinated not from private animosity nor any other reason than to desire to impair the effectiveness of military operations and enable the rebellion to establish itself into a government. The act was committed in a fortified city which had been invaded during the war and to the northward as well as the southward of which battles had many times been fought, which was the headquarters of all the armies of the United States from which daily and hourly went military orders. The President is the Commander-in-Chief of the Army and the president who was killed had many times made distinct military orders under his own hand, without the formality of employing the names of the Secretary of War or Commander-in-Chief of the Army for military reasons. I find no difficulty therefore in classing the offense as a Military one, and with this opinion arrive at the necessary conclusion, that the proper tribunal for the trial of those engaged in it was a military one.[8]

In the record of the trial of the conspiracy suspects, we have the following statement by the chief prosecutor, Judge Advocate General Joseph Holt (1807–1894): "How kindred to each other are the crimes of treason against a nation and the assassination of its chief magistrate. I think of those crimes the one seems to be, if not the necessary consequence, certainly a logical sequence from the other. The murder of the president of the United States … was pre-eminently a political assassination. Disloyalty to the government was its sole, its only inspiration."[9] This statement could seem to conflict with Judge Boynton's assertion that the assassination was a military crime, and thus triable by a military commission under military law. If there is confusion over whether the president is a military or a political officer, it derives from the Constitution. Article 2, section 2, states,

"The President shall be Commander in Chief of the Army and Navy of the United States."[10] There is no further elaboration of the president's powers regarding the military forces, or explanation of how he is to exercise his military powers.

In the Federalist Papers, Alexander Hamilton (1757–1804) explained how the president as commander-in-chief of the armed forces is limited in his power by the Constitution, and how it differs from that of the king of England in his time.

> It [the president's power] would amount to nothing more than the supreme command and direction of the military and naval forces, as first general and admiral of the confederacy; while that of the British King extends to the declaring of war and to the raising and regulating the fleets and armies—all which, by the Constitution under consideration, would appertain to the legislature.[11]

Later, Hamilton adds,

> The direction of war implies the direction of the common strength; and the power of directing and employing the common strength forms a usual and essential part in the definition of the executive authority.[12]

It is obvious that the Founding Fathers, in their resolve that the civilian authority should be superior to the military, granted the civilian executive officer—the president—ultimate power over the military. This was not intended to make the president a member of the armed forces, the equivalent of a general or admiral, for that would have defeated their purpose, to have civilian control over the military. They intended that the president should administer the armed forces, but should not be considered a soldier. The powers delegated to the Congress regarding war, are listed as:

> To Declare War, grant Letters of Marque and Reprisal, and make Rules concerning Captures on land and water;
> To Raise and Support Armies, but no Appropriation of Money to that use shall be for a longer term than two years;
> To provide and maintain a Navy;
> To Make Rules for the Government and Regulation of the land and naval forces;
> To Provide for calling forth the Militia to execute the Laws of the Union, Suppress Insurrections and repel Invasions;
> To provide for organizing, arming, and disciplining, the Militia, and for governing such part of them as may be employed in the Service of the United States, reserving to the States respectively, the Appointment of the Officers, and the Authority of training the Militia according to the Discipline proscribed by Congress.[13]

These are the basic war powers of the United States, and it can be seen that the Congress is given more of them than is the president. It is also clear that even though the president is designated the "commander-in-chief," he is given no military rank or decorations, as is common in other nations, and does not wear a uniform or any emblem of military authority. He is paid by a separate appropriation, not by the Pentagon. None of the cases involving other presidential assassinations or attempted assassinations were tried by military courts under military law. This suggests that with the exception of the Lincoln case, the idea of the president being the same as a uniformed officer was not proposed. John H. Surratt, Jr., was tried in a civil court in front of a jury. The army had hanged his mother, but trying him, using mostly the same witnesses and evidence, failed to bring a conviction.

The only president ever to put on a military uniform in the official exercise of his duties was George Washington (1732–1799). During the "Whiskey Rebellion," President Washington put on his Revolutionary War uniform and rode out to review the troops raised to enforce the federal taxes on whiskey, which Pennsylvania farmers were protesting. Although he accompanied the soldiers part of the way, and issued orders while with the troops, he turned over the field command to a subordinate officer, taking no part in any fighting.[14]

Whether the president can be considered to be a member of the armed forces, in the same sense as ordinary uniformed officers, is of secondary importance to the issue of whether the assassination conspiracy defendants were properly tried by a military commission. As the prisoners were being relegated to Fort Jefferson, another case of a similar nature was being decided. Four civilian men were arrested by the United States Army in South Carolina and charged with killing three soldiers. The defendants were tried by a military commission and sentenced to be executed. Their sentences commuted to life, they were imprisoned for a time at Fort Jefferson, during part of the same time that the Lincoln assassination conspiracy suspects were also confined there. The landmark case, *United States v. Commandant of Fort Delaware*, bears a direct relation to the case of the assassination suspects.

The decision of Judge Willard Hall (1780–1875), of the United States District Court for Delaware, read in part,

> In so small a body ... as the army, so associated, and with so much in common, there must be an *esprit de corps* that will not allow us to expect impartial justice in case of collision with citizens, while the broad ground of citizenship is not liable to such objection. This aspect of the case exhibits

nothing favoring a trial by military commission or alleged offenses by citizens against soldiers. On the contrary, all sound principles of law are opposed to subjecting the accused to the disadvantage of such a trial....

Looseness in admission of evidence, almost certain in proceedings before men not trained to preciseness in this respect, leads to misapprehension and confusion, lets in prejudice, suspicion and artifice, affords opportunity for perjury...

The rebellion had ceased, and the authority of the United States was acknowledged in [South Carolina, where the alleged offenses took place] ... the civil institutions of the state were in operation.... Nor would a temporary abeyance of civil judicature give jurisdiction to ... a military commission...

According to the law of the land the prisoners could not be tried before this Military Commission, and they ought not to, and cannot be held under the commuted sentences. Ordered that they be discharged.[15]

Judge Boynton overlooked or ignored the earlier decision of Judge Hall. Both cases were similar, in that they involved civilians tried by military commissions in areas where the civil courts were open and functioning. To quote author Thomas Bland Keys, "Judge Boynton's invalid opinion in Ex parte Mudd et al was a miscarriage of justice that deprived Dr. Mudd, Arnold, and Spangler [Michael O'Laughlen died at Fort Jefferson in the epidemic of yellow fever in 1867] of their Constitutional right of due process of law, and continued their illegal imprisonment at Fort Jefferson for another six months.... Judge Hall's decision in United States v. Commandant of Fort Delaware allows no other interpretation than that all eight civilians, who were charged with the murder of Lincoln and tried by the military commission, were deprived of due process of law."[16]

The Habeas Corpus Act of 1863 was only partially enforced by the Lincoln administration. Lincoln had suspended the writ of habeas corpus—effectively canceling the basic liberties listed in the Bill of Rights—in 1861. The president had assumed the authority for this action, which is provided for in the Constitution in times of rebellion or invasion, but exactly who has the authority to suspend the writ is not specifically stated. The act of 1863 legalized, after the fact, the president's newfound power. The act denied the authority of the military to try civilians.

Historian James G. Randall (1881–1953), in his comprehensive *Constitutional Problems Under Lincoln,* noted that the Habeas Corpus Act stated that the military must furnish lists of citizens arrested, who could then be brought before civil courts, where they were to be discharged if no indictments had been issued by grand juries. If no lists were provided to the courts within twenty days of arrest, the prisoner was to be released. The intent of the act was, while acknowledging the president's power to make arbitrary arrests in time of emergency, the supremacy of civil over military authority was to be upheld.

> Where there is no martial law, and where the ordinary civil courts are unimpeded, it has been generally recognized that military tribunals have no proper function to perform in the trial of civilians, and certainly not for offenses outside the military code.

The U.S. Supreme Court ruled in the case of Clement L. Vallandigham (1820–1871) that his trial by a military commission in 1863 could not be overturned because military commissions are not courts sanctioned by the Judiciary Act of 1789, and therefore their cases cannot be reviewed by the Supreme Court. The Milligan decision of 1866, however, reversed the Court's decision in the Vallandigham case, saying, "If there was law to justify this military trial [of Milligan] it is not our province to interfere; if there was not it is our duty to declare the nullity of the whole proceedings."

After showing that Stanton and Holt interpreted the Habeas Corpus Act as "extremely difficult of construction," and therefore not applying to trials by military commissions, Randall makes the observation, "Had this law been complied with, the effect would have been to restore the supremacy of the civil power; for the act contained provisions which, if enforced, would have greatly modified the president's control of prisoners.... It left the executive without restraint in all cases where martial law was instituted and where military commissions were used for the trial of citizens."[17]

Holt, in his official *Opinions of the Judge Advocate General of the Army*, noted the distinction between trials conducted by a civilian court and by a military commission:

> To subject military commissions partly to the laws and practice which govern civil courts, and partly to those which control courts martial, would be to destroy the harmony between the two different military tribunals, and to embarrass the administration of military justice. Such a course would tend also to defeat the purpose of Congress, which, in placing them in many respects on the same footing, evidently contemplated that the statutory rules of procedure which apply to the court martial should be applied, as far as practicable, to the military commission.

Holt also congratulated himself, after the fact, for following the mandate of the Supreme Court in the Milligan decision.

> These commissions, originating in the necessities of the rebellion, had been proved, by the experience of three years, indispensable for the punishment of public crimes, in regions where other courts had ceased to exist, and in cases

of which the local criminal courts could not legally take cognizance, or which, by reason of intrinsic defects of machinery, they were incompetent to pass upon.

And he stated forthrightly the purpose of trying the assassination suspects before a military commission instead of a civil court.

> But it was not until the two cases under consideration [of the assassination suspects and of Wirz, 1822–1865, commandant of the Confederate camp for prisoners of war at Andersonville, Georgia, where harsh conditions resulted in the deaths of as many as 14,000 Union captives, and hanged as a war criminal on November 10, 1865[18]] came on to be tried by the Military Commission, that its highest excellence was exhibited. It was not merely in that it was unencumbered by the technicalities and inevitable embarrassments attending the administration of justice before civil tribunals, or in the fact that it could so readily avail itself of the military power of the government for the execution of its processes and the enforcement of its orders, that its efficacy (though in these directions most conspicuous) was chiefly illustrated.... By no other species of tribunal, and by no other known mode of judiciary inquiry, could this result have been so successfully attained; and it may be truly said that without the aid and agency of the Military Commission, one of the most important chapters in the annals of the rebellion would have been lost to history, and the most complete and reliable disclosure of its inner and real life, alike treacherous and barbaric, would have failed to be developed.[19]

Note how Holt explains that a civil trial would be hampered by "technicalities and inevitable embarrassments," presumably referring to legal processes in harmony with the Constitution. In the following statement, Holt sweeps away the Milligan decision.

> The principle, well expressed by Major General Halleck, in General Order No. 1, of headquarters department of the Missouri, of January 1, 1862, that "many offenses which, in time of peace, are civil offenses, become, in time of war, military offenses, and are to be tried by a military tribunal, even in places where civil tribunals exist," has been followed by this government in a great number of cases; and offenses aimed at impairing the efficiency of the service, or the efforts of the government to suppress the rebellion, have been repeatedly brought to trial by military commissions when committed within our military and on the theatre of military operations, where the effect of the pressure of a vast civil war is, *ex necessitate*, to suspend for a time, for the preservation of the whole, some portion of the legal safeguards thrown around the citizen in time of peace. It is the fact that the state of Indiana was in this category (with the additional consideration that it had been and was being constantly threatened with invasion by the enemy) which conferred jurisdiction upon the military commission that has passed upon the cases of Dodd, Bowles, Milligan, Horsey, and other conspirators against the government.
>
> The amendments of the Constitution, which give the right of trial by jury to persons held to answer for capital or otherwise infamous crimes, except

when arising in the land or naval forces, are often referred to, as conclusive against the jurisdiction of military courts over such offenses when committed by citizens. But though the letter of the articles would give to such an argument, yet in construing the different parts of the Constitution together, such a literal interpretation of the amendments must be held to give way before the necessity for an efficient exercise of the WAR POWER which is vested in Congress by that instrument.[20]

Thus, in effect, it can be said that Holt is arguing that the suspension of the writ of habeas corpus sanctions arbitrary military rule over any area designated by the military as a theatre of operations, and that the basic protections of the Constitution's Bill of Rights do not apply in any case during the period designated by the executive and the military. To accept such a declaration is tantamount to a suspension of the entire Constitution and any other laws which the military may find to be hindering their operations, in any and all areas which they may designate. To argue that the Founding Fathers sanctioned or intended such a situation ever to arise is to totally ignore their careful and scrupulous effort to prevent the assumption of arbitrary power by any portion of the government which they created. It leaves, as we shall see in Chapter 9, the door wide open to the assumption by the executive branch and/or the military of arbitrary power of any sort. To accept that habeas corpus may be set aside at any time by the president, using the military forces to enforce this usurpation of power, is nothing less than to deny that the United States of America is a democracy, and that its people are protected against the suppression of their liberties by the sudden unchecked power of the would-be dictators.

General Henry W. Halleck (1815–1872), army chief of staff, had some interesting and contradictory things to say about these matters:

> Military commissions should as a general rule be resorted to only for cases which cannot be tried by a court-martial or by a proper civil tribunal. They are in other words tribunals of necessity, organized for the investigation and punishment of offenses which would otherwise go unpunished.
> Treason is an offense technically defined by the Constitution and is not triable by a military commission.
> Civil offenses cognizable by civil courts whenever such loyal courts exist will not be tried by a military commission. It should therefore be stated in every application for a commission whether or not there is any loyal court to which the civil offenses charged can be referred for trial.

In his General Order No. 1, General Halleck lists crimes which he says may be tried by military commissions; assassination is not listed among them.[21]

The Constitution, although often vaguely worded, does not say that one part of the document may be arbitrarily declared to override another.

In listing the powers of the Congress, including the war powers, it states that "Congress shall have power to ... make all laws which shall be necessary and proper for carrying into execution the foregoing powers, and all other powers vested by this Constitution in the Government of the United States, or in any Department or officer thereof."

Note the wording: "all laws which shall be necessary and proper." Is there any indication anywhere that the Founding Fathers felt that it was necessary and proper to deprive Americans of their basic rights, leaving them no ability to protest or challenge such power?

The argument over the jurisdiction of the military commission is not the only objection to the trial of the Lincoln assassination defendants. Even if we accept the contention that the trial was legal, there were several problems which arose over the testimony of certain witnesses, as well as questions about some of the evidence. Where the prosecution got into the greatest trouble was in trying to link the assassination to the leaders of the Confederacy.

After testifying at the trial of the conspirators, Charles A. Dunham (c.1832–1900) returned to Canada and again resumed his association with George N. Sanders. When questioned by Confederates in Canada about his published testimony, Dunham told them he had been misquoted. When he returned to Washington, he turned around and claimed that the Confederates in Canada had forced him to issue the denial. He even advertised a $500 reward for the arrest of Sanford Conover, whom he, using the name Wallace, said had stolen his identity. Conover and Wallace were aliases of the same man, Dunham.

Before the trial of the conspiracy suspects ended, the prosecutors received information from Canadian authorities that Dunham had lied about nearly everything he had said in his testimony, including his own name. They determined that Conover, Wallace, and Dunham were all the same man, and that his loyalty to the Union was totally unreliable. Incredibly, Dunham told the court that he had been misrepresented, and they believed him again! Furthermore, Dunham had coached other witnesses for the prosecution, in 1866, evidently paying them with money furnished by the judge advocate's office. William W. Cleary (1831–1897), writing to President Andrew Johnson after the trial, produced affidavits to prove that Confederate agents in Canada could not have met with Dunham on the dates to which Dunham had sworn. When a congressional committee questioned Dunham in early 1866, they forced him to admit to at least some of his lies. Witnesses Dunham had coached admitted to their perjury. Through it all, Dunham claimed he had been fooled by these witnesses.

Judge Advocate Joseph Holt finally admitted that it appeared that he had been fooled by Dunham.

Tried for perjury in February 1867, Dunham was convicted and sent to prison with a ten-year sentence. Dunham hoped to obtain his release by assisting Congressman Benjamin F. Butler (1818–1893) and his committee in their attempt to implicate President Johnson in the murder of Lincoln. Betraying Butler and Congressman James Mitchell Ashley (1824–1896) to Johnson, Dunham won favor with the president. Dunham went to the penitentiary in Albany, New York, but he received a presidential pardon shortly before Johnson left office in 1869.[22]

Another witness, Mrs. Mary Hudspeth, testified that in November 1864, she overheard two men conversing near her while riding a New York City streetcar. They were discussing going to Washington, one becoming "very angry because it had not fallen to him to go to Washington." She noticed that one man was wearing false whiskers and carrying a pistol. When the men got up and left the car, an envelope containing two letters fell on the floor and was found by Mrs. Hudspeth's daughter. One letter contained this passage: "Abe must die and now. You can choose your weapons. The cup, the knife, the bullet." Another quote, "Sanders is doing us no good in Canada," could be a reference to Confederate Commissioner George N. Sanders (1812–1873), an agent of the rebel spy mission in Canada. The other letter refers to a "Louis," whose wife is begging him to come home. One of the Booth conspiracy suspects was Lewis Powell, though there is no evidence that he was married.[23]

Other letters were introduced as evidence, hinting at Confederate involvement. One letter, written in code, dated April 15, 1865, stated "Old Abe is in hell," and suggested that there were plans to kill other Union leaders. A letter addressed to "Lon," was introduced, addressed to "J.W.B., National Hotel, Washington, D.C.," and beginning "Friend Wilkes." Referring to oil speculation, "Lon" advised, "When you sink your well, go deep enough; don't fail, everything depends on you and your helpers."[24] These letters were introduced at the beginning of the trial, which Stanton and Holt wanted closed to the public, with only a summary to be released to the press, carefully edited by Holt. Interestingly, the witness for the prosecution who supplied the letters were found to be questionable at best. Robert Purdy, who brought the "Lon" letter to the government's attention, was, upon investigation, found to be the probable author of the letter, and had also misrepresented himself, claiming to be a government detective. Although Holt knew the fraudulent nature of the letter before the conclusion of the trial, he used it anyway. Purdy acknowledged during his testimony that he had been charged with writing the "Lon" letter. Holt sought to discourage further investigation of Purdy.[25]

Stanton had issued a reward poster which stated that those accused of aiding the assassins would be tried by a military commission and executed. This was issued before the trial commenced, and even before the legal opinion of Attorney General Speed, which supported such a trial, had been issued. In connection with an earlier case involving a military trial, a high official of the Navy Department was quoted as saying, "Your civil courts are organized to acquit; we [the military] organize to convict!"[26]

Payments were made to individuals involved with the assassination trial from "The War Department Secret Service Fund." In a letter from a clerk at the War Department to E.B. French, second auditor at the General Accounting Office, dated July 26, 1870, we find the following information:

July 3, 1865	Richard Montgomery, Washington. May 9–22, June 8–14.
July 5, 1865	M. Bainbridge Ruggles, King George County, Va., $90. May 5–June 3.
July 5, 1865	A.R. Bainbridge, King George County, Va. $90. May 5–June 30.
August 7, 1865	John M. Lloyd, Surrattsville, Md., $150. May 12, June 30.
July 10, 1865	Louis J. Carland, Washington. $18. May 17, 18, 19, 30, 31, June 3.
August 11, 1865	Joseph Thomas Knott, Prince George's County, Md. $147. May 12, June 29.
August 14, 1865	William L. Bryant, King George County, Va. $84. May 12, June 7.

The letter mentions that "Secretary Stanton ... intended to apply to Congress for an appropriation to pay a certain amount which was connected with the conspiracy trial. This he never did." To this was added the admonition, "This must be confidential, of course."[27]

Richard Montgomery's work for Holt was called into question, as would others who testified about Confederate involvement in the assassination, as evidence arose that they were untrustworthy and their testimony probably fraudulent. Ruggles and Bainbridge were two of the Confederate soldiers who aided Booth and Herold in their escape. John M. Lloyd we have already met, his testimony against Mrs. Surratt being particularly devastating. Louis J. Carland was an employee of Ford's Theatre. Joseph Thomas Knott tended bar at the tavern in Surrattsville; his testimony at the trial was potentially damaging to Lloyd (see Chapter 6). William L. Bryant was another person who helped the fleeing Booth and Herold. Of course, it was and is common enough to compensate witnesses for travel, room and board expenses at a trial, but when we examine the amounts listed we must wonder. In 1865 dollars, these were large sums, especially Lloyd's share. Even if he had been wined and dined at the most expensive hotel in town for several days, Lloyd would not have needed $150. In fact, he was quartered at the Old Capitol Prison, where John T. Ford encountered him (see Chapter 6). Another prosecution witness, James B. Merritt, who presented testimony in support of Stanton and Holt's effort to tie the Confederate leaders to the assassination plot, was paid the princely sum of $6,768. Even this huge amount, far more than could be imagined for legitimate expenses at that time, did not satisfy Merritt, who had asked for more.

The most notorious of the false witnesses, Charles A. Dunham, was a fraud and committed perjury in testifying, a fact known to Stanton and Holt, but they never repudiated him, and blocked every move to have the trial dismissed or its harsh verdicts overturned. Richard Montgomery was commissioned a major in the army, and assigned to Holt's Bureau of Military Justice. Dunham's debts were paid by the U.S. government, and he also received additional money to cover his expenses, one such payment amounting to $240. Even as Dunham's papers proving that he had lied about virtually everything in his testimony, were being examined by Holt's subordinates, Holt himself was still describing Dunham as "a man of unusual intelligence and observation, and regarded by this Bureau as entirely reliable and trustworthy."[28]

It has been said that the government's reason for including Mrs. Mary E. Surratt among the defendants at the trial of the Lincoln assassination conspiracy suspects was to bring forth the missing conspirator, John H. Surratt, Jr., Mary's son. That John Surratt had been an active participant in Booth's conspiracy to kidnap President Lincoln was undeniable, even by John Surratt himself, though he denied involvement in the conspiracy to assassinate the president.[29]

If it is true that Stanton and Holt believed that prosecuting Mrs. Surratt might bring John Surratt to turn himself in to save his mother from execution, then that would seem to open the possibility that either Mrs. Surratt was entirely innocent, as she claimed, or that her involvement, if any, in the conspiracy was minor and that she should not have been given the extreme sentence.

Opposing that idea is the zeal displayed by the prosecution in building their case against Mrs. Surratt, including statements in the public press at the time of the trial, such as "Sufficient legal evidence exists to convince all those connected with the plot before any jury in the land," and "The government had a clear case against the accused; and before any decent court and jury, any fair lawyer could have got a verdict of guilty, which would not only have satisfied justice, but ... would have convinced the public mind."[30]

John Surratt himself commented on this in his later lecture. He said his friends "assured me there was no cause for fear [for his mother]. What else could I do but accept these unwavering assurances? Even had I thought otherwise, I could not have taken any action resulting in good." He maintained that his friends assured him that his mother's life was not in danger, and that he should remain in hiding. By the time he learned otherwise, it was too late to save her.[31] It seems most likely that John Surratt's surrender or capture would have made no difference in the government's case against his mother. All it would have accomplished was to have added one more rope to the gallows.

The issue of the legality of the trial of the Lincoln assassination suspects by a military commission was taken up at a moot court exercise at the T.C. Williams School of Law at the University of Richmond on February 12, 1993. Although a moot court has no standing as actual law, it gives law students a chance to present a case and gain experience in a realistic setting, supervised by law professors. This particular moot court dealt with an actual historical example—the case of Dr. Samuel A. Mudd. John Paul Jones, professor of law, stated, "The review of Dr. Mudd's case [was] the most thorough ever conducted."

The court consisted of Robinson O. Everett, former chief judge of the U.S. Court of Military Appeals and professor of law at Duke University; Edward D. Re, distinguished professor of law at St. John's School of Law; and Walter Thompson Cox, III, judge of the U.S. Court of Military Appeals and acting associate justice of the South Carolina Supreme Court. Counsel for the United States [prosecution] were John Jay Douglass, former commandant of the Judge Advocate General's School and professor of law at the University of Houston Law Center; and John S. Jenkins, associate dean and lecturer, George Washington University National Law Center, and former judge advocate general of the navy. Counsel for the petitioner [defense] were F. Lee Bailey, attorney at law and military trial lawyer; and Candida Ewing Staempfli Steel, attorney at law, former assistant corporation counsel for the District of Columbia, and Great-great-granddaughter of General Thomas Ewing, Jr., Dr. Mudd's lawyer at the 1865 trial.

Primary arguments for Dr. Mudd's defense centered on the question of jurisdiction and due process. The defense made use of the decision in *Ex parte Milligan*. The army attempted to prove that the serious nature

8. Justice?

of the crime and the conspiracy conducted in its planning was so grave that its purpose was to add new military impetus to the cause of the Confederacy. Citing ongoing military action after General Lee's surrender, the army concluded clear and present danger, especially in the District of Columbia. That danger was heightened by what was considered a major conspiracy to do away with the top level of the federal government. Arguments included commentary on Mudd's alleged role in what the army insisted was a plot to assassinate the commander-in-chief.

The cases for both sides were carefully prepared and expertly argued. In the end, the judges rejected the army's argument that they had jurisdiction. Doubts were even raised about the appropriateness of evidence presented accusing Dr. Mudd of conspiracy.

This moot court followed closely on the hearing conducted by the Army Board for the Correction of Military Records (ABCMR). This was a five-member panel of civilians empowered by the Department of the Army to consider revisions in military records. Ordinarily, this board would deal with recent cases, not one going back 127 years. Descendants of Dr. Samuel A. Mudd petitioned the army to review the case and overturn the conviction of Dr. Samuel Mudd. Leading this effort was Dr. Richard Dyer Mudd (1901–2002), grandson of Dr. Samuel Mudd. Dr. Richard Mudd had made the vindication of his grandfather a lifelong crusade, appealing to presidents of the United States, members of Congress, clergy,

Dr. Richard Dyer Mudd, the grandson of Dr. Samuel A. Mudd, spent many years working to have his grandfather's conviction and imprisonment removed from the record (photograph dated 1984, courtesy Saginaw Valley Historic Preservation Society, Thomas Mudd).

news media, virtually anyone who could bring pressure to bear upon the government in Dr. Mudd's behalf.

The board made it clear that they could not decide the question of the guilt or innocence of Dr. Mudd, but could rule on whether the army had had jurisdiction to try Mudd by a military commission. After reviewing the records of the original trial of 1865, listening to the presentations of Dr. Richard Mudd and various authorities in history and legal affairs, and considering the nature of the case, the board's decision was announced on July 24, 1992. It stated in part,

> The Board's research clearly shows that the civilian courts were fully open and operating in the District of Columbia in the Spring of 1865; that at the time President Lincoln was assassinated, Dr. Mudd was a civilian and a citizen of Maryland, a non-secessionist state; and that he had never served in the military or naval service.
>
> ... Furthermore, there is no evidence that the Capital was under siege or that any Confederate forces had invaded or were likely to invade the District of Columbia in the Spring of 1865.
>
> [The Board] therefore unanimously concludes that the military commission did not have jurisdiction to try him and that in doing so denied him his due process rights, particularly his right to trial by a jury of his peers. This denial constituted such a gross infringement of his Constitutionally protected rights, that his conviction should be set aside.

The board recommended "that the Archivist of the United States, the custodian of the Hunter Commission Report, correct the record in his possession by showing that Dr. Mudd's conviction was set aside pursuant to action taken under Title 10 USC 1552."

But this was not the end of the story. The ABCMR's decision was not an official order, only an advisory recommendation. The board did not have the authority to implement their recommendation. That authority lay with the leaders of the Department of the Army. An "Acting Assistant Secretary of the Army (Manpower and Reserve Affairs)," William Clark, denied the board's recommendation. His reason for refusing the board's unanimous recommendation are interesting, and have added to the controversy which has always surrounded Dr. Mudd's case. Clark's decision stated,

> It is not the role of the ABCMR to attempt to settle historical disputes. Neither is the ABCMR an appellate court. The precise issue which the ABCMR proposes to decide, the jurisdiction of the Military Commission over Dr. Mudd, was specifically addressed at the time in two separate habeas corpus proceedings, one before the Chief Justice of the Supreme Court, the other before a U.S. District Court. There was also an opinion by the Attorney General of the United States.

8. Justice?

The effect of the action recommended by the ABCMR would be to overrule all those determinations. Even if the issue might be decided differently today, it is inappropriate for a non judicial body, such as the ABCMR, to declare that the law 127 years ago was contrary to what was determined contemporarily by prominent legal authorities.

In a letter protesting the Clark decision, the author stated,

> The issue of the guilt or innocence of Dr. Samuel A. Mudd has been debated by students of the Lincoln assassination ever since that event. I will agree with Mr. Clark that the Board cannot determine that question, but neither can Mr. Clark, who, by his action has allowed to let stand Dr. Mudd's conviction, in effect affirming the original determination of guilt.... The failure to apply the Milligan decision to the Mudd case has a lot more to do with the politics of the time, and to the inflamed passions of the moment, than to sound legal reasoning.
>
> As to the issue that the Board cannot settle historical arguments, one need only ask why not? In referring this matter to the Board, the Army must have believed that the Board was the proper body to deal with the case. Why hold the hearing in the first place if that is not the Board's purpose? Who should have dealt with the case if not the Board?
>
> If the military commission of 1865 was a properly organized and Constitutional legal body, then Mr. Clark would be right in saying that the Board of 1992 cannot overturn its decision. But if it was not a legal body, as the Milligan decision clearly indicates, then its findings cannot be considered legally binding, not in 1865 and not in all the years since.[32]

No protests could move the Army in their determination to allow the convictions and punishments of the Lincoln assassination suspects to stand, not at the time, and not at any time since. Appeals to every authority, up to and including the highest, were denied.

> The White House, Washington
>
> To Dr. Richard D. Mudd   July 24, 1979
>
> I am aware of your efforts to clear the name of your grandfather, Dr. Samuel Mudd, who set the broken leg of President Lincoln's assassin, John Wilkes Booth, and who was himself convicted as a conspirator in the assassination. Your persistence in these efforts, extending over more than half a century, is a tribute to your sense of familial love and dedication and is a credit to the great principles upon which our nation was founded.
>
> ... Regrettably, I am advised that the findings of guilt and the sentence of the military commission that tried Dr. Mudd in 1865 are binding and conclusive judgments, and that there is no authority under law by which I, as President, could set aside his conviction.
>
> ... Nevertheless, I want to express my personal opinion that the declaration made by President [Andrew] Johnson in pardoning Dr. Mudd substantially discredits the validity of the military commission's judgment.... The Johnson pardon goes beyond a mere absolution of the crimes for which Dr. Mudd was convicted. The pardon states that Dr. Mudd's guilt was limited to aiding the

escape of [the] assassins and did not involve any other participation or complicity in the assassination plot itself ... but President Johnson went on to express his doubt concerning even Dr. Mudd's criminal guilt of aiding Lincoln's assassins in their escape...

A careful reading of the information provided to me about this case led to my personal agreement with the findings of President Johnson. I am hopeful that these conclusions will be given widespread circulation which will restore dignity to your grandfather's name...

Sincerely,

Jimmy Carter[33]

The White House, Washington   December 8, 1987

Dear Dr. Mudd:

I have investigated the situation with regard to your grandfather, Dr. Samuel Alexander Mudd. I know how much you have done and the effort you've put forth to get his name cleared of the charge against him. I regret to say I've learned that, as President, there is nothing I can do. Presidential power to pardon is all that is in a President's prerogatives and that, of course, was done by President Andrew Johnson.

Believe me, I'm truly sorry I can do nothing to help you in your long crusade. In my efforts to help, I came to believe as you do that Dr. Samuel Mudd was indeed innocent of any wrongdoing. But we'll have to accept that "full unconditional pardon" is what we must settle for.

Sincerely,

Ronald Reagan[34]

After the Army's decision to overrule their own Army Board for Correction of Military Records, and refusal to set aside the conviction of Dr. Mudd, the doctor's grandson, Dr. Richard D. Mudd, brought suit against the Army, in the person of Louis Caldera, secretary of the army. On October 29, 1998, U.S. District Judge Paul L. Friedman (1944–) found that the Army had failed to consider all of the evidence available, rendering their decision "arbitrary and capricious." This ruling did not deal with the question of the guilt or innocence of Dr. Samuel Mudd, but only with the Army's handling of the board recommendations. The court gave the Army thirty days in which to appeal the ruling, and that time passed without any action by the Army. The implications of this court decision are obvious: if Dr. Mudd was denied his rights by being tried by a military commission instead of a civil court, then so were the other seven defendants, who were all tried at the same time by the same military commission. This leaves the way open for other descendants of those tried to come forward, seeking some form of redress for the wrongful trial to which their ancestors were subjected in 1865.

On March 6, 2000, Army Assistant Secretary Patrick Henry again officially refused to accept the recommendations of the ABCMR that the record be changed to indicate Dr. Samuel Mudd was wrongfully convicted and imprisoned. The son of Dr. Richard D. Mudd, Thomas B. Mudd (1940–) appealed this decision before the United States Court of Appeals for the District of Columbia Circuit on September 3, 2002. The court issued its opinion on November 8, 2002. Excerpts from that opinion:

> The Appellant, Thomas B. Mudd ... seeks judicial review of the Army's refusal to reverse [Dr. Samuel Mudd's] conviction more than a century later. Appellant bases his claim on 10 U.S.C. s 1552 (a)(1) (2002), pursuant to which "(t)he Secretary of a military department may correct any military record ... when the Secretary considers it necessary to correct an error or remove an injustice." ... Appellant ... filed suit in the District Court, claiming that the action of the Secretary was arbitrary and capricious under the Administrative Procedure Act ("APA"), 5 U.S.C. S 706 (1)(A)(2002). The District Court heard the case twice, ... ultimately finding that the Secretary's decision was not arbitrary, capricious, or otherwise in violation of law. The District Court therefore granted summary judgment for the Army. Mudd II, 134 F. Supp. 2nd at 147.
> We agree that appellant cannot prevail on his claim. But we rely on different grounds than those advanced by the District Court. In our view, appellant's claim must be dismissed for want of standing. Under 10 U.S.C. s 1552 (g), "military record" pertains only to "an individual member or former member of the armed forces." Dr. Samuel Mudd was never a member of the armed forces. Therefore, even if appellant can establish Article III standing, his action must be still dismissed for want of prudential standing. Appellant's interest in correcting the military record that relates to his great-grandfather's conviction is not within the "zone of interests" protected by the statute covering the correction of military records.[35]

Ironically, in this denial of the Mudd appeal, the Army and the court recognized and cited that Dr. Samuel A. Mudd was not a member of the armed forces, a principal element in questioning the Army's right to try him under military law in the first place.

The author's argument to overturn the denial of the ABCMR's conclusion was expressed thusly:

President Clinton
The White House
Washington, DC   January 8, 1995
Dear Mr. President:
> ... the whole idea of such an important case being decided by a "lame duck" bureaucrat [William D. Clark, an acting assistant secretary in the G.H.W. Bush administration] is unworthy of the people and principles involved.
> ... It would be a great tragedy if a decision in the Samuel Mudd case came

too late for his grandson [Dr. Richard D. Mudd]. Please don't let that happen.[36]

The intention of this letter was to urge the president, in his capacity as commander-in-chief of the armed forces, to overrule the Clark decision and order the Secretary of the Army to implement the ABCMR's recommendations. The response from the White House was to refer this letter to the Department of Defense. No further action has been heard of from the White House.[37]

A letter from Stanton to President Johnson, dated February 15, 1867, sheds light on the legal problems facing the government in the wake of the Milligan decision:

> In view of the decision of the Supreme Court in Milligan's case respecting the limits and extent of the jurisdiction of military tribunals, this Department [War Department] is unable to determine what cases, if any, of those mentioned in the aforesaid reports can be acted upon by military authority. I should therefore recommend that they be referred to the Attorney General for his investigation and report to the end that the cases may be designated which are cognizant by the civil authorities, and such as are cognizant by military tribunals.[38]

It could be argued that this letter reflects Stanton's frustration with the Milligan decision, and his recognition that the trial of civilians under military law can no longer be accepted.

Is the Army afraid to admit they made a mistake? All of the people involved in the trial of the Lincoln assassination suspects are long dead. What difference could it make, generations later, to change the wording on a handful of yellowing old documents? Perhaps the answer to this question can be found in the following chapter, as we examine subsequent assumptions of power by presidents, and the use of military law, military commissions, and military courts to justify actions which go to the heart of our nation's laws, traditions, and concepts of justice.

9

HISTORY'S LONG SHADOW

The accused Lincoln assassination suspects were tried by a military commission under military law, and, according to the U.S. government, under the "Laws of War." What are known as the Laws of War are historical traditions, treaties and agreements between nations, addressing international conflicts, also described as the Law of Nations. In his legal opinion, Attorney General James Speed stated that "a military tribunal exists under and according to the Constitution in time of war.... Should Congress fail to create such tribunals, then, under the Constitution, they must be constituted according to the laws and usages of civilized warfare.... That the law of nations constitutes a part of the laws of the land must be admitted. The laws of nations are expressly made laws of the land by the Constitution, when it says that 'Congress shall have power to define and punish piracies and felonies committed on the high seas and offenses against the laws of nations.'" The quotation Speed cited does appear in the Constitution, so we must grant that the Founding Fathers recognized the existence of something called the Law of Nations, but anything more than that is an assumption, for the Constitution does not explain what was meant by "The Law of Nations."[1]

Laws of war are not exactly the same as the laws regulating the United States. Laws of War are not laws passed by the Congress, or by the state legislatures, or by local governments. They are not written down and published in huge, expensive sets of law books. Unlike our national laws, there is no system of courts to interpret the Laws of War. Much of what is called the Laws of War consists of precedent and practice. Since the nineteenth century, conventions have been held, and treaties agreed upon internationally, to set acceptable standards of behavior by the military in wartime. Nearly all of these treaties and agreements date after the 1860s.[2]

The first regulations governing the military of the United States were the Articles of War, established by the Continental Congress in 1775, before the United States existed as a sovereign nation. The new articles tended to follow British examples, modified over the years by the U.S. Congress as needed. The British adopted the establishment of courts-martial in 1686, with a panel of military officers conducting a hearing, and passing judgment on accused soldiers by a majority vote. George Washington (1732–1799), serving as an officer in the Virginia colonial militia in 1756, wrote that the British Articles of War existed to preserve "the rights and liberties of the people against the arbitrary proceedings of the military officers." During the American Revolution, the Continental Congress established military laws and procedures, clearly intending that they relate to the trial of soldiers, not of civilians. Among the instructions given by the Congress to General Washington was that he "mak(e) it your special care in discharge of the great trust committed unto you, that the liberties of America receive no detriment."[3]

In the Declaration of Independence, Thomas Jefferson (1743–1826) listed the reasons for the colonies' separation from the rule of the British king, among them being: "He has made judges dependent on his will alone.... He has affected to render the military independent of and superior to the Civil Power.... For depriving us, in many cases, of the benefits of Trial by Jury.... For taking away our Charters, abolishing our most valuable laws, and altering fundamentally the forms of our Governments."[4]

In a letter to James Madison (1751–1836), Jefferson mentioned, "a bill of rights providing for ... protection against standing armies, ... that eternal and unremitting force of the habeas corpus laws, and trials by jury in all matters of fact triable by the laws of the land and not by the law of nations. He added, "a bill of rights is what the people are entitled to against every government on earth, general or particular, and what no just government should refuse, or rest on inferences."[5]

The Massachusetts Bill of Rights, in 1780, declared, "No person can in any case be subject to law-martial, or to any penalties or pains, by virtue of that law, except those employed in the army or navy, and except the military in actual service, but by authority of the legislature."[6] Elbridge Gerry (1744–1814) stated that he "never expected to hear in a republic a motion to empower the Executive alone to declare war."[7] Lincoln's first attorney general, Edward Bates (1793–1869), observed that the president, though designated by the Constitution as commander-in-chief, may not be "skilled in the art of war and qualified to marshal a host in the field of battle," but commands in an administrative way, overseeing those who are "subject to the orders of the civil magistrate, and he and his army are always subordinate to the civil power."[8]

A work of British criminal law written in the early 18th century, called a "classic" in the field, Hale's *History of the Common Law,* stated that military law "is only to extend to members of the army, or to those of the opposed army, and never ... intended to be executed or exercised upon others, for others who had not listed under the army had no color or reason to be bound by military constitutions applicable to the army whereof they were not parts, but they were to be ordered and governed according to the laws of which they subject although it were a time of war."[9]

In another pre–Civil War work, Whiting's War *Powers of the President,* we find this statement: "All judicial convictions must be in accordance with the laws establishing the judiciary and regulating its proceedings. Whenever a person accused of crime is held by the government, not as a belligerent or prisoner of war, not merely as a citizen of the United States, then he is amenable to, and must be tried under and by virtue of, standing laws; and all rights guaranteed to other citizens in his condition must be conceded to him."[10]

The power assumed by President Lincoln, to suspend the writ of habeas corpus, thereby allowing the federal government to arrest and hold citizens without charges being brought against them, and subjecting those so arrested to be tried by military courts under military law, was challenged in two key cases, *Ex parte Marryman* in 1861 and *Ex parte Vallandigham* in 1864. Neither of these cases entirely settled the issues, both of whether the suspension power lies with the president or with Congress, or the question of whether American citizens can lawfully be tried by military courts or commissions when they are not members of the military, and when civilian courts are open and functioning. The definitive word was finally handed down by the U.S. Supreme Court in *Ex parte Milligan* in 1866, at least as far as the second question is concerned.[11]

Francis Lieber (1798–1872), aside from being renowned as an authority on military law, became indirectly involved in the trial of the Lincoln assassination conspiracy suspects, as a publication of his was used by the prosecution to support the authority of the government to conduct the trial under military law. Appended to the official record of the trial are excerpts from "Instructions for the Government of Armies of the United States in the Field." Lieber's "Instructions" were "approved by the president of the United States [Lincoln], he commands that they be published for the information of all concerned."[12] Lieber, writing well before the assassination, had some interesting things to say, some portions of which may make us wonder whether Stanton and Holt had actually read Lieber's "Instructions."

> Martial law is simply military authority exercised in accordance with the laws and usages of war.... As martial law is executed by military force, it is incumbent upon those who administer it to be strictly guided by the principles of justice, honor and humanity—virtues adorning a soldier even more than other men, for the very reason that he possesses the power of his arms against the unarmed....
>
> Military necessity does not admit of cruelty, that is, the infliction of suffering for the sake of suffering or for revenge, ... nor of tortures to extort confessions....
>
> A prisoner of war is a public enemy armed or attached to the hostile army for active aid, who has fallen into the hands of the captor, either fighting or wounded, on the field or in the hospital, by individual surrender or by capitulation....
>
> No belligerent has the right to declare that he will treat every captured man in arms of a levy *en masse* as a brigand or bandit....
>
> A prisoner of war is subject to no punishment for being a public enemy, nor is any revenge wreaked upon him by the intentional infliction of any suffering, or disgrace, by cruel imprisonment, want of food, by mutilation, death, or any other barbarity....
>
> The law of nations allows every sovereign government to make war upon another sovereign state, and, therefore, admits of no rules or laws different from those of regular warfare regarding the treatment of prisoners of war, although they may belong to the army of a government which the captor may consider as a wanton and unjust assailant....
>
> A spy is a person who secretly, in disguise or under false pretense, seeks information with the intention of communicating it to the enemy....
>
> The law of war ... makes no difference on account of the difference of sexes...
>
> The law of war does not allow proclaiming either an individual belonging to the hostile army, or a citizen, or a subject of the hostile government, an outlaw, who may be slain without trial by any captor, any more than the modern law of peace allows such international outlawry; on the contrary, it abhors such outrage. The sternest retaliation should follow the murder committed in consequence of such proclamation, made by whatever authority. Civilized nations look with horror upon offers of rewards for the assassination of enemies, as relapses into barbarism.[13]

As can be seen, Lieber's "Instructions" can and do cut both ways. Another quote from Lieber, made well before the Civil War, caused him problems later: "It is obvious that, whatever wise provisions a constitution may contain, nothing is gained if the power of declaring martial law be left in the hands of the executive ... that this cannot be done by the president alone, but by Congress only, need hardly be mentioned."[14] Although he changed his mind about this, and supported Lincoln's suspension of habeas corpus as necessary to save the Union, Lieber was embarrassed by his about-face, and retained his concern over the danger to liberties created by a large standing army: "Make our present large army a homogeneous, vast democratic army ... let some striking victory knit them well together, men to men, and then to the general, and every person vested in the analytical chemistry of History will tell you that a Bonaparte, dictating after a Lodi is unavoidable. No Congress, no Parliament can keep under an organized vast democratic army."[15] Shocked by the assassination of Lincoln, Lieber accepted Stanton's appointment as archivist of the Confederate papers and documents captured at the close of the war. Stanton's interest in the Confederate papers centered upon the hoped-for discovery of evidence of rebel complicity in the assassination of the president. But the task of sorting through the voluminous quantities of papers occupied Lieber and his staff for many months, outlasting the conspiracy trial, and, while furnishing much for historians, failed to produce any unambiguous evidence of the complicity of Jefferson Davis or other high officials of the Confederacy.[16]

Lieber's "Instructions" proved to be a major influence in the establishment of similar codes for other nations, and for the Hague Conferences of 1899 and 1907. The United States War Department issued its "Rules of Land Warfare" in 1914, also taking its inspiration from Lieber. But as with guarantees of liberty written into the Constitution, instructions and rules for war can often be brushed aside in the heat of the moment. After American suppression of the Philippine revolt in 1902, the setting aside of Lieber's efforts to instill humane treatment was explained in language which would haunt America's military in Vietnam, seventy years later. When asked whether the destruction of civilians' huts could be considered conforming to the rules of civilized warfare, an American officer stated, "These people are not civilized."[17]

In 1916 a bill was introduced in the U.S. Senate to allow military trials of those accused of sedition, or the incitement of rebellion against the government. With World War I in progress and America drifting toward entering the war, the bill was aimed at spies. Connecticut senator Frank Brandegee (1864–1924), a Republican, moved that the bill should be reviewed by the Judiciary Committee to decide if it violated the Constitution. Brandegee stated his opinion that the bill "simply bristles with constitutional questions and in my opinion is absolutely violative of every guaranty contained in the Constitution as to trial by jury and individual liberty." President Woodrow Wilson (1856–1924) agreed, writing that he was "wholly and unalterably opposed to such legislation (as) not only unconstitutional, but that in character it would put us nearly upon the level of the very people we are fighting and affecting to despise." Wilson's opposition killed the bill.[18]

On the night of June 13, 1942, a lone U.S. Coast Guardsman patrolling a stretch of beach near Amagansett, on New York's Long Island, encountered four men who offered him $260 to forget that he had seen them. Returning with his supervisor, he found that the mysterious men were gone, but the Coast Guardsmen discovered boxes of explosives, a German cigarette pack, and discarded German naval uniforms. The United States had been at war with Nazi Germany for six months, and here was evidence of the arrival of German spies on American soil. The leader of the four men was George John Dasch (1903–1992), whose American-accented English and familiarity with America after living there before the war resulted in his being made leader of the team. After arriving in America, however, Dasch decided to turn himself in to the FBI and alert them to the Nazi sabotage mission, which included a second team, landed near Jacksonville, Florida, which was to join forces with Dasch's team to sabotage American industrial, transportation, and power generation targets.

Dasch traveled to Washington, D.C., and alerted the FBI of his presence, expecting to be received as a hero. It took repeated efforts to convince the FBI that he was telling them the truth. Showing them the $82,000 the Germans had given him to finance his operations helped. Within two weeks of their initial landing, all eight German saboteurs had been arrested. FBI director J. Edgar Hoover (1895–1972) claimed sole credit for his bureau for foiling the Nazis, and his public statement alerted the Germans, who cancelled the planned landings of additional saboteurs.

President Franklin D. Roosevelt (1882–1945) determined to accept the recommendation of the War Department and try the Germans under military law by a military commission. As an army intelligence general put it, "The exigencies of the present situation appear to demand drastic action without too much deference to the technical rights, which might be accorded, under the Constitution." Because the Germans had been arrested before they could carry out any acts of sabotage, to try them as civilians in a civil court might bring a penalty of "only a two-year offense at most." President Roosevelt suggested trying them by court-martial, where the death penalty could be imposed. However, Attorney General Francis Biddle (1886–1968) advised against it, recommending trial by a military commission, whose rules of evidence would be less strict and whose verdict and sentence would not have to be unanimous. The legality of such a trial by military commission was questioned by some Justice Department lawyers, but it was considered that the American public needed to see a speedy and harsh treatment of the saboteurs to emphasize the seriousness of the threat of these enemy agents. Roosevelt issued his order on July 2, announcing that the "safety of the United States demands that all enemies who have entered upon the territory of the United States as part of an invasion or predatory incursion, or who have entered in order to commit sabotage, espionage, or other hostile or warlike acts, should be promptly tried in accordance with the law of war." Specifying the "law of war" rather than the Articles of War, or any other actual law established by the U.S. Congress, would eliminate the normal rules of procedure of the civil courts or even military courts, where the rights of the accused would be respected. Not only was this proclamation aimed at the eight Nazi agents (two of whom were naturalized American citizens) but anyone aiding the enemies of the United States, "or [who commit] violations of the law of war, shall be subject to the law of war and to the jurisdiction of military tribunals."[19] Thus, Roosevelt assumed powers nearly as sweeping as had Lincoln, eighty-one years before.

As had been the case at the trial of the Lincoln conspiracy suspects, defense attorneys found their objections overruled most of the time. One of the attorneys stated that it "was pretty apparent in the beginning that the commission was against us." The case was appealed to the U.S. Supreme Court. The argument was that the defendants had not committed any acts of sabotage, since they had been arrested before they had been able to act. The parallel with the Lincoln conspiracy suspects becomes obvious when the defense attorneys cited the *Ex parte Milligan* decision of 1866, holding that military courts and commissions are intended for use by the military against its own members, not civilians or foreigners. Attorney General Biddle maintained that "the president's power over enemies who enter this country in time of war, as armed invaders intending to commit hostile acts, must be absolute." The Supreme Court was not in a mood to accept a confrontation with the president in time of war.

It is doubtful that President Roosevelt had the time to carefully read and consider the transcript of the entire trial. Roosevelt managed the trial from behind the scenes, reminiscent of how Stanton had done so in the 1865 trial. Also, as in the Lincoln Conspiracy suspects' trial, the laws governing the case were the "Laws of War," rather than properly established American law. President Roosevelt maintained absolute authority throughout the whole case.[20]

The U.S. Supreme Court, in its decision *Ex parte Quirin*, stated,

> The law of war draws a distinction between the armed forces and the peaceful populations of belligerent nations and also between those who are lawful

and unlawful combatants. Lawful combatants are subject to capture and detention as prisoners of war by opposing military forces. Unlawful combatants are likewise subject to capture and detention, but in addition they are subject to trial and punishment by military tribunals for acts which render their belligerency unlawful.... An enemy combatant who without uniform comes secretly through the lines for the purpose of waging war by destruction of life or property, are [sic] familiar examples of belligerents who are generally deemed not to be entitled to the status of prisoners of war, but to be offenders against the law of war subject to trial and punishment by military tribunals.[21]

Richard Quirin was one of the would-be German saboteurs headed by Dasch. Upon their conviction by a military commission, all eight were sentenced to death. Two had their sentences commuted by President Roosevelt, including Dasch. The other six were executed on August 8, 1942. The Supreme Court had issued its decision on July 31, 1942, but held up release of the full opinion until October 29, 1942. Justice Robert H. Jackson (1892–1954) stated,

The Articles of War ... are clearly inapplicable to this case [*Ex parte Quirin*] and it is abundantly clear to me that it is well within the war powers of the president to create a non-statutory military tribunal of the sort here in question.... The right to convene such an advisory committee of his staff as a "military commission" for the discharge of his duties toward prisoners of war is one that follows from his position as commander in chief.

Justice Jackson did feel obliged to add that the president's power must be "discharged, of course, in the light of any obligation undertaken by our country under treaties or conventions or under customs and usages so generally accepted as to constitute the laws of warfare." Long after the case had been decided, Justice Jackson withdrew his opinion concurring with the majority in the Quirin case.[22]

It can be said that the case of the German saboteurs differs considerably from the case of the Lincoln assassination suspects. In 1942, the United States was legally at war with Germany, and the saboteurs were belligerents in that war, serving America's enemy. They were clearly enemy prisoners of war, and as such, could be dealt with as prisoners of war. The Lincoln conspiracy suspects, however, were not members of the rebel forces, and, it appears, not officially a part of the Confederate effort. One could argue that the government's attempt to tie the assassination suspects into the Southern government was intended to legitimize the government's case against them, as part of the effort to defeat the rebellion. The government did not, however, make such an effort in 1865. The similarities in the two cases center upon the issue of whether a military commission was the necessary and proper body to exercise jurisdiction over the cases.

As we have seen, the defense lawyers in the Lincoln conspirators trial argued that a military commission had no such authority. In the German saboteurs case it was also argued that the prisoners should have been tried in a federal civilian court, or at least, by a military court martial under the Articles of War. The Supreme Court's ruling in the Quirin case did not settle the matter for all time, since no legal ruling can ever be said to be binding eternally.[23]

In 1941, shortly after the Japanese attack on the United States, which plunged America into World War II, actions were taken against Japanese citizens in America, and against Americans of Japanese ancestry. Public uncertainty and fear, especially in the West Coast states, led to the internment of over 100,000 people, most of them lawful citizens of the United States. There can be no doubt that old-fashioned racism was at the heart of this action. Newspaper columnist Henry McLemore wrote, "Let us have no patience with the enemy or anyone whose veins carry his blood." Army lieutenant general John De Witt, who commanded army forces on the West Coast, stated, "The fact that no sabotage has taken place to date is a disturbing and confirming indication that such action will be taken." Such was the feeling of the time that eminent Americans, including Earl Warren (1891–1974), then California attorney general and later chief justice of the United States, supported and encouraged the internment and relocation. President Franklin D. Roosevelt signed the order on February 19, 1942, giving the U.S. Army the power to arrest, transport, and imprison Japanese and Japanese Americans in the states of Washington, Oregon, California, and part of Arizona, in camps in the California desert and other isolated areas inland, as far east as Arkansas.

The rationale for the mass relocation was the fear of espionage and sabotage by Japanese and Americans of Japanese ancestry in support of America's enemy, Imperial Japan. Although millions of Americans were of German and Italian descent, no similar mass roundup or internment of them was carried out. In the U.S. territory of Hawaii, where a large portion of the population were Japanese or Japanese American, no internment of these people was carried out, in spite of Hawaii being closer to Japan and far more vulnerable to Japanese invasion than the mainland. Furthermore, in the Hawaiian Islands, throughout the course of the war, not one act of sabotage was charged against any Japanese or Japanese American.[24]

In the Supreme Court cases which arose from the arrests, relocation, and seizure of properties of the Japanese and Japanese Americans, some statements were made which bear upon the issue of turning over the legal system to the military. In the case of *Hirabayashi v. United States*, Justice

Francis W. Murphy (1890–1949), although joining the majority to uphold the government curfew against "all persons of Japanese ancestry," stated, "broad guarantees of the Bill of Rights and other provisions of the Constitution protecting essential liberties" do not cease to exist because of "the mere existence of a state of war.... There are constitutional boundaries which it is our duty to uphold.... Disturbances based on color and ancestry are utterly inconsistent with our traditions and ideals. They are at variance with the principles for which we are now waging war."[25] In the case of *Korematsu v. United States*, Justice Murphy stated that in American law, the actions of individuals are "the sole basis for deprivation of rights," not inherited factors such as race or ethnic origin. In the same case, Justice Owen J. Roberts (1875–1955) also stated, "If any fundamental assumption underlies our system, it is that guilt is personal and not inheritable." Justice Jackson further issued a profound warning for the future:

> A military order, however unconstitutional, is not apt to last longer than the military emergency. Even during that period a succeeding commander may revoke it all. But once a judicial opinion rationalizes such an order to show that it conforms to the Constitution, or rather rationalizes the Constitution to show that the Constitution sanctions such an order, the Court for all time has validated the principle of racial discrimination in criminal procedure and of transplanting American citizens. The principle then lies about like a loaded weapon ready for the hand of any authority that can bring forward a plausible claim of an urgent need.[26]

The American Civil Liberties Union has called the mass arrests and internment of Japanese and American citizens of Japanese ancestry "the worst single wholesale violation of civil rights of American citizens in our history." President Roosevelt regretted "the burdens of evacuations and detentions which military necessity had imposed upon these people." But his regrets did not prevent him from approving the order for internment. Roosevelt's attorney general, Francis Biddle, reflecting on the president's motives, stated, "I do not think he was much concerned with the gravity or implication of this step.... He was never theoretical about things. What must be done to defend the country must be done." Secretary of the Interior Harold L. Ickes (1874–1952) stated, "The continued retention of these innocent people would be a blot upon the history of this country."[27]

Justice William O. Douglas (1898–1980), writing about his opinion in a related case, *Ex parte Endo*, said, "While the Army could evacuate the Japanese, it had no authority even in time of war to detain them in camps, as it was doing, absent evidence that those detained were not loyal to the United States." He later expressed regret for his affirmative vote in the Korematsu case: "It may be that military orders evacuating Americans of Japanese ancestry from the West Coast in World War II would never have been sustained except in the climate of war. My judgment is not the best because, as I have often said, my vote to affirm was one of my mistakes." He went on to explain how a champion of civil rights could be partially blinded in a moment of stress and confusion: "The Pentagon advised us [the Supreme Court] that the Japanese army could take everything west of the Rockies if they chose to land. Evacuation of the entire population would of course have been permissible by constitutional standards pertaining in time of war.... The Pentagon's argument was that if the Japanese army landed in areas thickly populated by Americans of Japanese ancestry, the opportunity for sabotage and confusion would be great. By doffing their uniforms they would be indistinguishable from the other thousands of people of like color and stature. It was not much of an argument, but it swayed a majority of the Court, including myself.... Locking up the evacuees after they had been removed had no military justification.... I have always regretted that I bowed to my elders and withdrew my opinion."[28] The military's argument described here was, of course, utter nonsense, since if it had been true, the same would have applied to the East Coast, regarding German and Italian invaders (which actually happened on a very small scale, as we have seen), but no serious arguments were put forward to intern the millions of Americans of German and Italian ancestry.

We can see that hysteria, fear, and prejudice, whether in Lincoln's time or much later, is a poison which can cloud the minds of even the greatest champions of individual rights and liberties.

The use of war, or warlike conditions, as justification for the laying aside of Constitutional provisions and/or guarantees of liberties, is not new. Even well before the Civil War, presidents began twisting the meaning of the Constitution to enable them to use the military to accomplish their ends. The quasi-war with France of 1798–1800 was cited by the U.S. State Department as precedent for the Vietnam War of 1961–1973, but this was seen to be reaching far beyond reality, even at the time. Congress openly debated the action against France before taking action, and President John Adams (1735–1826) was careful to include the Congress in his preparations. Congress took action to prepare for war, but there was no formal declaration. The initiation of war by the Congress did not have to be through a formal declaration, the Supreme Court ruled in 1801. "Congress is empowered to declare a general war, or Congress may wage a limited war; limited in place, in object, and in time," according to Justice Samuel Chase (1741–1811). It was recognized, though, that Congress had the authority to impose limits upon the president's conduct of a war, whether declared or not.

President Thomas Jefferson sent warships to the Mediterranean Sea to protect American ships and their crews from being seized by North African pashas and pirates. The President was careful to authorize the U.S. Navy to conduct a defensive action only, admitting that under the Constitution, he did not have the power to wage offensive war without the authorization of Congress.

President James K. Polk (1795–1849) ordered an American army to occupy territory which lay along the border with Mexico in 1846, and was claimed by both nations. Mexican forces clashed with American, and Polk and his supporters called it war.

Senator John Middleton Clayton (1796–1856) questioned the war, in words which would echo down to the 1960s.

> I do not see on what principle it can be shown that the president, without consulting Congress and obtaining its sanction for the procedure, has a right to send an army to take up a position, where, as it must have been foreseen, the inevitable consequence would be war.

Another critic, an obscure one-term congressman from Illinois named Abraham Lincoln (1809–1865), had this to say.

> Allow the president to invade a neighboring nation, whenever he shall deem it necessary to repel invasion, and you allow him to do so whenever he may choose to say he deems it necessary for such purpose—and you allow him to make war at pleasure.... This, our convention understood to be the most oppressive of all kingly oppressions; and they resolved to so frame the Constitution that no one man should hold the power of bringing the oppression upon us.

Years later, as president, Lincoln was faced with a unique and extraordinarily dangerous situation: a large-scale rebellion of one part of the United States. When that rebellion began, in mid–April, 1861, Congress was not in session. Lincoln acted promptly, calling for very large increases in the armed forces, a naval blockade of the rebelling section, and the suspension of the writ of habeas corpus. Unsure of the legality of his actions, Lincoln asked Congress to pass legislation approving of the measures he had taken to suppress the rebellion.[29]

By the 1960s, the United States had committed its armed forces to hostilities around the world many times. The Constitution of the United States very clearly places the power to declare war with the Congress. The only reference in the Constitution to war in connection with the president is in Article 2, section 2: "The President shall be Commander-in-Chief of the army and navy of the United States, and of the militia of the several states, when called into the actual service of the United States." No explanation is given as to what is meant by the title "commander-in-chief." We have already observed that no such military rank is recognized by the armed forces, and no uniform or badge of rank authorized for the president.[30] Only five times in American history has the Congress voted to declare war: 1812 against Britain; 1846 against Mexico; 1898 against Spain; 1917 against Germany; and 1941 against Germany, Italy, and Japan. Anything else involving the use of military force in combat is not and has not been a war in the legal meaning as understood by the Founding Fathers, under the Constitution.

During the 1960s, with America's involvement in combat in Southeast Asia, questions were asked regarding why the president did not ask for, nor the Congress authorize, a declaration of war. On February 26, 1966, Defense Secretary Robert S. McNamara (1916–2009) submitted the official policy on the question of declaring war:

> To declare war would ... increase the danger of misunderstanding of our true objectives in the conflict by the various Communist states, and increase the chances of their expanded involvement in it.... There is nothing in modern international law which requires a state to declare war before engaging in hostilities against another state. Absence of a formal declaration of war is not a factor which makes an international use of force unlawful.... A declaration of war is not necessary either to authorize the actions that have been taken by the United States in Vietnam or to provide an expression of congressional intent on the Vietnamese situation. The President has power under Article 2, section 2 of the Constitution as Commander in Chief to deploy U.S. military forces to Vietnam for the purpose of assisting South Vietnam to defend itself from armed aggression from North Vietnam. There have been at least 125 instances in which the president, without congressional authority, and in the absence of a declaration of war, has ordered the armed forces to take actions ... abroad.... Congressional intent is expressed by the joint resolution of Congress of August 10, 1964 ... explicitly approving all necessary steps, including the use of armed force, in the defense of freedom in Southeast Asia.

Congressman F. Edward Hebert (1901–1979), Democrat of Louisiana, a member of the House Armed Services Committee, stated, "As far as I'm concerned the Tonkin Gulf Resolution made it official. It was a declaration of war. On the basis of that resolution the president can do anything he needs or wants to do." An unnamed "military expert" was quoted as saying, "The only advantage of a declaration of war now would be to commit the U.S. to go in and win the war. That would mean action on the home front, too—prosecution of treasonable utterances and acts such as burning draft cards and the flag."[31] In other words, by this argument the president, not the Congress, now has the power to wage war, even without congressional authorization, and a congressional resolution is legally a law, with the same force and authority as a declaration of war, together with the possible suspension of habeas corpus. All this without the approval of Congress or any change in the Constitution. What would the Founding Fathers have thought of that?

The Gulf of Tonkin Resolution, as it came to be known, was officially the Southeast Asia Resolution, Public Law 88-408, passed by the Congress on August 10, 1964, by a vote of 416–0 in the House of Representatives and 88–2 in the Senate. This was a response to what was claimed to be an attack on U.S. Navy vessels in international waters in the Gulf of Tonkin, east of North Vietnam. The claim of attacks by North Vietnamese torpedo boats, and just how close the U.S. ships were to the coast, remains controversial to this day. Many have come to believe that no such attacks actually occurred.[32] Senator Wayne L. Morse (1900–1974), Democrat of Oregon, said, "We don't have a declaration of war because the president doesn't dare to recommend one. And I maintain that if you can't justify a war declaration, then you can't justify the war."[33] Morse was one of only two members of Congress to cast votes against the resolution.

The secretary of defense at the time, Robert S. McNamara, later wrote:

> Congress recognized the vast power the resolution granted to President Johnson, but it did not conceive of it as a declaration of war and did not intend it to be used, as it was, an authorization for an enormous expansion of U.S. forces in Vietnam—from 16,000 military advisors to 550,000 combat troops. Securing a declaration of war and specific authorization for the introduction of combat forces in subsequent years might well have been impossible; not seeking it was certainly wrong.

The U.S. Congress cannot claim that it did not understand that it was handing its war-declaring power over to the president, or that it was tricked into delegating its Constitutional responsibility for having the ultimate authority in deciding whether the United States should go to war. McNamara quotes the following exchange between Senator John Sherman Cooper (1901–1991), Republican of Kentucky, and Senator J. William Fulbright (1905–1995), Democrat of Arkansas, in debating the Tonkin Gulf Resolution:

> COOPER: Are we now giving the president advance authority to take whatever action he may deem necessary respecting South Vietnam and its defense, or with respect to the defense of any other country included in the [South East Asia Treaty Organization] treaty?
> FULBRIGHT: I think that is correct.

COOPER: Then, looking ahead, if the president decided that it was necessary to use such force as could lead to war, we will give that authority by this resolution?
FULBRIGHT: That is the way I would interpret it.[34]

The Tonkin Gulf Resolution was written, not by Congressmen, but by President Lyndon B. Johnson's (1908–1973) White House staff. Secretary McNamara and Senator Fulbright were the principal salesmen in getting the Congress to approve it. Johnson himself even admitted to having doubts afterwards regarding the North Vietnamese "attacks" on the U.S. destroyers, telling an aide, "Hell, those dumb stupid sailors were just shooting at flying fish." But Johnson wanted the resolution so that he could claim congressional approval of whatever he wanted to do in enlarging the war in Southeast Asia. Senator Morse had been tipped off by a Pentagon officer that the USS *Maddox*, one of the two destroyers involved in the incident, had been involved in South Vietnamese raids on the North Vietnamese coast. Thus, Secretary McNamara was either woefully ignorant of what had been happening in the Gulf, and was therefore not the appropriate person to brief Congress, or the secretary lied to the Congress.

Nearly two years later, Senate Foreign Relations Committee chairman William Fulbright had changed his tune. He changed from Johnson's salesman of a widening war policy into an increasingly more skeptical critic of that policy.[35] But by then it was too late. President Johnson, after tricking the Congress and the American public into transferring the decision for war to him and away from the Congress, as required by the Constitution, had escalated a relatively small military advisory mission into a full-scale war, which ultimately cost America over 58,000 dead, not to mention countless numbers of Vietnamese.

The debacle of the Vietnam War ultimately led to the adoption of the War Powers Act of 1973, which was, or should have been, the most important attempt to restore the Constitutional war-declaring function to the Congress since the Founding Fathers designed it that way. The Vietnam War was still under way, despite the American public's clearly stated preference for peace, expressed in voting for presidential candidates who promised a limited war leading to peace, in the elections of 1964, 1968, and 1972. President Richard M. Nixon (1913–1994), Johnson's successor, had campaigned in 1968 that he had "a secret plan" to end the war "in six months" after his election to the presidency. Yet, under Nixon, the war went on for another four years, only to end with a North Vietnamese victory. Nixon's policy had never offered much of a chance of winning the war, and virtually all of the dire predictions of what would happen if the North won did not materialize. Today, Americans are doing business in Vietnam and there is a growing tourist industry. All the sacrifices in blood and money had been for nothing.[36]

The War Powers Act, or Resolution, was an attempt to insure that the decision to commit U.S. military forces to combat was to be a mutual decision of the Congress and the president. It requires a President to consult with Congress whenever he feels it necessary to send troops into battle. Section 2 of the Resolution allows the commitment of the military "Only pursuant to (1) a declaration of war, (2) specific statutory authorization, or (3) a national emergency created by attack upon the United States, its territories or possessions, or its armed forces." The President must, "in every possible instance," consult Congress "before introducing United States Armed Forces into hostilities" or "imminent hostilities," and the president "shall consult regularly with Congress until United States Armed Forces are no longer engaged in hostilities or have been removed from such situations." If there is no congressional declaration of war, the president is required to notify the Speaker of the House of Representatives and the president pro tempore of the Senate that armed forces have been involved in hostilities. Such notification is to include the constitutional and legislative authority authorizing the action, and to provide an estimate of the scope and duration of the involvement. Additional such reports are required at least every six months. If the Congress is not in session when such involvement occurs, the president is to convene the Congress for notification. The President must discontinue the action within sixty days unless Congress authorizes the action or declares war. Furthermore, the Congress has the power to order the president to terminate the action whenever it chooses to do so.

President Nixon vetoed the War Powers Act, but Congress overrode the veto. Since its passage in 1973, over 100 presidential reports have been submitted, but only once was the Congress notified of the possibility of imminent hostilities, when President Gerald R. Ford (1913–2006) ordered U.S. Marines to rescue the crew of a freighter, the SS *Mayaguez*, which had been seized by Cambodia in 1975. Unfortunately, the War Powers Act's provisions do not automatically go into force. Congress must decide whether to invoke the act in each case, and it is much easier for the president, a single individual, to rally public support for military action, than it is for Congress, which probably would not be able to act with anything like unanimity, to stop a war begun by the president. Congressmen, by the nature of their office, are closer to the people than anyone else in the national government, and so are more vulnerable to the whims and shifting moods of the public, when called to act against a presidential and news media–fanned flame presented as a crisis.

One of the problems involved in implementing the War Powers Act is that presidents tend to use their own discretion in characterizing the nature of a military commitment. President Jimmy Carter (1924–) did report to the Congress on the military hostage rescue mission in Iran in 1980, but he did not inform Congress in advance because the mission was not an act of force. How the hostages were to be rescued without using force, deep within a nation openly hostile to the United States, would be difficult to imagine. The need for secrecy to insure the success of the mission was another reason for not notifying Congress in advance. President Ronald Reagan (1911–2004) did not report the sending of U.S. troops to El Salvador in 1981 because, in the administration's interpretation, the soldiers were "advisors" only, and would not be taking part in hostilities. It was recalled by some that the first American military forces sent to Vietnam were also "advisors." Efforts to invoke the War Powers Act over the invasion of Grenada in 1983 were not successful due to the failure of Congress to follow through strongly enough.[37]

It has become so commonplace since 1973 for the War Powers Act to be ignored by successive presidents, and rendered impotent by congressional disagreement and inaction, so that it appears that either the act must be revised to automatically go into effect whenever U.S. military forces are involved, or may become involved, in hostilities, or we must abandon the pretense of congressional involvement and simply accept the fact that the armed forces are entirely under the authority of the president alone and serve at his pleasure, with no checks and balances as required by the Founding Fathers. To admit that, of course, would be to admit that the United States is no longer a democracy governed by law.

In 2008, a bipartisan commission, after a year of study and discussion of the War Powers Act, concluded that it was ineffective and possibly unconstitutional. The commission, headed by former secretaries of state James A. Baker (1930–) and Warren Christopher (1925–2011), recommended the passage of a War Powers Consultation Act establishing a new joint congressional committee and requiring the president to consult the committee before sending the armed forces into "significant armed conflict." congressional approval would be required within 30 days of such a commitment. The proposal as reported could still be vetoed by the president and would still have to be implemented by a congressional vote each time a conflict arose, and response to terrorist attacks as well as covert actions would be exempted from the new act. Thus, even as this new proposal was being put forward, it bore within itself the seeds of its own failure. Christopher admitted that "it comes down to questions of congressional will ... to resist funding or to limit it.... There is nothing we can do by statute that will change that."[38] So far, no such revision has been enacted by Congress.

On September 11, 2001, hijacked aircraft were crashed into the World Trade Center's twin towers in New York City, and into the Pentagon building near Washington, D.C. Close to 3,000 people died in these nearly simultaneous attacks. The administration of George W. Bush (1946–) announced the commencement of a "war on terror" against persons and organizations designated by the administration as terrorists, whether or not they could be shown to have been involved in the attack . Bush told the American people, "This crusade—this war on terrorism—is going to take a while ... and the American people must be patient.... Our 'war on terror' begins with al Qaeda, but it does not end there. It will not end until every terrorist group of global reach has been found, stopped and defeated."[39] Thus was opened a Pandora's box full of military activity around the world, as well as what could be—and has been—called a full-scale assault on individual liberties at home.

Although there was no strong evidence that Iraq was involved in the 9/11 attacks on the U.S., the Bush administration called for an American invasion of Iraq, giving as a reason the threat that Iraq was making, or planning to make, weapons of mass destruction, especially nuclear weapons. As the U.S. administration sought to justify the war on Iraq before the United Nations, warnings came from the Central Intelligence Agency that Iraq's mobile biological labs, in which it was claimed the Iraqis were developing biological warfare weapons, were no such things. The administration, in its rush to war, was ignoring any information which might have weakened its case against Iraq.[40] UN weapons inspectors, investigating the claims of weapons of mass destruction, had already determined before the U.S. invasion of Iraq that no evidence could be found for such weapons development. The UN inspections were thorough, conducted without prior warnings, and were not interfered with by the Iraqis.[41]

The issue of why the administration of President G.W. Bush chose to steer the U.S. into a war in Iraq is beyond the scope of this book. We will only say that far more was involved than the supposed involvement of Iraq in the 9/11 attacks. The statement of Condoleezza Rice (1954–), U.S. secretary of state, before the 9/11 investigating commission, that "I don't think anybody could have predicted that these people would take an airplane and slam it into the World Trade Center, take another one and slam it into the Pentagon; that they would try and use an airplane as a missile," indicates either an inexplicable, most woeful, and entirely unforgivable failure to be aware of information which dated back at least seven years, or her statement is entirely false. Sibel Edmonds, a former translator for the Federal Bureau of Investigation, testified before the 9/11 Commission that the FBI knew of the planned attacks ahead of time. She stated later, "I gave [the 9/11 Commission] details of specific investigation files ... specific dates, specific target information, specific managers in charge of the investigation. I gave them everything so that they could go back and follow up. This is not hearsay. These things are documented." When the 9/11 Commission report was published it contained no mention of Edmonds or any prior warnings received by the FBI.[42]

Just as before, the old questions which had faced Abraham Lincoln, Franklin Roosevelt, and other past leaders boiled up again. Once more a congressional resolution was equated with a congressional declaration of war; again, arbitrary arrests and detention of "suspects," unlimited by Constitutional provisions for rights, were made; again, military commissions were ordered to try defendants under military law, dispensing with constitutional rights and presumption of innocence until proven guilty. A "state of war" existed, America was told. The nation was under attack by unscrupulous and evil terrorists, who would stop at nothing to achieve their wicked ends.

Generally patterning his order upon Roosevelt's in 1942, Bush proclaimed that those arrested as terrorists "shall not be privileged to seek any remedy or maintain any proceeding, directly or indirectly, or to have any such remedy or proceeding sought on the individual's behalf in (i) any court of the United States, or any state thereof, (ii) any court of any foreign nation or (iii) any international tribunal." Bush also reserved for himself, as Roosevelt had done, the sole power to review the records of all cases tried by military commissions.[43]

In 2006 the U.S. Congress passed HR 6166, the United States Military Commissions Act of 2006. The act was "to authorize trial by military commissions for violation of the law of war, and for other purposes." Certain provisions of the Uniform Code of Military Justice (UCMJ), the military's own handbook for legal actions by and involving the U.S. military, were exempted by the act:

> Article 10 of the U.C.M.J., relating to speedy trial, including any rule of courts-martial relating to speedy trial.

Articles 31 (a) (b) and (d) of the U.C.M.J., relating to compulsory self-incrimination.
Article 32 of U.C.M.J., relating to pretrial investigation.
Geneva Conventions: No alien unlawful enemy combatant subject to trial by military commission under this chapter may invoke the Geneva Conventions as a source of rights.
Jurisdiction: A military commission under this chapter shall have jurisdiction to try any offense made punishable by this chapter or the law of war when committed by an alien unlawful enemy combatant before, on, or after September 11, 2001. [This clause of the Military Commissions Act would seem to be in violation of the Constitution's Article 1, section 9, which prohibits ex post facto laws.]
Punishments: A military commission under this chapter may, under such limitations as the Secretary of Defense may proscribe, adjudge any punishment not forbidden by this chapter, including the penalty of death when authorized under this chapter or by the law of war.
Unlawful Enemy Combatant: defined as
(i) a person who has engaged in hostilities or who has purposefully and materially supported hostilities against the United States or its co-belligerents who is not a lawful enemy combatant including a person who is part of the Taliban, al-Qaida, or associated forces; or
(ii) a person who, before, on, or after the date of that enactment of the Military Commissions Act of 2006, has been determined to be an unlawful enemy combatant by a Combatant Status Review Tribunal or another competent tribunal established under the authority of the president or the Secretary of Defense.

So it appears that the act authorizes the president, through the military, to do just about anything he chooses to do to anyone he chooses. Other provisions of the act include:

Civilian defense attorneys may not be used unless the attorney has been determined to be eligible for access to classified information that is classified at the level Secret or higher. A finding of guilty by a particular commission requires only a two-thirds majority of the members of the commission present at the time the vote is taken [This could mean as few as two commission members].
The President has the authority for the United States to interpret the meaning and application of the Geneva Conventions and to promulgate higher standards and administrative regulations for violations of treaty obligations which are not grave breaches of the Geneva Conventions.
No court, justice, or judge shall have jurisdiction to consider an application for a writ of habeas corpus filed by or on behalf of an alien detained by the United States who has been determined by the United States to have been properly detained as an enemy combatant or is awaiting such determination.

The Military Commissions Act of 2009 revised some provisions of the 2006 act, but the American Civil Liberties Union stated that the amended act was "short of providing the due process required by the

Constitution." The debate continues over whether the Military Commissions Act restricts the right of habeas corpus for U.S. citizens or for legal resident aliens. Senator Patrick J. Leahy (1940–) criticized the act thusly: "Authorizing indefinite detention of anybody the government designates, without any proceeding and without any recourse—is what our worst critics claim the United States would do, not what American values, traditions and our rule of law would have us do." John P. Cerone, a law professor, states that the act "risks running afoul of the principle against ex post facto criminalization, as recognized in international law (Article 15 of the International Covenant on Civil and Political Rights) as well as U.S. constitutional law."

The Military Commissions Act changed the definition of actions listed under the War Crimes Act of 1996, exempting Americans from prosecution for war crimes unless they are defined as "grave breaches." Actions such as torture, cruel or inhuman treatment, murder, mutilation or maiming, intentionally causing serious bodily harm, rape, sexual assault or abuse, and taking hostages, would only be triable if the U.S. government designated the instances as "grave breaches." For good measure, the new definitions clause was made retroactive to November 26, 1997, thus making it an unconstitutional ex post facto law.

Jonathan Turley, a professor of constitutional law at George Washington University, stated: "The framers created a system where we did not have to rely on the good graces or good mood of the president. In fact, Madison said that he created a system essentially to be run by devils, where they could do no harm, because we didn't rely on their good motivations. Now we must."[44]

The United States has engaged its armed forces in combat, beginning in 2001, not through the legal and constitutional way of a congressional declaration of war, but by presidential order. Americans are told by their government and news media that they are at war. Hundreds of prisoners have been captured and detained, many for years, under authority of the "law of war." As was pointed out at the trial of the Lincoln assassination suspects in 1865, the "law of war" does not exist as a written set of laws established by the United States Congress. Certainly, when soldiers are deployed to combat zones and come under hostile fire, they have every right to conclude that they are at war. Their families and friends, attending the funerals at military cemeteries, have every right to assume that these lives have been lost in a lawful conflict which could not have been decided by any other means. But wishing and assuming does not make an action legal under the Constitution.

Is there an alternative? Must we discard our oldest and most sacred traditions in order to meet the challenges of today? That is a question with which Lincoln wrestled, along with later leaders, as we have seen. General William Odom, director of the National Security Agency in the Reagan administration, stated:

> ... Terrorism is not an enemy. It is a tactic. Because the United States itself has a long record of supporting terrorists and using terrorist tactics the slogans of today's war on terrorism merely makes the United States look hypocritical to the rest of the world. A prudent American President would end the present policy of "sustained hysteria" over potential terrorist attacks ... treat terrorism as a serious but not a strategic problem, encourage Americans to regain their confidence, and refuse to let al Qaeda keep us in a state of fright.[45]

A large-scale military effort, apart from the legality issue, is not the most effective way to counter the threat of terrorism. The Oxford Research Group stated in 2005 that "Al Qaida and its affiliates remain active and effective, with a stronger support base and a higher intensity of attacks than before 9/11.... Far from winning the 'war on terror,' the second George W. Bush administration is maintaining policies that are not curbing paramilitary movements and are actually increasing violent anti–Americanism." A study by the Rand Corporation reported on September 19, 2008, to the U.S. Congress's House Armed Services Committee that "by far the most effective strategy against religious groups has been the use of local police and intelligence services, which were responsible for the end of 73 percent of [terrorist] groups since 1968." Rand also stated that the U.S. military "should generally resist being drawn into combat operations in Muslim countries where its presence is likely to increase terrorist recruitment.... Moving away from military references would indicate that there was no battlefield solution to countering terrorism." Andrew Kohut, of the Pew Research Center, told the U.S. House of Representatives' Committee on Foreign Affairs in 2004 that "majorities or pluralities in seven of the nine countries surveyed said the U.S.–led war on terror was not really a sincere effort to reduce international terrorism. This was true not only in Muslim countries such as Morocco and Turkey, but in France and Germany as well. The true purpose of the war on terror, according to these skeptics, is American control of Middle East oil and U.S. domination of the world."[46]

America's experience in Vietnam should have taught us the futility of trying to win a guerrilla war through conventional military means. Troops who are not trained in guerrilla tactics, who are weighted down with heavy equipment, who are unfamiliar with the terrain, and who are motivated only by monetary incentives or career advancement, are at a huge disadvantage trying to defeat an enemy who knows how to travel light, to hide and strike from a direction and at a time when least expected, and who is inspired by nationalistic or religious motives or both. The United States should have learned that truth as long ago as our own revolution, when Americans using guerrilla tactics prevented the British army from suppressing the American revolution through the conventional military means of that time.

The question of what to do with terrorists if and when they are captured has plagued the U.S. "war on terror" from the beginning. What is the status of such captives? Are they "prisoners of war," entitling them to humane treatment as proscribed by the Geneva Conventions? Not if the "war on terror" is not a war in the legal sense, in that no declaration of war has been made by the U.S. Congress. Are they "enemy combatants," triable under provisions of the "law of war"? The "law of war" is not written down, and has not been established by the U.S. Congress, as mandated by the U.S. Constitution. The same questions of jurisdiction asked by the defense lawyers at the trial of the Lincoln assassination conspiracy suspects must be asked again. Also, do the "laws of war," whatever they are, apply when there is no legal declaration of war? Are the terrorist prisoners common criminals, triable in the civilian courts of the United States? Those who have been arrested on U.S. territory are, and could be (and a few have been) tried in this way. But the vast majority were taken prisoner abroad by U.S. military forces, their acts having been committed abroad. Can U.S. law be made to apply to foreigners on non–U.S. soil for crimes committed on foreign soil?

Ahmed Ghailani (1974–) was taken prisoner in July 2004, and held in various prisons abroad until his transfer to the U.S. military base at Guantánamo Bay, Cuba, in September 2006. He was tried in U.S. federal criminal court on charges of multiple murder and attempted murder—a total of 284 counts—and one count of conspiring to damage or destroy American property (U.S. embassies in Nairobi, Kenya, and Dar es Salaam, Tanzania). The jury found him not guilty on the 284 counts and guilty on the one remaining count. Public reaction to the verdict was largely disapproving. Senator Mitch McConnell (1942–) called for assurances that "terrorists will be tried from now on in the military commission system that was established for this very purpose at the secure facility at Guantanamo Bay, or detained indefinitely, if they cannot be tried without jeopardizing national security." Jack Goldsmith, who served in the G.W. Bush administration and now teaches at Harvard Law School, described unlimited detention and trial by military commission as "tradition-sanctioned, congressionally authorized, court-blessed, resource-saving, security-preserving, easier-than-trial option for long-term terrorist incapacitation.... It looks more appealing than ever."[47]

The Government's desire to put Khalid Sheikh Mohammed, described as "the mastermind of the 9/11 attacks," on trial in U.S. federal court, has been frustrated by the political fallout from the Ghailani trial outcome. Senator Lindsey O. Graham (1955–) stated, "It is inappropriate to give [Mohammed] the same constitutional rights as an American citizen." Attorney General Eric H. Holder Jr. (1951–) has stated, "The proposal ... to ban completely the use of civilian courts in prosecutions of terrorism-related activity obscures some basic facts and allows campaign slogans to overtake legal reality. There's no question that if such a plan advances, it would seriously harm our national security.... What's best for the case, when we can bring the strongest case, bring into court the evidence we can rely on, minimize the use of evidence we don't want to have presented" would be to use civilian courts.[48]

The eminent jurist and Lincoln scholar and author Frank J. Williams, offers these thoughts on the military justice system as it was and as it has evolved since Lincoln's time:

> Our Supreme Court has been more of a check on the executive and Congress than those during the Civil War and World War II.... The 2009 Military Commissions Act and the DOD [Department of Defense] regs that followed give unlawful enemy combatant detainees almost every due process right that our armed forces have by employing the *Uniform Code of Military Justice* in almost every instance. Our Supreme Court has found military tribunals in accord with the Constitution—if sanctioned by Congress which was done in at least two instances.... The resolution passed by Congress after 9/11 is more of a declaration of war than many other hostilities.... Despite the passage of time, the questions themselves are the same as those asked during the Civil War.... How can we insure that trials protect the civil liberties of the accused, while protecting our national security? ... There is no basis for believing that the framers of the Constitution intended that habeas corpus be suspended only after a formal declaration of war or during a civil war.... Whether such trials take place in Guantanamo, on United States soil, or anywhere else, the rights afforded during those trials are what matter. It is nearly impossible when a nation is at war to afford enemy combatants all rights available to civilian courts. For example, it is impossible to afford enemy combatants the right to a trial by a jury of his or her peers in a wartime climate. But this does not mean that all rights must or should be sacrificed.

In response to Justice Williams, your author stated:

The Constitution has nothing to say about "resolutions" or any other substitute for a declaration [of war]. Senator Wayne Morse's statement, "I maintain that if you can't justify a war declaration, then you can't justify the war" implies that Senator Morse must have believed that a resolution ... is not the same thing as a declaration of war.... The Cornell University Law School Legal Information Institute ... acknowledges that the Constitution "confers expansive powers on the president" but "does not define precisely the extent of those powers." They say that "the Founders gave the president the title [commander-in-chief] to preserve civilian supremacy over the military, not to provide additional powers outside of a congressional authorization or declaration of war."[49]

The reader should note that in the debate over whether the Gulf of Tonkin Resolution of 1964 was the equivalent of a congressional declaration of war, Secretary of Defense McNamara stated that the United States had not and should not declare war upon Vietnam. Read again the quotations of McNamara, both at the time and years later. In both cases he stated that war was not declared by Congress. Senator Wayne Morse agreed with him in that assertion. The Constitution refers to a declaration of war, not a resolution, and it very specifically declares that only Congress, and not the president, has the power to declare war. All of our history, and all of the structure and function of our government as created by our Founding Fathers, argues for this separation of powers as a firm and basic foundation for a government intended to serve the people, not to oppress them.

Many Americans who voted for Barack Obama (1961–) for President in 2008 hoped that he would renounce and shut down the wars started by the Bush administration in Iraq and Afghanistan immediately upon taking office. That did not happen. Instead, Obama embraced the two wars and made them his own. To be fair, we must acknowledge that Obama did not say that he would end the wars as soon as he took office. However, he must have known that a majority of the American people had grown tired of the wars, and were more concerned about poor economic conditions at home.

The cost of the wars plays a part in public opinion, given the poor results so far obtained. Even before Obama took office, it was revealed that the terrorists fighting in Iraq and Afghanistan were being paid by other nations, some of which profess to be friends of America. Pakistan pulled back its army from the regions of their country which border Afghanistan, thereby taking much of the pressure off of the terrorists operating from the mountainous border areas, and making the flow of aid, including financial aid, easier for the antigovernment people.

Whether the wars in Iraq and Afghanistan are legal or not, they have been, by any reasonable estimate, most unfavorable investments. Huge amounts of money from American taxpayers have been spent, to say nothing of the lives lost on both sides. Over a period of more than twelve years, it is fair to say that very little has been accomplished. Iraq saw the pullout of American forces, although it has not been confirmed that all of the American troops and private contractors are now gone from that country, and every day's news reports bring stories of attacks, bombings, mass casualties, mostly among civilians, making Iraq look like anything but a peaceful country. The removal of American forces is very reminiscent of our exit from Vietnam in 1973, when our troops were pulled out, leaving the war still going, expecting the South Vietnamese army to carry on without us. That war ended in 1975 with a victory for the North Vietnamese and the total collapse of the nation of South Vietnam. The difference in Afghanistan is that we are planning to continue to spend huge sums of money to support the faltering (and corrupt) government and armed forces of Afghanistan into the distant future.

The situation in Libya drew America into another war, at least briefly, and again raised the question about the president's war powers and how much, if any, support the Congress can give to such incursions. Rebels in Libya fought to overthrow the dictatorial government of Muammar el-Gaddafi (1942–2011), but were unable to succeed without outside help. While many Americans may have supported the anti–Gaddafi cause, there was much uneasiness about committing American forces to Libya. Again it was questioned whether such action was legal. The House of Representatives voted a resolution criticizing President Obama for exceeding the time allowed by law to commit American forces to combat without congressional approval, as required by the War Powers Act of 1973. The administration further clouded the issue by claiming that private meetings with individual members of Congress was the same thing as consulting the Congress. They also said that the operations were not the same as the "hostilities" stated in the War Powers Act. Whether this claim is correct or not, it subverts the intention of the War Powers Act by claiming that the president can interpret the act as he chooses.[50]

Summation

With the trial of those charged in the conspiracy to assassinate President Lincoln as our focal point, we have examined the problems that trial raised, and the weaknesses in our government, our society, and perhaps in human nature itself, that it exposed. We have advanced two basic ideas, that the president is a civilian administrator and not a uniformed member of the armed forces, as maintained by the prosecution; and the proposition that military law is for the military, and not for civilians in nonmilitary situations.

The United States of America was intended by its founders to have a government where law is supreme, and a structure where power is divided among the three branches of government in an even way to produce a balance, each branch being able to check abuses of the other two. Of course, over the passage of more than two centuries, situations have arisen which the Founders did not and could not have anticipated. They realized that such might be the case, and deliberately made the Constitution nonspecific and even vague. This provides the flexibility necessary to deal with the unanticipated. It does, however, also permit the stretching of both the words and spirit of the laws, sometimes in ways and directions beyond anything intended by the founders.

We have seen how even some of our most revered leaders, when faced with extraordinary problems, have been willing to stretch their Constitutional powers up to, and even beyond, the breaking point. Among the governmental systems of the world, that of the United States is very nearly the longest lasting. It can be said that the reason for this longevity is the spirit of a people who prize liberty above all. The American experiment is a gamble. However long the nation lasts and whatever problems and challenges may arise over the course of time, the desire of the people to be free, to have rights and liberties guaranteed, to have leaders who will likewise value those liberties over expediency or gain for the privileged, will remain strong enough to win the day. It is a gamble which involves considerable risk, for once lost, liberty is difficult to regain.

At the conclusion of the Constitutional convention in 1787, the aged Benjamin Franklin (1706–1790) who had said relatively little throughout the long hot summer of argument and compromise, drew the attention of the delegates to the chair in which the president of the convention, George Washington, had been sitting. On the back of the chair was carved a sun. "I have often in the course of the session, and the vicissitudes of my hopes and fears as to its issue, looked at that behind the president without being able to tell whether it was rising or setting. But now at length I have the happiness to know that it is a rising and not a setting sun." Franklin knew that, perhaps against the odds, he and his colleagues at the convention had been able to see the launching of the great experiment of self-government in a land of liberty and justice for all. How that experiment would play out over the decades and centuries to come he knew he would not live to see. Neither shall we. But as he was leaving Independence Hall he was asked by a woman what sort of a government the delegates of the convention had given the people. His answer has become a classic: "A republic, madam, if you can keep it."[1]

Afterword

This book has reached its conclusion, but, as the reader will undoubtedly be aware, the issues raised here are anything but resolved. This is a story which does not have, and cannot have, a conclusion. The Founding Fathers of America would doubtless be astonished if they could come back and see what has become of the little nation they invented so long ago; the toddler, ill housed, ill clothed, very poorly prepared to go it alone, surrounded by unsympathetic and predatory powers. It probably would please most of them that their infant has grown far beyond their wildest imaginings in size, resources, influence, and raw power. How they would react to today's America can only be guessed. The problems discussed in this book would, however, not only be familiar to them but also expected. They did what they could to provide protection for themselves and for those who would come afterwards. Although we are used to hearing them described as having been endowed with all the virtues anyone has ever possessed, we can see that they were not infallible. They were extraordinary beings, but also very human beings. The Constitution, and other objects both real and symbolic, which they left behind for us must be respected. We often hear it said that we could not do better than the founders did. Being honest with ourselves, we should accept that judgment. The founders would probably say that seeing their creation wracked by dissention and controversy does not surprise them. So it was in their time, so it is in ours, so it must be in all times to come. Debate, disagreement, however unpleasant or even hostile it may become, are nevertheless the distinguishing marks of democracy. If the founders could not admire all that their descendants have made of their creation, they would probably be gratified to see that the urge to be free is still alive, and they would undoubtedly cheer on its persistence.

The following quotations present the testimony of judges, lawyers,

Founding Fathers, past presidents, the U.S. Constitution, even the Bible, which support the need to prevent the accumulation of too much power in the Executive branch.

"Emergency powers are consistent with free government only when their control is lodged elsewhere than in the Executive who exercises them."
—Justice Robert H. Jackson

Presidential power "must stem either from an act of Congress or from the Constitution itself."
—Justice Hugo L. Black

"It seems rather contrary to an idea of a Constitution with three branches that the executive would be free to do whatever they want ... without a check."
—Justice Stephen G. Breyer

"In all criminal prosecutions, the accused shall enjoy the right to a speedy and public trial, by an impartial jury of the state and district wherein the crime shall have been committed, which district shall have been previously ascertained by law, and to be informed of the nature and cause of the accusation; to be confronted with the witnesses against him; to have compulsory process for obtaining witnesses in his favor, and to have the assistance of counsel for his defense."
—United States Constitution, Amendment 6

Congress has authorized the suspension of the writ of habeas corpus, as the Constitution permits; but the Constitution does not thereby permit the military to try, nor has Congress attempted to deliver over to the military for trial, judgment and execution, American citizens, not in the land or naval forces or in the militia in actual service, when accused of crime.... Congress ... have suspended the writ of habeas corpus; this goes to imprisonment—not trial, conviction, or punishment. This is the extreme limit to which the law-making power is permitted to go, and it is only in cases of strong necessity that this is permitted.... If you be proceeding in obedience to such Executive mandate, and if that give jurisdiction, still you proceed in a form and manner which the Constitution and law expressly forbid.
—Thomas Ewing, Jr., at the trial of the Lincoln assassination suspects

The complete independence of the courts of justice is peculiarly essential in a limited Constitution. By a limited Constitution I understand one which contains certain specified exceptions to the legislative authority; such, for instance, as that it shall pass no bills of attainder, no ex post facto laws, and the like. Limitations of this kind can be preserved in practice no other way than through the medium of courts of justice, whose duty it must be to declare all

acts contrary to the manifest tenor of the Constitution void. Without this, all the reservations of particular rights or privileges would amount to nothing.... There is no position which depends on clearer principles than that every act of a delegated authority, contrary to the tenor of the commission under which it is exercised, is void. No legislative act, therefore, contrary to the Constitution can be valid. To deny this would be to affirm that the deputy is greater than his principal; that the servant is above his master; that the representatives of the people are superior to the people themselves; that men acting by virtue of powers may do not only what their powers do not authorize, but what they forbid.
—Federalist No. 78 (Hamilton)

I had rather ask an enlargement of power from the nation, where it is found necessary, than to assume it by a construction which would make our powers boundless. Our peculiar security is in possession of a written constitution. Let us not make it a blank paper by construction.
—Thomas Jefferson

It is of great importance in a republic not only to guard the society against the oppression of its rulers, but to guard one part of the society against the injustice of the other part.... Justice is the end of government. It is the end of civil society. It ever has been and ever will be pursued until it be obtained, or until liberty be lost in the pursuit.
—Federalist No. 51 (Hamilton or Madison)

This conjunction of an immense military establishment and a large arms industry is new in the American experience. The total influence—economic, political, even spiritual—is felt in every city, every State house, every office of the Federal government. We recognize the imperative need for this development. Yet we must not fail to comprehend its grave implications. Our toil, resources and livelihood are all involved; so is the very structure of our society.

In the councils of government, we must guard against the acquisition of unwarranted influence, whether sought or unsought, by the military-industrial complex. The potential for the disastrous rise of misplaced power exists and will persist.

We must never let the weight of this combination endanger our liberties or democratic processes. We should take nothing for granted. Only an alert and knowledgeable citizenry can compel the proper meshing of the huge industrial and military machinery of defense with our peaceful methods and goals, so that security and liberty may prosper together.
—Dwight D. Eisenhower

Shall the throne of iniquity have fellowship with thee, which frameth mischief by a law?
—Psalms 94:20

Appendix I: Opinion of the Attorney General Regarding Suspension of the Writ of Habeas Corpus

by Edward Bates

From *The War of the Rebellion: A Compilation of the Official Records of the Union and Confederate Armies* (Washington: Government Printing Office, 1899), Series II, Vol. 2, pp. 20–30. [Excerpts.]

Attorney General's Office, July 5, 1861

Sir: You have required my opinion in writing upon the following questions:

First. In the present time of a great and dangerous insurrection has the president discretionary power to cause to be arrested and held in custody persons known to have criminal intercourse with the insurgents or persons against whom there is probable cause for suspicion of such criminal complicity?

Second. In such cases of arrest is the president justified in refusing to obey a writ of habeas corpus issued by a court or judge requiring him or his agent to produce the body of the prisoner and show the cause of his capture and detention to be adjudged and disposed of by such court or judge?

[The] separate departments of government ... are so co-ordinate and coequal—that is, neither being sovereign, each is independent in its sphere and not subordinate to the others, either of them or both of them together. We have three of these co-ordinate departments. Now if we allow one of the three to determine the extent of its own powers and also the extent of the powers of the other two that one can control the whole government and has in fact achieved the sovereignty.

Our fathers having divided the government into co-ordinate departments did not even try (and if they had tried would probably have failed) to create an arbiter among them to adjudge their conflicts and keep them within their respective bounds. They were left by design I suppose each independent and free to act out its own granted powers without any ordained legal superior professing the power to revise and reverse its action. And this with the hope that the three departments, mutually coequal and independent, would keep each other within their proper spheres by their mutual antagonism—that is, by the system of checks and balances to which our fathers were driven at the beginning by their fear of the unity of power....

To say that the departments of our Government are co-ordinate is to say that the judgment of one of them is not binding upon the other two as to the arguments and principles involved in the judgment. It binds only the parties to the case decided.... If the president be bound by the principles laid down by the judiciary so also is the judiciary bound by the principles laid down by the president; and thus we shall have a theory of constitutional government flatly contradicting itself.

The Government as a whole is limited, and limited in all its departments. It is the especial function of the judiciary to hear and determine cases, not to "establish principles" nor "settle questions," so as to conclude any person but the parties and privies to the case adjudged.

Of all the departments of the government the president is the most active and the most constant in action. He is called "the Executive," and so in fact he is, and much more also for the Constitution has imposed upon him many important duties and granted to him great powers which are in their nature not executive—such as the veto power, the power to send and receive ambassadors; the power to make treaties and the power to appoint officers. This last is not more an executive power when used by the president than it is when exercised by either House of Congress, by the courts of justice or by the people at large.

The President ... is charged with a greater range and variety of powers and duties than any other department. He is a civil magistrate, not a military chief; and in this regard we see a striking proof of the generality of the sentiment prevailing in this country at the time of the formation of our Government to the effect that the military ought to be held in strict subordination to the civil power.... The Constitution provides that "the president shall be Commander in Chief of the Army and Navy of the United States and of the militia of the several states when called into the actual service of the United States." And why is this? Surely not because the president is supposed to be or commonly is in fact a military man, a man skilled in the art of war and qualified to marshal a host in the field of battle. No, it is for quite a different reason; it is that whatever skillful soldier may lead our armies to victory against a foreign foe or may quell a domestic insurrection; however high he may raise his professional renown and whatever martial glory he may win still he is subject to the orders of the civil magistrate, and he and his army are always "subordinate to the civil power."

And hence it follows that whenever the president (the civil magistrate) in the discharge of his constitutional duty to "take care that the laws be faithfully executed" has occasion to use the army to aid him in the performance of that duty he does not thereby lose his civil character and become a soldier subject to military law and liable to be tried by a court-martial any more than does a civil court lose its legal and pacific nature and become military and belligerent by calling out the power of the country to enforce its decrees. The civil magistrates whether judicial or executive must of necessity employ physical power to aid them in enforcing the laws whenever they have to deal with disobedient and refractory subjects; and their legal power and right to do so is unquestionable. The right of the courts to call out the whole power of the country to enforce their judgments is as old as the common law; and the right of the president to use force in the performance of his legal duties is not only inherent in his office but has been frequently recognized and aided by Congress. One striking example of this is the act of Congress of March 3, 1807 (2 Stat., 445), which empowered the president without the intervention of any court to use the marshal, and if he be insufficient to use the Army summarily to expel intruders and squatters upon the public lands. And that power has been frequently exercised without as far as I know a question of its legality. To call as is sometimes done the judiciary the civil power and the President the military power, seems to me at once a mistake of fact and an abuse of language....

As to the first question: I am clearly of opinion that, in a time like the present when the very existence of the nation is assailed by a great and dangerous insurrection, the president has the lawful discretionary power to arrest and hold in custody persons known to have criminal intercourse with the insurgents or persons against whom there is probable cause for suspicion of such criminal complicity. And I think this position can be maintained in view of the principles already by a very plain argument.

The end, the suppression of the insurrection, is required of him [the president] the means and instruments to suppress it are lawfully in his hands; but the manner in which he shall use them is not prescribed and could not be prescribed without a foreknowledge of all the future changes and contingencies of the insurrection.

This is a great power in the hands of the Chief Magistrate; and because it is great and is capable of being perverted to evil ends its existence has been doubted or denied. It is said to be dangerous in the hands of an ambitious and wicked President because he may use it for the purposes of oppression and tyranny. Yes, certainly it is dangerous—all power is dangerous—and for the all-pervading reason that all power is liable to abuse; all the recipients of human power are men not absolutely virtuous and wise. Still, it is a power necessary to the peace and safety of the country and undeniably belongs to the Government and therefore must be exercised by some department or officer thereof.

Why should this power be denied to the president on the grounds of its inability to abuse and not denied to the other departments on the same grounds? Are they more exempt than he is from the frailties and vices of humanity? ... If it be said that a President may be ambitious and unscrupulous it may be said with equal truth that a legislature may be fractious and unprincipled and a court may be venal and corrupt.

... There is but one sentence in the Constitution which mentions the writ of habeas corpus (art. 1, sec. 9, clause 2), which is in these words: "The privilege of the writ of habeas corpus shall not be suspended unless when in cases of rebellion or invasion the public safety may require it."

... Does that mean that the writ itself shall not be issued, or that being issued the party shall derive no benefit from it? Suspended—does that mean delayed, hung up for a time or altogether denied? ...

I am aware that it has been declared by the Supreme Court that—

> If at any time the public safety should require the suspension of the powers vested by this act (meaning the judiciary act of 1789, section 14) in the courts of the United States, it is for the legislature to say so. That question depends upon political considerations, on which the legislature is to decide.

... The court does not speak of suspending the privilege of the writ, but of suspending the powers vested in the court by the act....

If the phrase "the suspension of the privilege of the writ of habeas corpus" we must understand a repeal of all power to issue the writ, then I freely admit that none but Congress can do it. But if we are at liberty to understand the phrase to mean that in case of a great and dangerous rebellion like the present the public safety requires the arrest and confinement of persons implicated in that rebellion, I as freely declare the opinion that the president has lawful power to suspend the privilege of persons arrested under such circumstances; for he is especially charged by the Constitution with the "public safety," and is the sole judge of the emergency which requires his prompt action.

This power in the president is no part of his ordinary duty in time of peace; it is temporary and exceptional, and was intended only to meet a pressing emergency when the judiciary is found to be too weak to insure the public safety; when (in the language of the act of Congress) there are "combinations too powerful to be suppressed by the ordinary course of judicial proceedings or by the powers vested in the marshals." Then and not till then has he the lawful authority to call to his aid the military power of the nation and with that power perform his great legal and constitutional duty to suppress the insurrection....

The power to do these things is in the hand of the president, placed there by the Constitution and the statute law as a sacred trust to be used by him in his best discretion in the performance of his great first duty— to preserve, protect and defend the Constitution. And for any breach of that trust he is responsible before the high court of impeachment and before no other human tribunal.

This, sir, is my opinion, the result of my best reflections upon the questions propounded by you. Such as it is it is submitted with all possible respect by your obedient servant,

Edward Bates
Attorney General.

Appendix II: The Constitution of the United States of America, Analysis and Interpretation

(Washington: U.S. Government Printing Office, 1973)

[See this publication for specific sources in the text. Only commentary in the notes is reproduced here.]

Article I—Legislative Department, Section 9—Denied to Congress, Cl. 3—Habeas Corpus

Clause 2. The Privilege of the Writ of Habeas Corpus shall not be suspended, unless when in cases of rebellion or invasion the public safety may require it.

This clause is the only place in the Constitution in which the Great Writ is mentioned, a strange fact in the context of the regard with which the right was held at the time the Constitution was written and stranger in the context of the role the right has come to play in the Supreme Court's efforts to constitutionalize federal and state criminal procedure.

Only the Federal government and not the States, it has been held obliquely, is limited by the clause. The issue that has always excited critical attention is the authority in which the clause places the power to determine whether the circumstances warrant suspension of the privilege of the Writ. In form, of course, clause 2 is a limitation of power, not a grant of power, and is in addition placed in a section of limitations. It might be argued, therefore, that the power to suspend lies elsewhere and that this clause limits that authority. This argument is opposed by the little authority there is in the subject. The clause itself does not specify and while most of the clauses of Sec. 9 are directed at Congress not all of them are. (Cf. Clauses 7, 8.) At the Convention the first proposal of a suspending authority expressly vested "in the legislature" the suspending power, but the author of this proposal did not retain this language when the matter was taken up, the present language then being adopted. Nevertheless, [p. 346] Congress' power to suspend was assumed in early commentary and stated in dictum by the Court. President Lincoln suspended the privilege on his own motion in the early Civil War period, but this met with such opposition (Including a finding by Chief Justice Taney on circuit that the president's action was invalid,) that he sought and received congressional authorization. Three other suspensions were subsequently ordered on the basis of more or less express authorization from Congress. The privilege of the Writ was suspended in nine counties in South Carolina in order to combat the Ku Klux Klan, pursuant to Act of April 20, 1871. It was suspended in the Philippines in 1905, pursuant to the act of July 1, 1902. Finally, it was suspended in Hawaii during World War II, pursuant to a section of the Hawaiian Organic Act.

When suspension operates, what is suspended? In *Ex parte Milligan,* the Court asserted that the Writ is not suspended but only the privilege, so that the Writ would issue and the issuing court on its return would determine whether the person applying can proceed, thereby passing on the constitutionality of the suspension and whether the petitioner is within the terms of the suspension.

Clause 3. No Bill of Attainder of ex post facto Law shall be passed.

Bills of Attainder

Bills of attainder ... are such special acts of the legislature, as inflict capital punishment upon persons supposed to be guilty of high offenses, such as treason and felony, without conviction in the ordinary course of judicial proceedings. If an act inflicts a milder degree of punishment than death, it is called a bill of pains and penalties.... In such cases, the legislature assumed judicial magistracy, [p. 365] pronouncing upon the guilt of the party without any of the common forms and guards of trial, and satisfying itself with proofs, when such proofs are within its reach, whether they are conformable to the rules of evidence, or not. In short, in all such cases, the legislature exercises the highest power of sovereignty, and what may be properly deemed an irresponsible despotic discretion, being governed solely by what it deems political necessity or expedience, and too often under the influence of unreasonable fears, or unfounded suspicions. The phrase "bill of attainder," as used in this clause and in clause 1 of sec. 10, applies to bills of pains and penalties as well as to the traditional bills of attainder.

The prohibition embodied in this clause is not to be strictly and narrowly construed in the context of traditional forms but is to be interpreted in accordance with the designs of the framers so as to preclude trial by legislature, a violation of the separation of powers concept. The clause thus prohibits all legislative acts, "no matter what their form, that apply either to named individuals or to easily ascertainable members of a group in such a way as to inflict punishment on them without a judicial trial...." [p. 366]

Ex Post Facto Laws

Definition.—At the time the Constitution was adopted, many persons understood the terms *ex post facto* laws to embrace all retrospective laws, or laws governing or controlling past transactions, whether ... of a civil or a criminal nature. But ... the Supreme Court decided that the phrase, as used in the Constitution, applied only to penal and criminal statutes.... Every law which makes criminal an act which was innocent when done, or which inflicts a greater punishment than the law annexed to the crime when [p. 368] committed, is an *ex post facto* law within the prohibition of the Constitution. [p. 369].... A change of the place of trial of an alleged offense after its commission is not an ex post facto law. If no place of trial was provided when the offense was committed, Congress may designate the place of trial thereafter. A law which alters the rule of evidence to permit a person to be convicted upon less or different evidence than was required when the offense was committed is invalid ... [p. 370]

Article II—Executive Department, Section 2— Powers and Duties of the President, Cl. 1— Commander-in-Chief.

The president shall be Commander in Chief of the Army and Navy of the United States and of the Militia of the several states, when called into the actual service of the United States.... [p. 448]

Analysis and Interpretation of the Constitution   185

Development of the Concept.

Surprisingly little discussion of the Commander-in-Chief clause is found in the Convention or in the ratifying debates. From the evidence available, it appears that the Framers vested the duty in the president because experience in the Continental Congress had disclosed the inexpediency of vesting command in a group and because the lesson of English history was that danger lurked in vesting command in a person separate from the responsible political leaders. But the principal concern here is the nature of the power granted by the clause.

The Limited View.—The purely military aspects of the Commander-in-Chiefship were those which were originally stressed. Hamilton said the office "would amount to nothing more than the supreme command and direction of the Military and naval forces, as first general and admiral of the confederacy." [Joseph] Story wrote in his Commentaries: "The propriety of admitting the president to be commander in chief, so far as to give orders, and have a general superintendence, was admitted. But it was urged, that it would be dangerous to let him command in person, without any restraint, as he might make a bad use of it. The consent of both houses of Congress ought, therefore, to be required, before he should take the actual command. The answer then given was, that though the president might, there [p. 449] was no necessity that he should, take the command in person; and there was no probability that he would do so, except in extraordinary emergencies, and when he was possessed of superior military talents" [p. 450]....

In brief, the powers claimable for the president under the Commander-in-Chief clause at a time of wide-spread insurrection were equated with his powers under the clause at a time when the United States is engaged in a formally declared foreign war. And since Lincoln performed various acts especially in the early months of the Civil War which, like increasing the Army and Navy, admittedly fell within the Constitutional provinces of Congress, it seems to have been assumed during World War I and II that the Commander-in-Chiefship carried with it the power to exercise like powers practically at discretion, not merely in wartime but even at a time when war became a strong possibility. No attention was given the fact that Lincoln had asked Congress to ratify and confirm his acts, which Congress promptly did, with the exception of his suspension of the habeas corpus privilege which was regarded by many as attributable to the president in the situation then existing, by virtue of his duty to take care that the laws be faithfully executed. Nor was this the only respect in which war or the approach of war was deemed to operate to enlarge the scope of power claimable by the president as Commander-in-Chief in wartime [p. 452].

Presidential Theory of the Commander-in-Chief in World War II—and Beyond.

In his message of September 7, 1942, to Congress, in which he demanded that Congress forthwith repeal certain provisions of the Emergency Price Control Act of the previous January 30th, President Roosevelt formulated his conception of his powers as "Commander in Chief in wartime" as follows:

I ask the Congress to take this action by the first of October. Inaction on your part by that date will leave me with an inescapable responsibility to the people of this country to see to it that the war effort is no longer imperiled by threat of economic chaos.

In the event that the Congress should fail to act, and act adequately, I shall accept the responsibility, and I will act.

At the same time that farm prices are stabilized, wages can and will be stabilized also. This I will do.

The President has the powers, under the Constitution and under congressional acts, to take measures necessary to avert a disaster which would interfere with the winning of the war.

I have given the most thoughtful consideration to meeting this issue without further reference to the Congress. I have determined, however, on this vital matter to consult with the Congress....

The American people can be sure that I will use my powers with a full sense of my responsibility to the Constitution and to my country. The American people can also be sure that I shall not hesitate to use every power vested in me to accomplish the defeat of our enemies in any part of the world where our own safety demands such defeat.

When the war is won, the powers under which I act automatically revert to the people—to whom they belong. [p. 453]

Evacuation of the West Coast Japanese.—On February 19, 1942, President Roosevelt issued an executive order, "by virtue of the authority vested in me as President of the United States, and Commander in Chief of the Army and Navy," providing, as a safeguard against subversion and sabotage, power for his military commanders to designate areas from which "any person" could be excluded or removed and set up facilities for such persons elsewhere. Pursuant to this order, more than 112,000 residents of the Western States, all of Japanese descent and more than two out of every three of whom were [p. 454] natural born citizens, were removed from their homes and herded into temporary camps and later into "relocation centers" in several states.

It was apparently the original intention of the Administration to rest its measures concerning this matter on the general principle of military necessity and the power of the Commander-in-Chief in wartime. But before any action of importance was taken under the order, Congress ratified and adopted it by the act of March 21, 1942, by which it was made a misdemeanor to knowingly enter, remain in, or leave prescribed military areas contrary to the orders of the Secretary of War or of the commanding officer of the area. The cases which subsequently arose in consequence of the order were decided under the order plus the act. The question at issue, said Chief Justice Stone for the Court, "is not one of congressional power to delegate to the president the promulgation of the Executive order, but whether, acting in cooperation, Congress and the Executive have constitutional ... [power] to impose the curfew restriction here complained of." [p. 455]

The Postwar Period.—The end of active hostilities did not terminate either the emergency or the federal governmental response to it. President Truman proclaimed the termination of hostilities on December 31, 1946, and Congress enacted a joint resolution which repealed a great variety of wartime statutes and set termination dates for others in July, 1947. Signing the resolution, the president said that the emergencies declared in 1939 and 1940 continued to exist and that it was "not possible at this time to provide for terminating all war emergency powers." The hot war was giving way to the Cold War.... The Court held constitutional the new [extension of wartime laws] on the ground that cessation of hostilities did not conclude the government's powers but that the power continued to remedy the evil arising out of the emergency.... Justice Jackson ... noted that he found the war power "the [p. 458] most dangerous one to free government in the whole catalogue of powers" and cautioned that its exercise should "be scrutinized with care." [p. 459]

The power of Congress to control the president's discretion.—The most far-reaching proposal considered in Congress was a bill which purported to reestablish congressional control over the war power by providing that the president could not use the armed forces of the United States abroad in the absence of a declaration of war, except to repel an attack or an imminent threat of attack on the United States or on the armed forces of the United States outside the United States, to protect the evacuation of United States citizens from areas in which hostilities have commenced, or pursuant to some specific statutory authority, and even the exceptions could not be sustained beyond thirty days in the absence of appropriate congressional action. Proponents argued that Congress had the power to limit the president's discretion as a "necessary and proper" adjunct of its powers [p. 463] to declare war and to provide for and regulate the armed forces and because under Article I, sec. 8, cl. 18, Congress also has power to make all "necessary and proper" laws to carry into effect the "powers vested by this Constitution in the Government of the United States, or in any department or officer thereof." Opponents have asserted that as Commander-in-Chief the president has independent powers to utilize military forces not only to protect the Nation from attack but to further the Nation's interests and that this power is not subject to significant congressional limitation. Moreover, Congress' power to declare war, in this view, says little about the other myriad resorts to force short of all out war, so that Congress does not actually have the degree of "necessary and proper" power which others have deemed to find in the power to effectuate the authority to declare war.... But whether one or the other, the dispute has established precedents of practice and policy rather than constitutional rules.

The President as Commander of the Armed Forces.

While the president customarily delegates supreme command of the forces in active service, there is no constitutional reason why he should do so, and he has been known to resolve personally important questions of military policy. Lincoln early in 1862 issued orders for a general advance in the hopes of stimulating McClellan to action; Wilson in 1918 settled the question of an independent American command on the Western Front; Truman in 1945 ordered that the bomb be dropped on Hiroshima and Nagasaki. As against an enemy in the field the president possesses all the powers which are accorded by international law to any supreme commander. "He may invade the hostile country, and subject it to the sovereignty and authority of the United States." In the absence of attempts by Congress to limit his power, he may establish and prescribe the jurisdiction and procedure of military commissions, and of tribunals in the nature of such commissions, in territory occupied by Armed Forces of the United [p. 464] States, and his authority to do this sometimes survives cessation of hostilities.... He is the ultimate tribunal for the enforcement of the rules and regulations which Congress adopts for the government of the forces, and which are enforced through courts-martial. Indeed, until 1830, courts-martial were convened solely on his authority as Commander-in-Chief....

The power of Congress to "make rules for the government and regulation of the land and naval forces (Art. I, sec. 8, cl. 14) did not prevent President Lincoln from promulgating in April, 1863, a code of rules to govern and conduct in the field of the armies of the United States which was prepared at his instance by a commission headed by Francis Lieber and which later became the basis of all similar codifications [p. 465] both here and abroad.

The Commander-in-Chief a civilian officer.—Is the Commander-in-Chief a military or civilian office in the contemplation of the Constitution? Unquestionably the latter. An opinion by a New York surrogate deals adequately, though not authoritatively, with the subject: "The President receives his compensation for his services as Chief Executive of the Nation, not for the individual parts of his duties. No part of his compensation is paid from sums appropriated for the military or naval forces, and it is equally clear under the Constitution that the president's duties as Commander-in-Chief represents only a part of duties *ex officio* as Chief Executive (Article II, sections 2 and 3 of the Constitution) and that the latter's office is a civil office. The President does not enlist in, and he is not inducted or drafted into, the armed forces. Nor is he subject to court-martial or other military discipline. On the contrary, Article II, section 4 of the Constitution provides that "The President, (Vice President) and All Civil Officers of the United States shall be removed from Office on Impeachment for, and Conviction of Treason, Bribery or other high crimes and misdemeanors." ... The last two war presidents, President Wilson and President Roosevelt, both clearly recognized the civilian nature of the president's position as Commander in Chief. President Roosevelt, in his Navy Day Campaign speech at Shibe Park, Philadelphia, on October 27, 1944, pronounced this principle as follows:—"It was [p. 466] due to no accident and no oversight that the framers of our Constitution put the command of our armed forces under civilian authority. It is the duty of the Commander in Chief to appoint the Secretaries of War and Navy and the Chiefs of Staff." It is also to be noted that the Secretary of War, [now Secretary of Defense] who is the regularly constituted organ of the president for the administration of the military establishment of the Nation, has been held by the Supreme Court of the United States to be merely a civilian officer, not in military service. (*United States v. Burns*, 79 U.S. 246, 1871). On the general principle of civilian supremacy over the military, by virtue of the Constitution, it has recently been said: "The supremacy of the civil over the military is one of our great heritages." (*Duncan v. Kahanamoko*, 324 U.S. 833, 1945, 13 L.W. 4205 at page 4210.)

Appendix III: Opinion of the Constitutional Power of the Military to Try and Execute the Assassins of the President

by *Attorney General James Speed*
(Washington: Government Printing Office, 1865)

Opinion. Attorney General's Office, Washington, July—, 1865.

Sir: You ask me whether the persons charged with the offense of having assassinated the president can be tried before a military commission, or must they be tried before a civil court.

The President was assassinated at a theatre in the city of Washington. At the time of the assassination a civil war was flagrant, the city of Washington was defended by fortifications regularly and constantly manned, the principal police of the city was by federal soldiers, the public offices and property in the city were all guarded by soldiers, and the President's House and person were or should have been under the guard of soldiers. Martial law had been declared in the District of Columbia, but the civil courts were open and held their regular sessions, and transacted business as in times of peace.

Such being the facts, the question is one of great importance—important, because it involves the constitutional guarantees thrown about the rights of the citizen, and because the security of the army and the government in time of war is involved; important, as it involves a seeming conflict betwixt the laws of peace and of war.

Having given the question propounded the patient and earnest consideration its magnitude and importance require, I will proceed to give the reasons why I am of the opinion that the conspirators not only may but ought to be tried by a military tribunal.

A civil court of the United States is created by a law of Congress under and according to the Constitution. To the Constitution and the law we must look to ascertain how the court is constituted, the limits of its jurisdiction, and what its mode of procedure.

A military tribunal exists under and according to the Constitution in time of war. Congress may prescribe how all such tribunals are to be constituted, what shall be their jurisdiction and mode of procedure. Should Congress fail to create such tribunals, then, under the Constitution, they must be constituted according to the laws and usages of civilized warfare. They may take cognizance of such offenses as the laws of war permit; they must proceed according to the customary usages of such tribunals in time of war, and inflict such punishments as are sanctioned by the practice of civilized nations in time of war. In time of peace neither Congress nor the military can create any military tribunals, except such as are made in pursuance of that clause of the Constitution which gives to Congress the power "to make rules for the government of the land and naval forces." I do not think that Congress can, in time of war or peace, under this clause of the Constitution, create military tribunals for the adjudication of offenses committed by persons not engaged in, or belonging to, such forces. This is a proposition too plain for argument. But it does not follow that because such military tribunals cannot be created by Congress under this clause, that they cannot be created at all. Is there no other power conferred by the Constitution upon Congress or the military under which such tribunals may be created in time of war?

That the law of nations constitutes a part of the laws of the land, must be admitted. The laws of nations are expressly made laws of the land by the Constitution, when it says that "Congress shall have power to define and punish piracies and felonies committed on the high seas and offenses against the laws of nations." To *define* is to give the limits or precise meaning of a word or thing in being; to make, is to call into being. Congress has power to *define*, not to make, the laws of nations; but Congress has the power to make rules for the government of the army and navy. From the very face of the Constitution, then, it is evident that the laws of nations do constitute a part of the laws of the land. But very soon after the organization of the federal government, Mr. Randolph, then Attorney General, said: "The law of nations, although not specifically adopted by the Constitution, is essentially a part of the law of the land. Its obligation commences and runs with the existence of a nation, subject to modification on some points of indifference." (See opinion Attorney General, vol. 1, page 27.) The framers of the Constitution knew that a nation could not maintain an honorable place amongst the nations of the world that does not regard the great and essential principles of the law of nations as a part of the law of the land. Hence Congress may define those laws, but cannot abrogate them, or, as Mr. Randolph says, may "modify on some points of indifference."

That the laws of nations constitute a part of the laws of the land is established from the face of the Constitution, upon principle and by authority.

But the laws of war constitute much the greater part of the law of nations. Like the other laws of nations, they exist and are of binding force upon the departments and citizens of the government, though not defined by any law of Congress. No one that has ever glanced at the many treatises that have been published in different ages of the world by great, good, and learned men, can fail to know that the laws of war constitute a part of the law of nations, and that those laws have been prescribed with tolerable accuracy.

Congress can declare war. When war is declared, it must be, under the Constitution, carried on according to the known laws and usages of war amongst civilized nations. Under the power to define those laws, Congress cannot abrogate them or authorize their infraction. The Constitution does not permit this government to prosecute a war as an uncivilized and barbarous people.

As war is required by the frame-work of our government to be prosecuted according to the known usages of war amongst the civilized nations of the earth, it is important to understand what are the obligations, duties, and responsibilities imposed by war upon the military. Congress, not having defined, as under the Constitution it might have done, the laws of war, on whom the exercise of such powers devolve, over whom, and to what extent do those powers reach, and in how far the citizen and the soldier are bound by the legitimate use thereof.

The power conferred by war is, of course, adequate to the end to be accomplished, and not greater than what is necessary to be accomplished. The law of war, like every other code of laws, declares what shall not be done, and does not say what may be done. The legitimate use of the great power of war, or rather the prohibitions upon the use of that power, increase or diminish as the necessity of the case demands. When a city is besieged and hard pressed, the commander may exert an authority over the non-combatants which he may not when no enemy is near.

All wars against the domestic enemy or to repel invasions are prosecuted to preserve the government. If the invading force can be overcome by the ordinary civil police of a country, it should be done without bringing upon the country the terrible scourge of war; if a commotion or insurrection can be put down by the ordinary process of law, the military should not be called out. A defensive foreign war is declared and carried on because the civil police is inadequate to repel it; a civil war is waged because the laws cannot be peacefully enforced by the ordinary tribunals of the country through civil process and by civil officers. Because of the utter inability to keep the peace and process and maintain order by the customary officers and agencies in time of peace, armies are organized and put into the field. They are called out and invested with the powers of war to prevent total anarchy and to preserve the government. Peace is the normal condition of a country, neither being without law, but each having laws appropriate to the conditions of society. The maxim *inter arma silent leges* is never wholly true. The object of war is to bring society out of its abnormal condition; and the laws of war aim to have that done with the least possible injury to persons or property.

Anciently, when two nations were at war, the conqueror had or asserted the right to take from his enemy his life, liberty, and property: if either was spared, it was a favor or act of mercy. By the laws of nations, and of war as a part thereof, the conqueror was deprived of this right.

When two governments, foreign to each other, are at war, or when a civil war becomes territorial, all of the people of the respective belligerents become by the law of nations the enemies of each other. As enemies they cannot hold intercourse, but neither can kill or injure the other except under a commission from their respective governments. So humanizing have been and are the laws of war, it is a high offense against them to kill an enemy without such commission. The laws of war demand that a man shall not take human life except under a license from his government; and under the Constitution of the United States no license can be given by any department of the government to take human life in war, except according to the law and usages of war. Soldiers regularly in the service have the license of the government to deprive men, the active enemies of their government, of their liberty and lives; their commission so to act is as perfect and legal as that of a judge to adjudicate, but the soldier must act in obedience to the laws of war, as the judge must in obedience to the civil law. A civil judge must try criminals in the mode prescribed in the Constitution and the law; so, soldiers must kill or capture according to the laws of war. Non-combatants are not to be disturbed or interfered with by the armies of either party except in extreme cases. Armies are called out and organized to meet and overcome the active, acting public enemies.

But enemies with which an army has to deal are of two classes:

1st. Open, active participants in hostilities, as soldiers who wear the uniform, move under the flag, and hold the appropriate commission from their government. Openly assuming to discharge the duties and meet the responsibilities and dangers of soldiers, they are entitled to all belligerent rights, and should receive all the courtesies due to soldiers. The true soldier is proud to acknowledge and respect those rights, and ever cheerfully extends those courtesies.

2nd. Secret, but active participants, as spies, brigands, bushwhackers, jayhawkers, war rebels, and assassins. In all wars, and especially in civil wars, such secret, active enemies rise up to annoy and attack an army, and they must be met and put down by the army. When lawless wretches become so impudent and powerful as not to be controlled and governed by the ordinary tribunals of a country, armies are called out, and the laws of war invoked. Wars never have been and never can be conducted upon the principle that an army is but a *posse comitatus* of a civil magistrate.

An army, like all other organized bodies, has a right, and it is its first duty, to protect its own existence, and the existence of all its parts, by the means and in the mode usual among civilized nations when at war. Then the question arises, do the laws of war authorize a different mode of proceeding and the use of different means against secret active enemies from those used against open active enemies?

As has been said, the open enemy or soldier in time of war may be met in battle and killed, wounded, or taken prisoner, or so placed by the lawful strategy of war as that he is powerless. Unless the law of self-preservation absolutely demands it, the life of a wounded enemy or a prisoner must be spared. Unless pressed thereto by the extremest necessity, the laws of war condemn and punish with great severity harsh or cruel treatment to a wounded enemy or a prisoner.

Certain stipulations and agreements, tacit or express, betwixt the open belligerent parties, are permitted by the laws of war, and are held to be of very high and sacred character. Such is the tacit understanding, or it may be usage, of war, in regard to flags of truce. Flags of truce are resorted to as a means of saving human life, or alleviating human suffering. When not used with perfidy, the laws of war require that they should be respected. The Romans regarded ambassadors betwixt belligerents as persons to be treated with consideration and respect. Plutarch, in his Life of Caesar, tells us that the barbarians in Gaul having sent some ambassadors to Caesar, he detained them, charging fraudulent practices, and led his army to battle, obtaining a great victory.

When the senate decreed festivals and sacrifices for the victory, Cato declared it to be his opinion that Caesar ought to be given into the hands of the barbarians, that so the guilt which this breach of faith might otherwise bring upon the state might be expiated by transferring the curse on him who was the occasion of it.

Under the Constitution and laws of the United States, should a commander be guilty of such a flagrant breach of law as Cato charged upon Caesar, he would not be delivered to the enemy, but would be punished after a military trial. The many honorable gentlemen who hold commissions in the army of the United States, and have been deputed to conduct war according to the laws of war, would keenly feel it as an insult to their profession of arms for any one to say they could not or would not punish a fellow soldier who was guilty of wanton cruelty to a prisoner, or perfidy towards the bearers of a flag of truce.

The laws of war permit capitulation of surrender and paroles. They are agreements betwixt belligerents, and should be scrupulously observed and performed. They are contracts wholly unknown to civil tribunals. Parties to such contracts must answer any breaches thereof to the customary military tribunals in time of war. If an officer of rank, possessing the pride that becomes a soldier and a gentleman, who should capitulate to surrender the forces and property under his command and control, be charged with a fraudulent breach of the terms of surrender, the laws of war do not permit that he should be punished without a trial, or, if innocent, that he shall have no means of wiping out the foul imputation. If a paroled prisoner is charged with a breach of his parole, he may be punished if guilty, but not without a trial. He should be tried by a military tribunal constituted and proceeding as the laws and usages of war prescribe.

The law and usage of war contemplate that soldiers have a high sense of personal honor. The true soldier is proud to feel and to know that his enemy possesses personal honor, and will conform and be obedient to the laws of war. In a spirit of justice, and with a wise appreciation of such feelings, the laws of war protect the character and honor of an open enemy. When by the fortunes of war one open enemy is thrown into the hands and power of another, and is charged with dishonorable conduct and a breach of the laws of war, he must be tried according to the usages of war. Justice and fairness say that an open enemy to whom dishonorable conduct is imputed, has a right to demand a trial. If such a demand can be rightfully made, surely it cannot be rightfully refused. It is to be hoped that the military authorities of this country will never refuse such a demand, because there is no act of Congress that authorizes it, and they are a part of the law of the land.

One belligerent may request the other to punish for breaches of the laws of war, and, regularly, such a request should be made before retaliatory measures are taken. Whether the laws of war have been infringed or not, is of necessity a question to be decided by the laws and usages of war, and is cognizable before a military tribunal. When prisoners of war conspire to escape or are guilty of a breach of appropriate and necessary rules of prison discipline, they may be punished, but not without trial. The commander who should order every prisoner charged with improper conduct to be shot or hung, would be guilty of a high offense against the laws of war, and should be punished therefore, after a regular military trial. If the culprit should be condemned and executed, the commander would be as free from guilt as if the man had been killed in battle.

It is manifest, from what has been said, that military tribunals exist under and according to the laws and usages of war in the interest of justice and mercy. They are established to save human life, and to prevent cruelty as far as possible. The commander of an army in time of war has the same power to organize military tribunals and execute their judgments that he has to set his squadrons in the field and fight battles. His authority in each case is from the law and usage of war.

Having seen that there must be military tribunals to decide questions arising in time of war betwixt belligerents who are open and active enemies, let us next see whether the laws of war do not authorize such tribunals to determine the fate of those who are active, but secret, participants in the hostilities.

In Mr. Wheaton's Elements of International Law, he says, "the effect of a state of war, lawfully declared to exist, is to place all the subjects of each belligerent power in a state of mutual hostility. The usage of nations has modified this maxim by legalizing such acts of hostility only as are committed by those who are authorized by the express or implied command of the state; such are the regularly commissioned naval and military forces of the nation and all others called out in its defense, or spontaneously defending themselves, in case of necessity, without any express authority for that purpose. Cicero tells us in his offices, that by the Roman feudal law no person could lawfully engage in battle with the public enemy without being regularly enrolled, and taking the military oath. This was a regulation sanctioned both by policy and religion. The horrors of war would indeed be greatly aggravated, if every individual of the belligerent states were allowed to plunder and slay indiscriminately the enemy's subjects without being in any manner accountable for his conduct. *Hence it is that, in land wars, irregular bands of marauders are liable to be treated as lawless banditti, not entitled to the protection of the mitigated usages of war as practiced by civilized nations."* (Wheaton's Elements of International Law, page 406, 3rd Edition.) [Emphasis by J. Speed].

In speaking upon the subject of banditti, Patrick Henry said, in the Virginia convention, "the honorable gentleman has given you an elaborate account of what he judges tyrannical legislation, and an *ex post facto* law— (in the case of Josiah Phillips;) he has misrepresented the facts. That man was not executed by a tyrannical stroke of power, nor was he a Socrates; he was a fugitive murderer, and an outlaw; a man who commanded an *infamous banditti,* and at *a time when the war was at the most perilous stage* he committed the most cruel and shocking barbarities; he was an enemy to the human name. Those who declare war against the human race may be struck out of existence as soon as apprehended. He was not executed according to those beautiful legal ceremonies which are pointed out by the laws in criminal cases. The enormity of his crimes did not entitle him to it. I am truly a friend to legal forms and methods, but, sir, the occasion warranted the measure. A pirate, an outlaw, or a common enemy to all mankind, may be put to death at any time. It is justified by the *law of nature and nations."* (3rd volume Elliott's Debates on Federal Constitution, page 140.) [Emphasis by P. Henry].

No reader, not to say student, of the law of nations, can doubt but that Mr. Wheaton and Mr. Henry have fairly stated the laws of war. Let it be constantly borne in mind that they are talking of the law in a state of war. These banditti that spring up in time of war are respecters of no law, human or divine, of peace or of war, are *hostes humani generis,* and may be hunted down like wolves. Thoroughly desperate and perfectly lawless, no man can be required to peril his life in venturing to take them prisoners—as prisoners, no trust can be reposed in them. But they are occasionally made prisoners. Being prisoners, what is to be done with them? If they are public enemies, assuming and exercising the right to kill, and are not regularly authorized to do so, they must be apprehended and dealt with by the military. No man can doubt the right and duty of the military to make prisoners of them, and being public enemies, it is the duty of the military to punish them for any infraction of the laws of war. But the military cannot ascertain whether they are guilty or not without the aid of a military tribunal.

In all wars, and especially in civil wars, secret but active enemies are almost as numerous as open ones. That fact has contributed to make civil wars such scourges to the countries in which they rage. In nearly all foreign wars the contending parties speak different languages, and have different habits and manners; but in most civil wars that is not the case; hence there is a security in participating secretly in hostilities that induces many to thus engage. War prosecuted according to the most civilized usage is horrible, but its horrors are greatly aggravated by the immemorial habits of plunder, rape, and murder practiced by secret, but active participants. Certain laws and usages have been adopted by the civilized world in wars between nations that are not of kin to one another, for the purpose and to the effect of arresting or softening many of the necessary cruel consequences of war. How strongly bound are we, then, in the midst of a great war, where brother and personal friend are fighting against brother and friend, to adopt and be governed by those laws and usages.

A public enemy must or should be dealt with in all wars by the same laws. The fact that they are public enemies, being the same, they should deal with each other according to those laws of war that are contemplated by the Constitution. Whatever rules have been adopted and practiced by the civilized nations of the world in war to soften its harshness and severity, should be adopted and practiced by us in this war. That the laws of war authorized commanders to create and establish military commissions, courts, or tribunals, for the trial of offenders against the laws of war, whether they be active or secret participants in the hostilities, cannot be denied. That the judgments of such tribunals may have been sometimes harsh, and sometimes even tyrannical, does not prove that they ought not to exist, nor does it prove that they are not constituted in the interest of justice and mercy. Considering the power that the laws of war give over secret participants in hostilities, such as banditti, guerrillas, spies, etc., the position of a commander would be miserable indeed if he could not call to his aid the judgments of such tribunals; he would become a mere butcher of men, without the power to ascertain justice, and there can be no mercy where there is no justice. War in its mildest form is horrible; but take away from the contending armies the ability and right to organize what is now known as a Bureau of Military Justice, they would soon become monster savages, unrestrained by any and all ideas of law and justice. Surely no lover of mankind, no one that respects law and order, no one that has the instinct of justice, or that can be softened by mercy, would, in time of war, take away from the commanders the right to organize military tribunals of justice, and especially such tribunals for the protection of persons charged or suspected with being foes and participants in the hostilities. It would be a miracle if the records and history of this war do not show occasional cases in which those tribunals have erred; but they will show many, very many cases in which human life would have been taken but for the interposition and judgments of those tribunals. Every student of the laws of war must acknowledge that such tribunals exert a kindly and benign influence in time of war. Impartial history will record the fact that the Bureau of Military Justice, regularly organized during this war, has saved human life and prevented human suffering. The greatest suffering, patiently endured by our soldiers, and the hardest battles gallantly fought during this protracted struggle, are not more creditable to the American character than the establishment of this bureau. This people have such an educated and profound respect for law and justice—such a love of mercy—that they have, in the midst of this greatest of civil wars, systematized and brought into regular order tribunals that before this war existed under the law of war, but without general rule. To condemn the tribunals that have been established under this bureau is to condemn and denounce the war itself, or, justifying the war, to insist that it shall be prosecuted according to the harshest rules, and without the aid of the laws, usages, and customary agencies for mitigating those rules. If such tribunals had not existed before, under the laws and usages of war, the American citizen might as proudly point to their establishment as to our inimitable and inestimable constitutions. It must be constantly borne in mind that such tribunals and such a bureau cannot exist except in time of war, and cannot then take cognizance of offenders or offenses where the civil courts are open, except offenders and offenses against the laws of war.

But it is insisted by some, and doubtless with honesty, and with a zeal commensurate with their honesty, that such military tribunals can have no constitutional existence. The argument against their constitutionality may be shortly, and I think fairly, stated thus:

Congress alone can establish military or civil judicial tribunals. As Congress had not established military tribunals, except such as have been created under the articles of war, and which articles are made in pursuance of that clause in the Constitution which gives to Congress the power to make rules for the government of the army and navy, any other tribunal is and must be plainly unconstitutional, and all its acts void.

This objecting thus stated, or stated in any other way, begs the question. It assumes that Congress alone can establish military judicial tribunals. Is that assumption true?

We have seen that when war comes, the laws and usages of war come also, and that during the war they are a part of the laws of the land. Under the Constitution, Congress may define and punish offenses against those laws, but in default of Congress's defining those laws and prescribing a punishment for their infraction, and the mode of proceeding to ascertain whether an offense has been committed, and what punishment is to be inflicted, the army must be governed by the laws and usages of war as understood and practiced by the civilized nations of the world. It has been abundantly shown that these tribunals are constituted by the army in the interest of justice and mercy, and for the purpose and to the effect of mitigating the horrors of war.

But it may be insisted that though the laws of war, being a part of the law of nations, constitute a part of the laws of the land, that those laws must be regarded as modified so far and whenever they come in direct conflict with plain constitutional provisions. The following clauses of the Constitution are principally relied upon to show the conflict betwixt the laws of war and the Constitution:

"The trial of all crimes, except in cases of impeachment, shall be by jury; and such trial shall be held in the State where the said crime shall have been committed; but when not committed within any state, the trial shall be at such place or places as the Congress may by law have directed." (Art. III of the original Constitution, sec. 2.)

"No person shall be held to answer for a capital or otherwise infamous crime unless on a presentment or, indictment of a grand jury, except in cases arising in the land or naval forces, or in the militia when in actual service, in time of war or public danger; nor shall any person be subject for the same offense to be twice put in jeopardy of life or limb, nor shall be compelled, in any criminal case, to be witness against himself, nor be deprived of life, liberty, or property, without due process of law; nor shall private property be taken for public use without just compensation." (Amendments to the Constitution, Art. V)

"In all criminal prosecutions, the accused shall enjoy the right to a speedy and public trial by an impartial jury of the State and district wherein the crime shall have been committed, which district shall have been previously ascertained by law, and be informed of the nature and cause of the accusation; to be confronted with the witnesses against him, to have compulsory process for obtaining witnesses in his favor; and to have the assistance of counsel for his defense." (Art. VI of the amendments to the Constitution.)

These provisions of the Constitution are intended to fling around the life, liberty, and property of a citizen all the guarantees of a jury trial. These constitutional guarantees cannot be estimated too highly, or protected too sacredly. The reader of history knows that for many weary ages the people suffered for the want of them; it would not only be stupidity, but madness in us not to preserve them. No man has a deeper conviction of their value or a more sincere desire to preserve and perpetuate them than I have.

Nevertheless, these exalted and sacred provisions of the Constitution must not be read alone and by themselves, but must be read and taken in connexion [sic] with other provisions. The Constitution was framed by great men, men of learning and large experience, and it is a wonderful monument of their wisdom. Well versed in the history of the world, they knew that the nation for which they were forming a government would, unless all history was false, have wars, foreign and domestic. Hence the government framed by them is clothed with the power to make and carry on war. As has been shown when war comes, the laws of war come with it. Infractions of the laws of nations are not denominated *crimes,* but *offenses.* [Emphasis on these two words by J. Speed.] Hence the expression in the Constitution that "Congress shall have power to define and punish** *offenses* against the law of nations." Many of the *offenses* against the law of nations for which a man may, by the laws of war, lose his life, his liberty, or his property, are not *crimes.* It is an offense against the law of nations to break a lawful blockade, and for which a forfeiture of the property is the penalty, and yet the running of a blockade has never been regarded as a crime; to hold communication or intercourse with the enemy is a high offense against the laws of war, and for which those laws prescribe punishment, and yet it is not a *crime;* to act as a spy is an offense against the laws of war, and the punishment for which in all ages has been death, and yet it is not a crime; to violate a flag of truce is an offense against the laws of war, and yet not a crime of which a civil court can take cognizance; to unite with banditti, jayhawkers, guerrillas, or any other unauthorized marauders is a high offense against the laws of war; the offense when the band is organized or joined. The atrocities committed by such a band do not constitute the offense, but make the reasons, and sufficient reasons they are, why such banditti are denounced by the laws of war. Some of the offenses against the laws of war are crimes, and some are not. Because they are crimes they do not cease to be offenses against those laws; nor because they are not crimes or misdemeanors do they fail to be offenses against the laws of war. Murder is a crime, and the murderer as such must be proceeded against in the form and manner prescribed in the Constitution; in committing the murder an offense may also have been committed against the laws of war; for that offense he must answer to the laws of war, and the tribunals legalized by that law.

There is, then, an apparent but no real conflict in the constitutional provisions. *Offenses* against the laws of war must be dealt with and punished under the Constitution as the laws of war, they being a part of the law of nations direct; *crimes* must be dealt with and punished as the Constitution, and the laws made in pursuance thereof, may direct.

Congress has not undertaken to define the code of war nor to punish offenses against it. In the case of a spy, Congress has undertaken to say who shall be deemed a spy, and how he shall be punished. But every lawyer knows that a spy was a well known offender under the laws of war, and that under and according to those laws he could have been tried and punished without an act of Congress. This is admitted by the act of Congress, when it says that he shall suffer death "according to the law and usages of war." The act is simply declaratory of the law.

That portion of the Constitution which declares that "no person shall be deprived of his life, liberty, or property without due process of law," has such direct reference to, and connexion [sic] with, trials for *crime* or *criminal* prosecutions that comment upon it would seem to be unnecessary. Trials for offenses against the laws of war are not embraced or intended to be embraced in those provisions. If this is not so, then every man that kills another in battle is a murderer, for he deprived a "person of life without that due process of law" contemplated by this provision; every man who holds another as a prisoner of war is liable for false imprisonment, as he does so without that due process of law contemplated by this provision; every soldier that marches across a field in battle array is liable to an action of trespass, because he does it without that same due process. The argument that flings around offenders against the laws of war these guarantees of the Constitution would convict all soldiers of our army of murder; no prisoners could be taken and held; the army could not move. The absurd consequences that would of necessity flow from such an argument show that it cannot be the true construction—it cannot be what was intended by the framers of the instrument. One of the prime motives for the Union and a federal government was to confer the powers of war. If any provisions of the Constitution are so in conflict with the power to carry on war as to destroy and make it valueless, then the instrument, instead of being a great and wise one, is a miserable failure, a *felo de se*. [Emphasis by J. Speed.]

If a man would sue out his writ of *habeas corpus,* and the return shows that he belonged to the army or navy, and was held to be tried for some offense against the rules and articles of war, the writ should be dismissed and the party remanded to answer to the charges. So, in time of war, if a man should sue out a writ of *habeas corpus,* and it is made appear that he is in the hands of the military as a prisoner of war, the writ should be dismissed and the prisoner remanded to be disposed of as the laws and usages of war require. If the prisoner be a regular unoffending soldier of the opposing party to the war, he should be treated with all the courtesy and kindness consistent with his safe custody; if he has offended against the laws of war, he should have such trial and be punished as the laws of war require. A spy, though a prisoner of war, may be tried, condemned, and executed by a military tribunal without a breach of the Constitution. A bushwacker, a jayhawker, a bandit, a war rebel, an assassin, being public enemies, may be tried, condemned, and executed as offenders against the laws of war. The soldier that would fail to try a spy or bandit after his capture would be as derelict in duty as if he were to fail to capture; he is as much bound to try and to execute, if guilty, as he is to arrest; the same law that makes it his duty to pursue and kill or capture makes it his duty to try according to the usages of war. The judge of a civil court is not more strongly bound under the Constitution and the law to try a criminal than is the military to try an offender against the laws of war. [Emphasis by J. Speed.]

The fact that the civil courts are open does not affect the right of the military tribunal or hold as a prisoner and to try. The civil courts have no more right to prevent the military, in time of war, from trying an offender against the laws of war than they have a right to interfere with and prevent a battle. A battle may be lawfully fought in the very view and presence of a court; so a spy, a bandit, or other offender against the law of war may be tried, and tried lawfully, when and where the civil courts are open and transacting the usual business.

The laws of war authorize human life to be taken without legal process, or that legal process contemplated by those provisions in the Constitution that are relied upon to show that military judicial tribunals are unconstitutional. Wars should be prosecuted justly as well as bravely.

One enemy in the power of another, whether he be an open or a secret one, should not be punished or executed without trial. If the question be one concerning the laws of war, he should be tried by those engaged in the war—they and they only are his peers. The military must decide whether he is or not an active participant in the hostilities. If he is an active participant in the hostilities, it is the duty of the military to take him a prisoner without warrant or other judicial process, and dispose of him as the laws of war direct.

It is curious to see one and the same mind justify the killing of thousands in battle because it is done according to the laws of war, and yet condemning that same law when, out of regard for justice and with the hope of saving life, it orders a military trial before the enemy are killed. The love of law, of justice, and the wish to save life and suffering, should impel all good men in time of war to uphold and sustain the existence and action of such tribunals. The object of such tribunals is obviously intended to save life, and when their jurisdiction is confined to offenses against the laws of war, that is their effect. They prevent indiscriminate slaughter; they prevent men from being punished or killed upon mere suspicion.

The law of nations, which is the result of the experience and wisdom of ages, has decided that jayhawkers, banditti, etc., are offenders against the laws of nature, and of war, and as such amenable to the military. Our Constitution has made those laws a part of the law of the land. Obedience to the Constitution and the law, requires that the military should do their whole duty; they must not only meet and fight the enemies of the country in open battle, but they must kill or take the secret enemies of the country, and try and execute them according to the laws of war. The civil tribunals of the country cannot rightfully interfere with the military in the performance of their high, arduous, and perilous, but lawful duties. That Booth and his associates were secret public enemies, no mind that contemplates the facts can doubt. The exclamation used by him when he escaped from the box on to the stage, after he had fired the fatal shot, *sic semper tyrannis*, and his dying message, "say to my mother that I died for my country," show that he was not an assassin from private malice, but that he acted as a public foe. Such a deed is expressly laid down by Vattel, in his work on the law of nations, as an offense against the laws of war, and a great crime. "I give, then, the name of assassination to a treacherous murder, whether the perpetrators of the deed be the subjects of the party whom we cause to be assassinated or of our own sovereign, or that it be executed by any other emissary introducing himself as a suppliant, a refugee, or a deserter, or, in fine, as a stranger." (Vattel, 339.) [Emphasis by J. Speed.]

Neither the civil nor the military department of the government should regard itself as wiser and better than the Constitution and the laws that exist under or are made in pursuance thereof. Each department should, in peace and in war, confining itself to its own proper sphere of action, diligently and fearlessly perform its legitimate functions, and in the mode prescribed by the Constitution and the law. Such obedience to and observance of law will maintain peace when it exists, and will soonest relieve the country from the abnormal state of war.

My conclusion, therefore, is, that if the persons who are charged with the assassination of the president committed the deed as public enemies, as I believe they did, and whether they did or not is a question to be decided by the tribunal before which they are tried, they not only can, but ought to be tried before a military tribunal. If the persons charged have offended against the laws of war, it would be as palpably wrong for the military to hand them over to the civil courts, as it would be wrong in a civil court to convict a man of murder who had, in time of war, killed another in battle.

I am, sir, most respectfully, your obedient servant.

James Speed, Attorney General
To the President.

Appendix IV: Digest of Opinions of the Judge Advocate General of the Army

Edited by Major W. Winthrop, Judge Advocate, U.S. Army, Third Edition, Published by the Authority of the Secretary of War (Washington: Government Printing Office, 1868)

[Excerpts.]

Military Commission, I—Origin, Constitution, Procedure, etc.

11. To subject military commissions partly to the laws and practice which govern civil courts, and partly to those which control courts-martial, would be to destroy the harmony between the two different military tribunals, and to embarrass the administration of military justice. Such a course would tend also to defeat the purpose of Congress, which, in placing them in many respects on the same footing, evidently contemplated that the statutory rules of procedure which apply to the court-martial should be applied, as far as practicable, to the military commission.

14. Extract from the published official report of this Bureau to the Secretary of War, of November 13, 1865: ...

"These commissions, originating in the necessities of the rebellion, had been proved by the experience of three years, indispensable for the punishment of public crimes, in regions where other courts had ceased to exist, and in cases in which the local criminal courts could not legally take cognizance, or which, by reason of intrinsic defects of machinery, they were incompetent to pass upon."

"But it was not until the two cases under consideration" (of the Assassins and of Wirz) "came on to be tried by the Military Commission, that its highest excellence was exhibited. It was not merely in that it was unencumbered by the technicalities and inevitable embarrassments attending the administration of justice before civil tribunals, or in the fact that it could so readily avail itself of the military power of the government for the execution of its processes and the enforcement of its orders, that its efficacy (though in these directions most conspicuous) was chiefly illustrated.... By no other species of tribunal, and by no other known mode of judicial inquiry, could this result have been so successfully attained; and it may truly be said that without the aid and agency of the Military Commission, one of the most important chapters in the annals of the rebellion would have been lost to history, and the most complete and reliable disclosure of its inner and real life, alike treacherous and barbaric, would have failed to be developed."

Military Commission, II—(Jurisdiction in case of Citizens.)

2. A military commission is not restricted in its jurisdiction to offenses committed in the State or district where it sits, as are the ordinary criminal courts of the country. The jurisdiction of a military commission, like that of a general court-martial, is not confined to the place of the commission of the offense, but is co-extensive with the limits of the federal domain, and extends to any military department in which, on account of facilities for obtaining testimony, or for other good reason, it may be convenient to bring a case to trial. A military commission derives its authority from the unwritten or common law of war. Its jurisdiction cannot be limited to offenses made penal only by the laws of the United States or of the State in which the offense was committed.

14. Where a military commission was invested, by the original order of the general convening it, "with jurisdiction in all cases, civil, criminal, and in equity, usually triable in courts established by law," *held* that such a tribunal was not authorized to be created, either by law or usage, and

recommended that it be ordered by the Secretary of War to be dissolved.

25. *Held* (June, 1864) that the murder of Union soldiers, for the disloyal and treasonable purpose of resisting the government in its efforts to suppress the rebellion, was a military offense, quite other than the ordinary offense of murder, cognizable by the criminal courts; and that citizens who had been guilty thereof, though in a State where the courts are open, might properly be brought to trial before a military commission. In such case, the circumstances conferring jurisdiction should be indicated in the charge and distinctly set forth in the specifications.

30. The principle, well expressed by Major General Halleck, in General Order No. 1, of headquarters department of the Missouri, of January 1, 1862, that "many offenses which, in time of peace, are civil offenses, become, in time of war, military offenses, and are to be tried by a military tribunal, even in places where civil tribunals exist," has been followed by this government in a great number of cases; and offenses aimed at impairing the efficiency of the service, or the efforts of the government to suppress the rebellion, have been repeatedly brought to trial by military commissions when committed within our military lines and on the theatre of military operations, where the effect of the pressure of a vast civil war is, *ex necessitate,* to suspend for a time, for the preservation of the whole, some portion of the legal safeguards thrown around the citizen in time of peace. It is the fact that the State of Indiana was in this category (with the additional consideration that it had been and was being constantly threatened with invasion by the enemy) which conferred jurisdiction upon the military commission that had passed upon the cases of Dodd, Bowles, Milligan, Horsey, and other conspirators against the government. [These convictions overturned by the U.S. Supreme Court in ex parte Milligan, 1866].

The amendments of the Constitution, which give the right of *trial by jury* to persons held to answer for capital or otherwise infamous crimes, except when arising in the land and naval forces, are often referred to, as conclusive against the jurisdiction of military courts over such offenses when committed by citizens. But though the letter of the articles would give color to such an argument, yet in constructing the different parts of the Constitution together, such a literal interpretation of the amendments must be held to give way before the necessity for an efficient exercise of the war power which is vested in Congress by that instrument.

A striking illustration of the recognition of this principle by the legislation of the country since an early period of our history is furnished by the 57th article of war, in the fact that it has from the beginning rendered amenable to trial by court-martial, for certain offenses, not only military persons, but all persons whatsoever.

This article, establishing this jurisdiction, was adopted by the Congress of the Confederation, and its terms and effect remained unchanged at the time of the formation of the Constitution. In 1806 a slight modification was introduced in its language—the substitution of the word "whosoever" for the words "all persons";—and thus a Congress, composed probably of many of the founders of the republic, substantially reaffirmed the Jurisdiction previously conferred.

Military Commission, IV—(Jurisdiction in Case of an Enemy.)

4. Guerrillas are triable by military commission for "violation of the laws and customs of war" in the commission of acts of violence, robbery, etc.

Military Commission, V—(Judgment and Sentence.)

1. Every case ... of a death sentence by a military commission must be submitted to the president for his approval before it can be acted upon.

2. Under a charge of a violation of the common law of war, a military commission may inflict such punishment as in its discretion may be deemed adequate and proper.

Appendix V: Instructions for the Government of Armies of the United States in the Field

by Francis Lieber

From *The War of the Rebellion: A Compilation of the Official Records of the Union and Confederate Armies.* (Washington: Government Printing Office, 1899), Series III, Vol. 3, pp. 148–164. [Excerpts.]

Section I.—Martial Law—Military jurisdiction—Military necessity—Retaliation.

4. Martial law is simply military authority exercised in accordance with the laws and usages of war. Military oppression is not martial law; it is the abuse of the power which that law confers. As martial law is executed by military force, it is incumbent upon those who administer it to be strictly guided by the principles of justice, honor, and humanity—virtues adorning a soldier even more than other men, for the very reason that he possesses the power of his arms against the unarmed.

12. Whenever feasible, martial law is carried out in cases of individual offenders by military courts; but sentences of death shall be executed only with the approval of the chief executive, provided the urgency of the case does not require a speedier execution, and then only with the approval of the chief commander.

13. Military jurisdiction is of two kinds: First, that which is conferred and defined by statute; second, that which is derived from the common law of war. Military offenses under the statute law must be tried in the manner therein directed; but military offenses which do not come within the statute must be tried and punished under the common law of war. The character of the courts which exercise these jurisdictions depends upon the local laws of each particular country.

In the armies of the United States the first is exercised by courts-martial; while cases which do not come within the Rules and Articles of War, or the jurisdiction conferred by statute on courts-martial, are tried by military commissions.

15. ... Men who take up arms against one another in public war do not cease on this account to be moral beings, responsible to one another and to God.

16. Military necessity does not admit of cruelty—that is, the infliction of suffering for the sake of suffering or for revenge, nor of maiming or wounding except in fight, nor of torture to extort confessions.... In general, military necessity does not include any act of hostility which makes the return to peace unnecessarily difficult.

20. Public war is a state of armed hostility between sovereign nations or governments. It is a law and requisite of civilized existence that men live in political, continuous societies, forming organized units, called states or nations, whose constituents bear, enjoy, and suffer, advance and retrograde together, in peace and in war.

Section III.—Deserters—Prisoners of War—Hostages—Booty on the battle-field.

49. A prisoner of war is a public enemy armed or attached to the hostile army for active aid, who has fallen into the hands of the captor, either fighting or wounded, on the field or in the hospital, by individual surrender or by capitulation.

52. No belligerent has the right to declare that he will treat every captured man in arms of a levy en masse as a brigand or bandit.

56. A prisoner of war is subject to no punishment for being a public enemy, nor is any revenge wreaked upon him by the intentional infliction of any suffering, or disgrace, by cruel imprisonment, want of food, by mutilation, death, or any other barbarity.

67. The law of nations allows every sovereign government to make war upon another sovereign State, and, therefore, admits of no rules or

laws different from those of regular warfare, regarding the treatment of prisoners of war, although they may belong to the army of a government which the captor may consider as a wanton and unjust assailant.

68. Unnecessary or revengeful destruction of life is not lawful.

75. Prisoners of war are subject to confinement or imprisonment such as may be deemed necessary on account of safety, but they are to be subjected to no other intentional suffering or indignity. The confinement and mode of treating a prisoner may be varied during his captivity according to the demands of safety.

80. ... the modern law of war permits no longer the use of any violence against prisoners in order to extort the desired information, or to punish them for having given false information.

Section V.—Safe conduct—Spies— War-traitors—Captured messengers— Abuse of the flag of truce.

88. A spy is a person who secretly, in disguise or under false pretense, seeks information with the intention of communicating it to the enemy.

90. A traitor under the law of war, or a war-traitor, is a person in a place or district under martial law who, unauthorized by the military commander, gives information of any kind to the enemy, or holds intercourse with him.

102. The law of war, like the criminal law regarding other offenses, makes no difference on account of the difference of sexes, concerning the spy, the war-traitor, or the war-rebel.

Section IX.—Assassination.

148. The law of war does not allow proclaiming either an individual belonging to the hostile army, or a citizen, or a subject of the hostile government an outlaw, who may be slain without trial by any captor, any more than the modern law of peace allows such international outlawry; on the contrary, it abhors such outrage. The sternest retaliation should follow the murder committed in consequence of such proclamation, made by whatever authority. Civilized nations look with horror upon offers of rewards for the assassination of enemies as relapses into barbarism.

Chapter Notes

Chapter 1

1. George S. Bryan, *The Great American Myth* (New York: Carrick & Evans, 1940), pp. 168–85; Abraham Lincoln, *Speeches and Writings: 1859–1865*, Literary Classics of the United States (New York: Library of America, 1989), p. 687.

2. Marquis de Chambrun, "Personal Recollections of Mr. Lincoln," *Scribner's Magazine*, January 1893, pp. 26–38; Salmon P. Chase, *Inside Lincoln's Cabinet: The Civil War Diaries of Salmon P. Chase*, ed. David Donald (New York: Longmans, Green, 1954), pp. 266–68; Bryan, pp. 195–98; *New York Herald*, April 16, 1865; Thomas R. Turner, "Public Opinion and the Assassination of Abraham Lincoln," *Lincoln Herald* 78, no. 1 (Spring 1976), pp. 17–24.

3. Benjamin P. Thomas and Harold M. Hyman, *Stanton: The Life and Times of Lincoln's Secretary of War* (New York: Alfred A. Knopf, 1962), pp. 397–401.

4. Constitution of the United States, Article I, section 9; Lincoln, pp. 237, 252–53, 456–58, 466–67, 512–13, 526; John Rhodehamel and Louise Taper, eds., *"Right or Wrong, God Judge Me": The Writings of John Wilkes Booth* (Urbana: University of Illinois Press, 1997), pp. 124–25; Joseph Story, *Commentaries on the Constitution of the United States* (1833; reprint, Durham: Carolina Academic Press, 1987), p. 483; Mark E. Neely, Jr., *The Fate of Liberty* (New York: Oxford University Press, 1991), p. 5; Phillip Shaw Paludan, *The Presidency of Abraham Lincoln* (Lawrence: University Press of Kansas, 1994), pp. 71–76, 79–82, 191–92; "Habeas Corpus," Wikipedia, http://en.wikipedia.org/wiki/Habeas_corpus; Anthony Wright, *Citizens and Subjects: An Essay on British Politics* (London: Routledge, 1994); Kermit L. Hall, ed., *The Oxford Companion to the Supreme Court of the United States* (New York: Oxford University Press, 2005), p. 415; *Oxford English Dictionary*, 4, Oxford University Press, p. 849.

5. Sidney Cromwell, *Political Opinions in 1774 and 1863: A Letter to a Victim of Arbitrary Arrests and "American Bastilles"* (New York: Anson D.F. Randolph, 1863), pp. 14–15.

6. Thomas Goodrich, *The Darkest Dawn* (Bloomington: Indiana University Press, 2005), p. 153, quote of Sarah Hill of Norristown, Pennsylvania.

7. Thomas Reed Turner, *Beware the People Weeping* (Baton Rouge: Louisiana State University Press, 1982), pp. 56–63.

8. Thomas and Hyman, pp. 360–80.

9. David Homer Bates, *Lincoln in the Telegraph Office* (New York: The Century Co., 1907), pp. 392, 399; Louis A. Warren, ed., "Stanton at Lincoln's Bedside," *Lincoln Lore* 575 (April 15, 1940); Roy Z. Chamlee, Jr., *Lincoln's Assassins* (Jefferson, NC: McFarland, 1990), pp. 147, 232–33.

10. Gamaliel Bradford, "Union Portraits, 5. Edwin M. Stanton," *Atlantic Monthly*, August 1915, pp. 180–91; Chamlee, pp. 26, 233–34; L.E. Chittenden, *Recollections of President Lincoln and His Administration* (New York: Harper and Brothers, 1891), pp. 178, 180–81, 186, 192; Leonard Grover, "Lincoln's Interest in the Theatre," *The Century Magazine*, April 1909, pp. 942–50; Dumas Malone, ed., *Dictionary of American Biography* (New York: Charles Scribner's Sons, 1964), pp. 517–21; Frederick W. Seward, *Reminiscences of a War-Time Statesman and Diplomat 1830–1915* (New York: G.P.

Putnam's Sons, 1916), pp. 256–57; Moorfield Storey, "Dickens, Stanton, Sumner, and Storey," *Atlantic Monthly*, April 1930, pp. 463–65; Thomas and Hyman, pp. 63–65, 383, 385, 396–98, 400; Louis A. Warren, ed., "Edwin McMasters Stanton," *Lincoln Lore* 990 (March 29, 1948); Warren, "Stanton at Lincoln's Bedside"; Gideon Welles, "Lincoln and Johnson," *The Galaxy* 14, nos. 4–5 (April–May 1872), pp. 521–32, 663–73.
    11. Howard H. Peckham, "James Tanner's Account of Lincoln's Death," *The Abraham Lincoln Quarterly* 2, no. 4 (December 1942), pp. 176–83; "Tanner Also Present," *Washington Post*, April 16, 1905; Maxwell Whiteman, ed., *While Lincoln Lay Dying* (Philadelphia: The Union League of Philadelphia, 1968).
    12. L.C. Baker, *History of the United States Secret Service* (Philadelphia: L.C. Baker, 1867), pp. 20–21, 39–44, 45–70, 72–84, 127, 145, 174–78, 195–96, 202–29, 378–83, 465–75, 494–95, 507–08, 525, 530; James O. Hall, "An Interview with James O. Hall," *Journal of the Lincoln Assassination* 4, no. 2 (August 1990), pp. 29–30; Jacob Mogolever, *Death to Traitors* (Garden City, NY: Doubleday, 1960), pp. 21, 27, 29–32, 34, 37, 46–47, 49–50, 58, 73, 83, 88, 100, 109, 110, 215, 332–85.
    13. R.D. Hunt and J.R. Brown, *Brevet Brigadier Generals in Blue* (Gaithersburg, MD: Olde Soldier Books, 1997); "A New Version of the Greatest Manhunt," *New York Times Magazine*, December 7, 1930; Osborn H. Oldroyd, *The Assassination of Abraham Lincoln* (Washington, D.C.: O.H. Oldroyd, 1901), pp. 66–68; Stanton to Major O'Beirne, April 16, 1865, in RG 110, National Archives.
    14. Oldroyd, pp. 84–88; Steven G. Miller, "Rollcall for the Garrett's Farm Patrol," *Surratt Courier* 19, no. 9 (September 1994), pp. 3–5; Louis A. Warren, ed., "A $100,000 Reward," *Lincoln Lore* 314 (April 15, 1935).
    15. Francis X. Busch, *Enemies of the State* (Indianapolis: Bobbs-Merrill, 1954), pp. 22–23.
    16. Thomas and Hyman, pp. 400–01.

Chapter 2

    1. Benn Pitman, ed., *The Assassination of President Lincoln and the Trial of the Conspirators* (New York: Moore, Wilstach & Baldwin, 1865), pp. 18–21.
    2. Busch, pp. 30–34.
    3. Pitman, pp. 17–21.
    4. Ezra J. Warner, *Generals in Blue* (Baton Rouge: Louisiana State University Press, 1964), pp. 158–59, 209–10, 243–44, 257–58; Malone, Vol. 5, pp. 263–64, 283, 400–01; Chamlee, pp. 174ff, 216, 247, 249–52, 441; Robert and Katharine Morsberger, *Lew Wallace: Militant Romantic* (New York: McGraw-Hill, 1980), pp. 172–75, 192–93; Lew Wallace, *An Autobiography* (New York: Harper & Brothers, 1906), pp. 850–51; Hunt and Brown, pp. 125, 486.
    5. Theodore Roscoe, *The Web of Conspiracy* (Englewood Cliffs, NJ: Prentice-Hall, 1959), pp. 443–44; Stanton to Col. H.L. Burnett, War Department Records, File "B," Doc. 490, JAO, National Archives; Oldroyd, p. 127.
    6. Joan Chaconas, "Historic Fort McNair," *Surratt Society News* 9, no. 6 (June 1984), pp. 5–6; John B. Ellis, *The Sights and Secrets of the National Capital* (San Francisco: H.H. Bancroft & Co., 1869), pp. 462–65; Michael W. Kauffman, "Fort Lesley McNair and the Lincoln Conspirators," *Lincoln Herald* 80, no. 4 (Winter 1978), pp. 176–88; Phyllis I. McClellan, *Silent Sentinel on the Potomac, Fort McNair, 1791–1991* (Bowie, MD: Heritage Books, 1993), pp. 1–51; *Washington: City and Capital* (Washington, D.C.: Government Printing Office, 1937), p. 878.
    7. Pitman, pp. 22–23.
    8. Samuel Bland Arnold, *Memoirs of a Lincoln Conspirator*, ed. Michael W. Kauffman (Bowie, MD: Heritage Books, 1995), pp. 22, 39, 41–43, 48; Sketches of Samuel B. Arnold, War Dept., File "S" 554 (JAO) 1865, Microcopy 599, Reel 3, frames 611–17, National Archives; R.R. Jones, and James Kipp, Affidavits, War Department file "A" 195 (JAO) 1865, Microcopy 599, reel 2, frames 655–59, National Archives; George A. Atzerodt, Confession of G.A. Atzerodt, War Department file "W" 550, (JAO) 1865, Microcopy 599, reel 3, frames 611–17, National Archives.
    9. John A. Bingham, "Argument..." in Pitman, pp. 352–54, 364–65, 367, 372.
    10. David E. Herold, Voluntary Statement, April 27, War Dept. file "H" R.B. (JAO) p. 38, Microcopy 599, reel 4, frames 442–85, National Archives.
    11. Richard D. Mudd, *Dr. Samuel Alexander Mudd and His Descendants* (Saginaw: Richard D. Mudd, 1989), p. ii; Samuel

A. Mudd, Summary of Statement Made in Bryantown, MD, April 21 and 22, War Dept. Records, Microcopy 599, Reel 4, frame 46, National Archives; Samuel A. Mudd, Statement of Dr. S.A. Mudd, April 21, 1865, War Dept. file "M" R.B. (JAO) p. 60, 1865, Microcopy 599, Reel 5, frames 212–25, National Archives.
12. S.B. Arnold, *Memoirs*, pp. 22–23, 25, 27, 29, 49; Louis J. Weichmann, *A True History of the Assassination of Abraham Lincoln and of the Conspiracy of 1865*, ed. Floyd E. Risvold (New York: Alfred A. Knopf, 1975), pp. 44–45.
13. Betty J. Ownsbey, *Alias "Paine": Lewis Thornton Powell, the Mystery Man of the Lincoln Conspiracy* (Jefferson, NC: McFarland, 1993), pp. 3–9, 10–15, 23–33, 76–85; William A. Tidwell, with James O. Hall and David W. Gaddy, *Come Retribution: The Confederate Secret Service and the Assassination of Lincoln* (Jackson: University Press of Mississippi, 1988), pp. 339–41, 413–15, 421.
14. Samuel Carter III, *The Riddle of Dr. Mudd* (New York: G.P. Putnam's Sons, 1974), pp. 73, 94, 112; Clara E. Laughlin, *The Death of Lincoln* (New York: Doubleday, Page, 1909), pp. 317–21; Edman Spangler, Examination of Edman Spangler, War Dept. Records, file "S" R.B. (JAO), p. 78. 1865, Microcopy 599, Reel 6, frames 201–04, National Archives.
15. James O. Hall, *The Surratt Family and John Wilkes Booth* (Clinton, MD: The Surratt Society [1976]), pp. 1–10, 14–15, 17, 18–20; Guy W. Moore, *The Case of Mrs. Surratt* (Norman: University of Oklahoma Press, 1954), pp. 4–19; Mary E. Surratt, Statement of Mrs. Mary E. Surratt, April 28, 1865, War Dept. Records, file "S" R.B. (JAO) p. 78. 1865, Microcopy 599, Reel 6, frames 170–200. National Archives; Mary E. Surratt, Statement of Mrs. Mary E. Surratt, April 17, 1865, War Dept. Records, file "S" R.B. (JAO) p. 79. 1865, Microcopy 599, Reel 6, frames 233–57. National Archives; Anna E. Surratt, Statement, April 28, 1865, War Dept. Records, file "S" R.B. (JAO) p. 79. 1865, Microcopy 599, Reel 6, frames 212–26, National Archives.

Chapter 3

1. Thomas Ewing, Jr., "Argument on the Plea to the Jurisdiction of the Military Commission," in Pitman, p. 266; John A. Bingham, "Argument..." in Pitman, p. 355.
2. James Speed, *Opinion on the Constitutional Power of the Military to Try and Execute the Assassins of the President* (Washington, D.C.: Government Printing Office, 1865), pp. 4–11; Edward Bates, "Diary," *Annual Report of American Historical Society* 4 (1930), p. 483; James Grant Wilson and John Fiske, eds., *Appleton's Cyclopedia of American Biography* (New York: D. Appleton, 1887), Vol. 5, pp. 625–26.
3. Thomas and Hyman, pp. 423–24.
4. Bingham in Pitman, pp. 361–62.
5. Lincoln, p. 371.
6. Reverdy Johnson, "Argument on the Jurisdiction of the Military Commission," in Pitman, pp. 251–62.
7. Levi C. Turner to James A. Hardie, June 4, 1864, in *The War of the Rebellion: A Compilation of the Official Records of the Union and Confederate Armies* (Washington, D.C.: Government Printing Office, 1899), Series II, Vol. 7, pp. 194–95 [hereinafter called O.R.]; Henry W. Halleck to James H. Carlton, February 4, 1864, O.R., Series I, Vol. 34, part 2, pp. 245–46.
8. Ewing in Pitman, pp. 264–67.
9. Bingham, in Pitman, pp. 351–72.
10. "Military and Martial Law," *North American Review* 102, no. 211 (April 1866), pp. 334–56.
11. Francis Lieber, "Instructions for the Government of the Armies of the United States in the Field," in Pitman, pp. 410–19.
12. John W. Curran, "Lincoln Conspiracy Trial and Military Jurisdiction Over Civilians," *Notre Dame Lawyer* 9, no. 1 (Nov. 1933), pp. 26–49; Neely, pp. 40–41, 64–65, 168.
13. John C. Brennan, "More on the Three Versions of the 1865 Trial Testimony," *Surratt Courier* 11, no. 2 (February 1986), pp. 5–7; John C. Brennan, "The Three Versions of the Testimony in the 1865 Conspiracy Trial," *Surratt Society News* 8, no. 3 (March 1983), pp. 3–6; Otto Eisenschiml, *Why Was Lincoln Murdered?* (Boston: Little, Brown, 1937), pp. 110, 115, 117, 249, 282, 457; *New York Times*, May 10, 1865; Ben Perley Poore, *The Conspiracy Trial for the Murder of the President* (Boston: J.E. Tilton and Company, 1865), Vol. I, p. 223.
14. Neely, pp. 167–73.
15. Lincoln, pp. 467–69.
16. Constitution of the United States of America; James G. Randall, *Constitutional Problems Under Lincoln* (Urbana: University of Illinois Press, 1964), pp. 163–67.

Chapter 4

1. Malone, ed., Vol. I, pp. 277–78; Wilson and Fiske, eds., Vol. I, p. 263.
2. Chamlee, pp. 167, 201, 226, 324–25, 335–36, 365, 411, 434.
3. Ibid., pp. 192–93, 201, 205, 374–75, 391.
4. Malone, p. 298.
5. Chamlee, pp. 76, 149; Henry L. Burnett, "Some Incidents in the Trial of President Lincoln's Assassins," in James Grant Wilson and Titus Munson, eds., *Personal Recollections of the War of the Rebellion* (New York: Commandery of the Loyal Legion of the United States, 1883–91, 1891), pp. 183–237, 258.
6. Poore, Vol. III, p. 84–86 [Montgomery], pp. 116–17.
7. Carman Cumming, *Devil's Game: The Civil War Intrigues of Charles A. Dunham* (Urbana: University of Illinois Press, 2004), pp. 20–34, 95–122, 130, 145–59, 160–80.
8. Poore, Vol. I, pp. 22–23 [Von Steinacker].
9. Oldroyd, pp. 124–27; Poore, Vol. I, pp. 18–20; Samuel B. Arnold, Statement, April 18, 1865, National Archives Microcopy 619, Reel 458, frames 0305–12; Edman Spangler, Examination, M-599, Reel 6, frames 0201–4; Dr. Samuel A. Mudd, Statement, April 21, 1865, M-599, Reel 5, frames 0212–38; Mary E. Surratt, Statement, April 17, 1865, M-599, Reel 6, frames 0233–57, 0170–0200; George A. Atzerodt, Statement, April 25, 1865, M-599, Reel 3, frames 0596–0602.
10. Poore, Vol. I, pp. 115–18 [Lloyd]; Vol. I, pp. 309–10 [Jett]; Vol. I, p. 316 [Conger]. Vol. II, pp. 92–3 [Doherty].
11. Poore, Vol. I, pp. 471–79 [Bell]; Vol. I, p. 480 [Robinson]; Vol. II, p. 6 [A. Seward].
12. Poore, Vol. III, pp. 196–97 [Norton]; Vol. I, pp. 63–65 [Lee].
13. Poore, Vol. I, pp. 419–21; Arnold, *Memoirs*, p. 51.
14. Poore, Vol. I, pp. 420–21 [W.H. Terry]. Arnold, Statement. Poore, Vol. I, p. 139 [Van Tine], Vol. I, p. 166 [D. Stanton].
15. Poore, Vol. II, p. 161 [Washington]; pp. 150–52 [M. Simms]; Vol. I, p. 436 [Thomas].
16. Poore, Vol. I, pp. 69–78.
17. Poore, Vol. II, pp. 44, 89–91, 185–88, 499.
18. Poore, Vol. II, p. 461 [Ritterspaugh]; Vol. I, pp. 205–06 [J. Simms]; Vol. I, pp. 227–28 [Burroughs].
19. Edward Steers, Jr., "General Conspiracy," in Steers, ed., *The Trial* (Lexington: University Press of Kentucky, 2003), pp. xxxiv–xxxv; Pitman, pp. 44–45.

Chapter 5

1. Poore, Vol. I, pp. 11–13.
2. Chamlee, p. 246.
3. Roscoe, pp. 436–37; *Boston Journal*, June 7, 1865.
4. Charles F. Cooney, ed., "At the Trial of the Lincoln Conspirators," *Civil War Times Illustrated* 12, no. 5 (August 1973), p. 25.
5. Poore, Vol. I, pp. 52, 58, 61, 62.
6. Roscoe, p. 479; Poore, Vol. I, p. 54; Bernard C. Steiner, *Life of Reverdy Johnson* (Baltimore: The Norman Remington Co., 1914), p. 115.
7. Malone, Vol. 3, pp. 237–39; Lorie Ann Porter, "Not So Strange Bedfellows: Thomas Ewing II and the Defense of Samuel Mudd," *Lincoln Herald* 90, no. 3 (Fall 1988), pp. 91–101.
8. Samuel Carter III, *The Riddle of Dr. Mudd* (New York: G.P. Putnam's Sons, 1974), pp. 42, 171–72; Chamlee, pp. 208, 236, 270, 386, 390, 459–60, 538; Rossiter Johnson, ed., *The Biographical Dictionary of America* (Boston: American Biographical Society, 1906); Otto Eisenschiml, *In the Shadow of Lincoln's Death* (New York: Wilfred Funk, 1940), pp. 145–47.
9. William E. Doster, *Lincoln and Episodes of the Civil War* (New York: G.P. Putnam's Sons, 1915), pp. 257, 259; Hunt and Brown, p. 169.
10. Chamlee, pp. 431–32.
11. John W. Clampitt, "The Trial of Mrs. Surratt," *North American Review* 131, no. 286 (September 1880), pp. 223–40; "Frederick A. Aiken," *The Washington Post*, December 24, 1878, p. 2; Michael W. Kauffman, "John Wilkes Booth and the Murder of Abraham Lincoln," *Blue & Gray Magazine* 7, no. 4 (April 1990), pp. 8–25, 46–62; Christine R. Christensen, "Finding Frederick," *Lincoln Herald* 113, no. 2 (Summer 2011), pp. 83–107.
12. John Howard Brown, ed., *The Twentieth Century Biographical Dictionary of Notable Americans* (Boston: The Biographical Society, 1904); Chamlee, pp. 236, 306, 421–22; Poore, Vol. III, p. 347.

13. Poore, Vol. II, p. 467 [Walsh]; p. 468 [Nokes]; Vol. III, pp. 26–27 [McKim].
14. Poore, Vol. III, p. 475 [Ford]; pp. 45–46 [Lamb]; p. 52 [Carland]; pp. 21–22 [Gifford].
15. Poore, Vol. II, pp. 515–17 [Richter]; pp. 506–07 [McAllister]; p. 507 [Briscoe].
16. Poore, Vol. III, pp. 143–53.
17. Poore, Vol. II, pp. 204–05.
18. Poore, Vol. III, pp. 64–65 [Craig]; pp. 62–64 [Hall]; pp. 340–41 [Wharton]; Pitman, pp. 236–39; Patricia L. Faust, ed., *Historical Times Illustrated Encyclopedia of the Civil War* (New York: HarperCollins, 1991), p. 12.
19. Poore, Vol. II, p. 252 [J.C. Thomas]; p. 382 [J.A. Bloyce]; Vol. III, pp. 451–52 [M. Mudd]; Vol. II, pp. 386–89 [G. Mudd].
20. Turner, *Beware,* pp. 184–85.
21. Cooney, p. 31.
22. Poore, Vol. II, p. 483 [Knott]; Vol. III, pp. 68–69 [Lusby]; pp. 455–59 [Fitzpatrick]; Vol. II, pp. 344–45 [Howell]; pp. 174–79 [Wiget].
23. Joan L. Chaconas, "Unpublished Atzerodt Confession Revealed Here for the First Time," Surratt Courier, Vol. 13, no. 10, October, 1988, pp. 1–3. National Archives Microcopy, M-599, reel 3, frames 596–602. Michael W. Kauffman, American Brutus (New York: Random House, 2004), p. xiv.

Chapter 6

1. James O. Hall, "John M. Lloyd: 'Star Witness,'" *Surratt Society News* 2, no. 3 (March 1977), p. 3; Laurie Verge, "That Man Lloyd," *Surratt Courier* 13, no. 4 (April 1988), pp. 2–3; James O. Hall, "Why John M. Lloyd Was in Upper Marlboro," *Surratt Society News* 5, no. 9 (September 1980), pp. 5–6; *Boston Evening Journal,* May 15, 1865.
2. Poore, Vol. I, pp. 69–72, 75–76; Weichmann, pp. 11–29.
3. Poore, Vol. I, pp. 115–119.
4. Poore, Vol. I, pp. 136–37, 372.
5. Holt to W.D. Kelley, March 30, 1869, in Weichmann, p. 395.
6. Ekin to Weichmann, June 7, 1877, in Weichmann, p. 398.
7. Kautz to Weichmann, April 27, 1885, in Weichmann, p. 398.
8. T.M. Harris, *Assassination of Lincoln* (Boston: American Citizens Company, 1892), quoted in Weichmann, p. 400.
9. Wallace, p. 848.
10. "Lloyd, John M.," http://www.spartacus.schoolnet.co.uk/USACWlloyd.htm.
11. Poore, Vol. I, pp. 70–71.
12. Statement of John M. Lloyd, April 23, 1865, National Archives, M-599, Reel 5, frames 147–61; Pitman, p. 121.
13. St. Marie to Joseph Holt, May 23, 1865, Bureau of Military Justice Records, National Archives; Joseph George, Jr., "H.B. Ste. Marie and His Role in the Arrest of John H. Surratt," *Lincoln Herald* 85, no. 4 (Winter 1983), pp. 269–79.
14. War Department Archives, National Archives. The report is undated.
15. Deposition of Gilbert J. Raynor, April 19, 1865, War Department Records, Judge Advocate General's files.
16. Deposition of D.H.L. Gleason, April 18, 1865, War Department Records, Judge Advocate General's files.
17. Letter from "Clara" to Weichmann, New York, February 15, 1865, War Department Archives.
18. Adjutant General's Office, Roll 6, no. 499–500.
19. Weichmann, p. 86.
20. John H. Surratt Jr., "The Rockville Lecture," in Weichmann, p. 435, Alfred Isacsson, "The Status of Weichmann Studies," *Surratt Courier* 11, no. 1 (January 1986), pp. 1, 6–10.
21. "Defends Mrs. Surratt," *Washington Post,* January 7, 1908.
22. Chamlee, pp. 75, 189.
23. War Department Files, Bureau of Military Justice, File "W," JAO, National Archives.
24. Weichmann to Col. H.L. Burnett, May 5, 1865, Judge Advocate General's files, War Department Records.
25. *Trial of John H. Surratt* (Washington, D.C.: Government Printing Office, 1867), pp. 814–15.
26. John T. Ford, "Behind the Curtain of a Conspiracy," *North American Review* 148, no. 389 (April 1889), pp. 484–93.
27. Poore, Vol. I, pp. 117, 121, 122.
28. *Trial of John H. Surratt,* pp. 276–77, 280–81, 290, 293.
29. Poore, Vol. II, p. 483.
30. Michael W. Kauffman, *American Brutus* (New York: Random House, 2004), p. 233.
31. O.R., Series I, Vol. 46, Part III, p. 937.
32. Cottingham to Colonel Burnett, May 14, 1865; Affidavit of J.W. Ridenour, December 1, 1865, Bureau of Military Justice Records, National Archives.

33. Verge, "That Man Lloyd."
34. Weichmann to Stanton, August 4, 1865, War Department Records.
35. Weichmann "to the Special Commission appointed for the distribution of the awards for the capture of the assassins," December 27, 1865, War Records Division, National Archives.
36. Lloyd Lewis, *Myths After Lincoln* (New York: Harcourt, Brace, 1929), pp. 225–26.
37. Joseph George, Jr., "The Days Are Yet Dark," *Records of the American Catholic Historical Society of Philadelphia* 95, nos. 1–4 (1984), pp. 67–81.
38. Pitman, *Trial of John H. Surratt*, p. 432.
39. George, "The Days Are Yet Dark."
40. Weichmann, p. xviii.
41. Weichmann to Oldroyd, July 22, 1901, Oldroyd Manuscripts, Lilly Library, Indiana University, Bloomington.
42. Weichmann to Oldroyd, August 18, 1901, Oldroyd Manuscripts.
43. Weichmann to Oldroyd, August 21, 1901, Oldroyd Manuscripts.
44. "L.J. Weichmann Goes to Rest," Anderson (Indiana) *Herald*, June 6, 1902.
45. Weichmann to the Special Commission.

Chapter 7

1. Pitman, pp. 246–49.
2. Cooney, "At the Trial of the Lincoln Conspirators."
3. Clampitt, "The Trial of Mrs. Surratt."
4. Ibid.; Ford, "Behind the Curtain of a Conspiracy"; James O. Hall, "The Mercy Recommendation for Mrs. Surratt," *Surratt Courier* 15, no. 8 (August 1990), pp. 4–5; Allen Thorndike Rice, ed., "New Facts About Mrs. Surratt," *North American Review* 147, no. 380 (July 1888), pp. 83–94.
5. Chamlee, pp. 194, 444, 450, 466, 540–42; David M. Jordan, *Winfield Scott Hancock: A Soldier's Life* (Bloomington: Indiana University Press, 1988), pp. 176–81, 218, 255–306.
6. Chamlee, pp. 199, 215, 217, 380, 444; A.M. Gambone, *Major-General John Frederick Hartranft* (Baltimore: Butternut and Blue, 1995), pp. 1–9, 41, 97, 136, 147, 161–62, 244–47; Roscoe, pp. 435, 437, 478, 488, 492–93.
7. John A. Gray, "The Fate of the Lincoln Conspirators," *McClure's Magazine* 37, no. 6 (October 1911), pp. 626–36.

8. Chamlee, pp. 447, 455, 461–62, 468–70, 480; Ownsbey, pp. 6, 86, 138–40, 148, 201–07; Elizabeth Steger Trindal, *Mary Surratt: An American Tragedy* (Gretna, LA: Pelican, 1996), pp. 206–14; Wilson and Fiske.
9. Clampitt, "The Trial of Mrs. Surratt."
10. Chamlee, pp. 470–71; Gray, "The Fate of the Lincoln Conspirators"; "The Execution," *Washington Evening Star*, July 7, 1865, p. 2; James O. Hall, "The Prop Knockers," *Surratt Courier* 11, no. 9 (September 1986), p. 1, 5–8; Trindal, pp. 220–26.
11. *Fort Jefferson National Monument* (Washington, D.C.: U.S. Department of the Interior, National Park Service, U.S. Government Printing Office, 1969); Albert Mauncy, "The Gibraltar of the Gulf of Mexico," *The Florida Historical Quarterly* 21, no. 4 (April 1943), pp. 303–31; Arnold, *Memoirs*, pp. 65–68, 73–76, 77, 83, 93–94, 99–105, 110–14, 116–18, 121–24, 164; A. O'D, "Thirty Months at the Dry Tortugas," *The Galaxy* 7, no. 2 (February 1869), pp. 282–88; Stephen Z. Starr, *Colonel Grenfell's Wars* (Baton Rouge: Louisiana State University Press, 1971), pp. 44–45, 55, 57–58, 63, 95, 97, 107, 123–25, 128–31, 145–47, 248, 291–92, 301–13, 324–26.

Chapter 8

1. Catherine Soanes and Sara Hawker, *Compact Oxford English Dictionary of Current English*, 3d ed. (Oxford: Oxford University Press, 2005), p. 551.
2. Allan Nevins, "The Case of the Copperhead Conspirator," http://www.soc.umn.edu/~samaha/cases/milligan_copperhead_conspirator.htm.
3. The Decisions of the Supreme Court of the United States at December Term, 1866, Ex parte In the Matter of Lambdin P. Milligan, Petitioner, *Cases Argued and Decided in the Supreme Court of the United States* (Rochester: The Lawyers Co-operative, 1884), 18 Law; Ed. U.S. 70–73, Wallace 3–6, p. 281.
4. Nevins, "The Case of the Copperhead Conspirator."
5. Carter, pp. 280–81, 294.
6. Nettie Mudd, ed., *The Life of Dr. Samuel A. Mudd* (New York: Neale, 1906), p. 299.
7. Joseph G. Gambone, "*Ex parte Milligan*: The Restoration of Judicial Prestige?" *Civil War History* 16, no. 3 (September

1970), pp. 246–59; *New York Herald*, December 20, 1866; *Harper's Weekly*, January 19, 1867; *New York World*, January 5, 1867; *Washington National Intelligencer*, December 18, 1866; *Washington Evening Star*, December 18, 1866.
  8. *Ex parte Mudd*, 17 Federal Cases 954, case no. 9,899, District Court, S.D. Florida, September 1868.
  9. Poore, Vol. 2, p. 140.
  10. Constitution of the United States, Article 2, section 2.
  11. Federalist No. 69.
  12. Federalist No. 74.
  13. Constitution, Article 1, section 8.
  14. John Ferling, *The Ascent of George Washington* (New York: Bloomsbury Press, 2009), pp. 336–37; Louis Fisher, *Presidential War Power*, 2d ed., rev. (Lawrence: University Press of Kansas, 2004), pp. 22–23; "U.S. Army Ranks," http://www.army.mil/symbols/armyranks.html; U.S. Army Center of Military History, Historical Resources Branch, letter to author, November 5, 2012, Frederick Hatch Papers. The army historians say flatly: "The President of the United States is not a member of the armed forces."
  15. 25 Federal Cases 590–591, case no. 14,842; U.S. House of Representatives, "Murder of Union Soldiers," Report No. 23, 39th Congress, 2nd session, 35–37; "Judge Hall's Decision," *Wilmington* (Delaware) *Gazette*, November 23, 1866.
  16. Thomas Bland Keys, "Were the Lincoln Conspirators Dealt Justice?" *Lincoln Herald* 80, no. 1 (Spring 1978), pp. 38–46.
  17. Randall, pp. 163–68, 174–76.
  18. Faust, p. 837.
  19. Major W. Winthrop, ed., *Digest of Opinions of the Judge Advocate General of the Army* (Washington, D.C.: Government Printing Office, 1868), pp. 223–24.
  20. Winthrop, pp. 229–30.
  21. Henry W. Halleck, Letter to Brigadier General Pope, December 31, 1861; General Orders No. 1, January 1, 1862, reprinted in Burrus Carnahan, "The Role of Military Commissions," *Surratt Courier* 27, no. 3 (March 2002), pp. 5–7.
  22. Chamlee, p. 327; Cumming, pp. 199–212, 258; Joseph E. Messmer, "Sanford Conover—Charles A. Dunham—Forger," *Civil War History* 4, no. 4 (December 1958), pp. 438–40; William A. Tidwell, *April '65* (Kent: Kent State University Press, 1995), pp. 150–54.

  23. Benn Pitman, ed., *The Assassination of President Lincoln and the Trial of the Conspirators* (New York: Moore, Wilstach & Baldwin, 1865), p. 40.
  24. Pitman, pp. 41–43.
  25. Joseph George Jr., "Subornation of Perjury at the Lincoln Conspiracy Trial?" *Civil War History* 38, no. 3 (September 1992), pp. 232–41.
  26. Joseph George Jr., "Military Trials of Civilians Under the Habeas Corpus Act of 1863," *Lincoln Herald* 98, no. 4 (Winter 1996), pp. 126–38.
  27. John Potter, Ds. Clk., War Dept., to E.B. French, July 26, 1870. David Rankin Barbee examined these records at the General Accounting Office on February 27, 1943. Note in Barbee Papers, Box 6, folder 347, Georgetown University, Washington, D.C.
  28. Joseph George, Jr., "The Conspiracy Trial's 'Suppressed Testimony,'" *Lincoln Herald* 111, no. 2 (Summer 2009), pp. 94–127.
  29. Chamlee, p. 457; John H. Surratt, Jr., "Lecture," *Washington Evening Star*, December 7, 1870.
  30. *New York World*, May 16, 1865, p. 4; May 26, p. 1; May 27, p. 4; June 2, p. 8; *Albany Argus*, June 15, 1865, p. 2.
  31. John Surratt, "Lecture."
  32. Army Board for Correction of Military Records, Transcript of Hearing in the Matter of Samuel A. Mudd, M.D., Deceased, Index No. 101.01, Board dates 22 January 1992, Docket Number: AC91-05511; George McNamara, "History Again, the Rehearing of Dr. Samuel A. Mudd," *Journal of the Lincoln Assassination* 7, no. 1 (April 1993), pp. 2–8; Frederick Hatch, Letter to Michael P.W. Stone, Under Secretary of the Army, September 20, 1992, Frederick Hatch Papers. Published in *Journal of the Lincoln Assassination* 6, no. 3 (December 1992), pp. 46–47.
  33. President Jimmy Carter, Letter to Dr. Richard D. Mudd, July 24, 1979. Dr. Richard D. Mudd Papers, Georgetown University, Washington, D.C.
  34. President Ronald Reagan, Letter to Dr. Richard D. Mudd, December 8, 1987.
  35. Edward Steers Jr., "Judge Friedman's Ruling in the Case of Dr. Mudd," *Surratt Courier* 24, no. 1 (January 1999), pp. 4–5; United States District Court for the District of Columbia, Richard D. Mudd, M.D., Plaintiff, v. Louis Caldera, Secretary of the Department of the Army, et al., Defendants; Civil Action No. 97-2946 (PLF); United

States Court of Appeals for the District of Columbia Circuit, Thomas B. Mudd ... Appellant, v. Thomas H. White, Secretary of the Army, et al., Appellees; Appeal ... No. 97cv02946.

36. Frederick Hatch, Letter to President Clinton, January 8, 1995. Frederick Hatch Papers.

37. James A. Dorskind, Letter to Frederick Hatch, February 9, 1995. Frederick Hatch Papers.

38. Letter, E.M. Stanton to A. Johnson, February 15, 1867, Department of Justice Archives.

Chapter 9

1. "Laws of War," Wikipedia, http://en.wikipedia.org/wiki/Law_of_war; Speed, *Opinion*, pp. 3–4; Constitution of the United States of America, Article I, section 8.

2. "Laws of War," Wikipedia.

3. Louis Fisher, *Military Tribunals and Presidential Power* (Lawrence: University Press of Kansas, 2005), pp. 1–7.

4. Thomas Jefferson, The Declaration of Independence, in *Thomas Jefferson: Writings*, ed. Merrill D. Peterson, Literary Classics of the United States (New York: Library of America, 1984), pp. 19–24.

5. Thomas Jefferson, Letter to James Madison, December 20, 1787, ibid., pp. 915–16.

6. Quoted in Fisher, *Military Tribunals...*, p. 9.

7. Quoted in Fisher, ibid., p. 16.

8. 10 Op. Att'y Gen. 74, 79 (1861), quoted in Fisher, ibid., p. 17.

9. Ed. of 1820 by Runnington, p. 42, quoted in Curran, Lincoln Conspiracy Trial and Military Jurisdiction Over Civilians."

10. Whiting, *War Powers of the President* (Boston, 1862), p. 124, quoted in Curran, Lincoln Conspiracy Trial and Military Jurisdiction Over Civilians."

11. *Ex parte Merryman*, Taney 246, Fed. Cas. No. 9487 (1861); *Ex parte Vallandigham* 1 Wall 243 (1864); *Ex parte Milligan*, S.C. 4 Wall. 2–142; Curran, Lincoln Conspiracy Trial and Military Jurisdiction Over Civilians."

12. E.D. Townsend, Assistant Adjutant General, General Orders No. 100, War Department, Adjutant General's Office, Washington, April 24, 1863; in Ben Pitman, ed., *The Assassination of President Lincoln and the Trial of the Conspirators* (New York: Moore, Wilstach & Baldwin, 1865), p. 410.

13. Francis Lieber, "Instructions for the Government of Armies of the United States in the Field," excerpted in Pitman, pp. 410–18. See Appendix IV.

14. Francis Lieber, *On Civil Liberty and Self Government* (Philadelphia, 1853), I, 130–1 (3d ed.), 108.

15. Frank Freidel, *The Life of Francis Lieber* (Baton Rouge: Louisiana State University Press, 1947), p. 322.

16. Freidel, pp. 370–75.

17. Fisher, *Military Tribunals...*, pp. 78–81.

18. Fisher, ibid., pp. 86–87.

19. Andrew Curry, "Liberty and Justice," *U.S. News and World Report*, December 10, 2001, pp. 52–53; George Lardner, Jr., "Nazi Saboteurs Captured!" *The Washington Post Magazine*, January 13, 2002, pp. 12–16, 23–24; Fisher, *Military Tribunals...*, pp. 91–100.

20. Lardner, "Nazi Saboteurs Captured!"; Fisher, *Military Tribunals...*, pp. 124–25.

21. "*Ex parte Quirin*" [317 U.S. 1 (1942)], Wikipedia, http://en.wikipedia.org/wiki/Ex_parte_Quirin.

22. Ibid.

23. For example, the U.S. Supreme Court ruled in 1896 that "separate but equal" school facilities segregating races was legal, yet the court in 1954 overturned that earlier ruling.

24. Fisher, *Military Tribunals...*, pp. 139–41; Samuel Eliot Morison, Henry Steele Commager, and William E. Leuchtenburg, *The Growth of the American Republic, Vol. 2*, 7th ed. (New York: Oxford University Press, 1980), p. 561.

25. *Hirabayashi v. United States*, 320 U.S. 81 (1943); Fisher, p. 140.

26. *Korematsu v. United States*, 323 U.S. 214 (1944); Fisher, p. 141–42.

27. Doris Kearns Goodwin, *No Ordinary Time* (New York: Touchstone Books, 1994), pp. 321–22, 514.

28. William O. Douglas, *The Court Years, 1939–1975* (New York: Random House, 1980), pp. 35, 38–39, 279–80.

29. Fisher, *Presidential War Power*, pp. 24–26, 33–34, 41–43, 47–48.

30. U.S. Constitution, Article 2, section 2; John H. Eicher and David J. Eicher, *Civil War High Commands* (Stanford: Stanford University Press, 2001). Eicher lists presidents under the heading "Principal Execu-

tives of the United States Government during the Civil War Era" (p. 70), and not among the officers of the armed forces: "Revised Regulations of 10 Aug. 1861, War Dept.: Art. 1, Sec. 4, Rank of officers ... 1. Lt. Gen. [Lieutenant General] 2. Maj. Gen. [Major General] 3. Brig Gen. [Brigadier General]," etc. There is no mention of the president as a member of the armed forces (p. 19).

31. "Why No War Declaration," and "Why War Declaration 'Seems Undesirable': The Official View," *U.S. News and World Report*, May 22, 1967, pp. 31–33.

32. "Gulf of Tonkin Resolution," Wikipedia, http://en.wikipedia.org/wiki/Gulf_of_Tonkin_Resolution.

33. "Why No War Declaration?"

34. Robert S. McNamara, with Brian Van De Mark, *In Retrospect: The Tragedy and Lessons of Vietnam* (New York: Times Books, 1995), pp. 127–28, 138–39.

35. Stanley Karnow, *Vietnam: A History* (New York: Penguin, 1984), pp. 390–91, 500.

36. Karnow, pp. 683–84; Anthony Summers, *The Arrogance of Power* (New York: Penguin, 2001), pp. 294–96.

37. Donald C. Bacon, Roger H. Davidson, and Morton Keller, *The Encyclopedia of the United States Congress* (New York: Simon & Schuster, 1995), pp. 2097–2102; Richard F. Grimmett, CRS Report for Congress, *RL 32267: The War Powers Resolution: After Thirty Years*.

38. Karen De Young, "Ex Secretaries Suggest New War Powers Policy," *Washington Post*, July 9, 2008, p. A-10.

39. "War on Terror," Wikipedia, http://en.wikipedia.org/wiki/War_on_Terror.

40. Joby Warrick, "Warnings on WMD 'Fabricator' Were Ignored, Ex-CIA Aide Says," *Washington Post*, June 25, 2006, p. A-1.

41. Walter Pincus, "Bush Memoir Makes Selective Use of Iraq Data," *Washington Post*, November 16, 2010, p. A-29.

42. Peter Lance, *Cover Up: What the Government Is Still Hiding About the War on Terror* (New York: Regan Books, 2004), pp. 179, 202; Douglas Jehl, "CIA Chief Orders 'Curveball' Review," *New York Times*, April 8, 2005, p. A-8. Information questioning the 9/11 attacks and the origin of the "War on Terror" may be found in the following sources: David Ray Griffin, *The New Pearl Harbor* (Northampton, MA: Olive Branch Press 2004) and *The 9/11 Commission Report: Omissions and Distortions* (Northampton, MA: Olive Branch Press, 2005); Richard A. Clarke, *Against All Enemies* (New York: Free Press, 2004); Michael C. Ruppert, *Crossing the Rubicon* (Gasbriola Island, BC: New Society Publishers, 2004); James Bamford, *A Pretext for War* (New York: Anchor Books, 2005); Jim Marrs, *The Terror Conspiracy* (New York: The Disinformation Co., 2006); Bob Graham, with Jeff Nussbaum, *Intelligence Matters* (Lawrence: University Press of Kansas, 2004).

43. 66 Fed. Reg. 57835–36, sec. 7 (2001); Fisher, *Military Tribunals*, pp. 168–69.

44. "Military Commissions Act of 2006," Wikipedia, http://en.wikipedia.org/wiki/Military_Commissions_Act_of_2006.

45. "War on Terror," Wikipedia.

46. Ibid.

47. Peter Finn, "Terror Detainee Largely Acquitted," *Washington Post*, November 11, 2010, p. A-1; Peter Finn and Anne E. Kornblut, "Verdict in Terror Case a Setback for Advocates of Civilian Trials," *Washington Post*, November 19, 2010, p. A-2.

48. Carrie Johnson, "Terror Trials by Military Flawed, Too," *Washington Post*, March 14, 2010, p. A-2; Spencer S. Hsu, "Holder Criticizes Exclusive Use of Military Commissions," *Washington Post*, April 16, 2010, p. A-11.

49. Frank J. Williams to Frederick Hatch, March 4, 2013, Frederick Hatch Papers. Frederick Hatch to Frank J. Williams, March 19, 2013, ibid.; Cornell University Law School Legal Information Institute, "Commander in Chief Powers," http://www.law.cornell.edu/wex/commander_in_chief_powers.

50. Greg Miller, "Iraq War Helps Fund Al-Qaeda, Officials Say," *Washington Post*, May 20, 2007, p. A-10; David A. Fahrenthold, "Legislators Call Obama's Actions in Libya Illegal," *Washington Post*, May 26, 2011, p. A-6; David A. Fahrenthold, "House Reprimands Obama Over Military Effort in Libya," *Washington Post*, June 4, 2011, p. A-3; Scott Wilson, "Obama Says Hill's Approval Not Needed for Libya Action," *Washington Post*, June 16, 2011, p. A-1.

Summation

1. Walter Isaacson, *Benjamin Franklin: An American Life* (London: The Folio Society, 2008), p. 383.

BIBLIOGRAPHY

Books

Arnold, Samuel Bland. *Memoirs of a Lincoln Conspirator.* Ed. Michael W. Kauffman. Bowie, MD: Heritage Books, 1995.
Bacon, Donald C., Roger H. Davidson, and Morton Keller. *The Encyclopedia of the United States Congress.* New York: Simon & Schuster, 1995.
Baker, L.C. *History of the United States Secret Service.* Philadelphia: L.C. Baker, 1867.
Bates, David Homer. *Lincoln in the Telegraph Office.* New York: Century, 1907.
Brown, John Howard, ed. *The Twentieth Century Biographical Dictionary of Notable Americans.* Boston: Biographical Society, 1904.
Bryan, George S. *The Great American Myth.* New York: Carrick & Evans, 1940.
Burnett, Henry L. "Some Incidents in the Trial of President Lincoln's Assassins." In James Grant Wilson and Titus Munson, eds., *Personal Recollections of the War of the Rebellion.* New York: Commandery of the Loyal Legion of the United States, 1883–1891.
Busch, Francis X. *Enemies of the State.* Indianapolis: Bobbs-Merrill, 1954.
Carter, Samuel, III. *The Riddle of Dr. Mudd.* New York: Putnam's, 1974.
Cases Argued and Decided in the Supreme Court of the United States. Rochester: Lawyers Co-Operative, 1884. 18 Law Ed. U.S. 70–73, Wallace 3–6.
Chamlee, Roy Z., Jr. *Lincoln's Assassins.* Jefferson, NC: McFarland, 1990.
Chase, Salmon P. *Inside Lincoln's Cabinet: The Civil War Diaries of Salmon P. Chase.* Ed. David Donald. New York: Longmans, Green, 1954.
Chittenden, L.E. *Recollections of President Lincoln and His Administration.* New York: Harper, 1891.
Cromwell, Sidney. *Political Opinions in 1774 and 1863: A Letter to a Victim of Arbitrary Arrests and American Bastilles.* New York: Anson D.F. Randolph, 1863.
Cumming, Carman. *Devil's Game: The Civil War Intrigues of Charles A. Dunham.* Urbana: University of Illinois Press, 2004.
Doster, William E. *Lincoln and Episodes of the Civil War.* New York: Putnam's, 1915.
Douglas, William O. *The Court Years, 1939–1975.* New York: Random House, 1980.
Edwards, William C., and Edward Steers, Jr., eds. *The Lincoln Assassination: The Evidence.* Urbana: University of Illinois Press, 2009.
Eicher, John H., and David J. Eicher. *Civil War High Commands.* Stanford: Stanford University Press, 2001.
Eisenschiml, Otto. *In the Shadow of Lincoln's Death.* New York: Wilfred Funk, 1940.
_____. *Why Was Lincoln Murdered?* Boston: Little, Brown, 1937.

Bibliography

Ellis, Dr. John B. *The Sights and Secrets of the National Capital.* San Francisco: H.H. Bancroft, 1869.
Faust, Patricia L., ed. *Historical Times Illustrated Encyclopedia of the Civil War.* New York: HarperCollins, 1991.
Ferling, John. *The Ascent of George Washington.* New York: Bloomsbury Press, 2009.
Fisher, Louis. *Military Tribunals and Presidential Power.* Lawrence: University Press of Kansas, 2005.
____. *Presidential War Power.* Lawrence: University Press of Kansas, 2004.
Fort Jefferson National Monument. Washington, D.C.: U.S. Department of the Interior, National Park Service, U.S. Government Printing Office, 1969.
Freidel, Frank. *The Life of Francis Lieber.* Baton Rouge: Louisiana State University Press, 1947.
Gambone, A.M. *Major-General John Frederick Hartranft.* Baltimore: Butternut and Blue, 1995.
Goodrich, Thomas. *The Darkest Dawn.* Bloomington: Indiana University Press, 2005.
Goodwin, Doris Kearns. *No Ordinary Time.* New York: Touchstone Books, 1994.
Grimmett, Richard F. *CRS Report for Congress, RL 32267: The War Powers Resolution: After Thirty Years* [2003].
Hall, James O. *The Surratt Family and John Wilkes Booth.* Clinton, MD: Surratt Society [1976].
Hall, Kermit L. *The Oxford Companion to the Supreme Court of the United States.* New York: Oxford University Press, 2005.
Hamilton, Alexander, John Jay, and James Madison. *The Federalist Papers.* Great Books of the Western World, Vol. 43. Chicago: Encyclopaedia Britannica, 1952.
Harris, T.M. *Assassination of Lincoln.* Boston: American Citizens, 1892.
Hunt, Roger D., and J.R. Brown. *Brevet Brigadier Generals in Blue.* Gaithersburg, MD: Olde Soldier Books, 1997.
Isaacson, Walter. *Benjamin Franklin: An American Life.* London: Folio Society, 2008.
Jefferson, Thomas. *Writings.* Ed. Merrill D. Peterson. Literary Classics of the United States. New York: Library of America, 1984.
Johnson, Rossiter, ed. *The Biographical Dictionary of America.* Boston: American Biographical Society, 1906.
Jordan, Daniel M. *Winfield Scott Hancock: A Soldier's Life.* Bloomington: Indiana University Press, 1988.
Karnow, Stanley. *Vietnam: A History.* New York: Penguin, 2001.
Kauffman, Michael W. *American Brutus.* New York: Random House, 2004.
Lance, Peter. *Cover-Up: What the Government Is Still Hiding About the War on Terror.* New York: Regan Books, 2004.
Laughlin, Clara E. *The Death of Lincoln.* New York: Doubleday, Page, 1909.
Lewis, Lloyd. *Myths After Lincoln.* New York: Harcourt, Brace, 1929.
Lieber, Francis. *On Civil Liberty and Self Government.* Philadelphia, 1853.
Lincoln, Abraham. *Speeches and Writings, 1859–1865.* Literary Classics of the United States. New York: Library of America, 1989.
Malone, Dumas, ed. *Dictionary of American Biography.* New York: Scribner's, 1964.
McClellan, Phyllis I. *Silent Sentinel on the Potomac: Fort McNair, 1791–1991.* Bowie, MD: Heritage Books, 1993.
McNamara, Robert S., with Brian Van De Mark. *In Retrospect: The Tragedy and Lessons of Vietnam.* New York: Times Books, 1995.
Mogolever, Jacob. *Death to Traitors.* Garden City, NY: Doubleday, 1960.
Moore, Guy W. *The Case of Mrs. Surratt.* Norman: University of Oklahoma Press, 1954.

Morrison, Samuel Eliot, Henry Steele Commager, and William E. Leuchtenburg. *The Growth of the American Republic*. New York: Oxford University Press, 1980.
Morseberger, Robert, and Katherine Morseberger. *Lew Wallace: Militant Romantic*. New York: McGraw-Hill, 1980.
Mudd, Nettie, ed. *The Life of Dr. Samuel A. Mudd*. New York: Neale, 1906.
Mudd, Richard D. *Dr. Samuel Alexander Mudd and His Descendants*. Saginaw: Richard D. Mudd, 1989.
Neely, Mark E., Jr. *The Fate of Liberty*. New York: Oxford University Press, 1991.
Oldroyd, Osborn H. *The Assassination of Abraham Lincoln*. Washington: O.H. Oldroyd, 1901).
Ownsbey, Betty J. *Alias "Paine": Lewis Thornton Powell, the Mystery Man of the Lincoln Conspiracy*. Jefferson, NC: McFarland, 1993.
Palludan, Phillip Shaw. *The Presidency of Abraham Lincoln*. Lawrence: University Press of Kansas, 1994.
Pitman, Benn, ed. *The Assassination of President Lincoln and the Trial of the Conspirators*. New York: Moore, Wilstach & Baldwin, 1865.
Poore, Ben Perley, ed. *The Conspiracy Trial for the Murder of the President*. Boston: J.E. Tilton, 1865.
Randall, James G. *Constitutional Problems Under Lincoln*. Urbana: University of Illinois Press, 1964.
Rhodehamel, John, and Louise Taper. *"Right or Wrong, God Judge Me": The Writings of John Wilkes Booth*. Urbana: University of Illinois Press, 1997.
Roscoe, Theodore. *The Web of Conspiracy*. Englewood Cliffs, NJ: Prentice-Hall, 1959.
Seward, Frederick W. *Reminiscences of a War-Time Statesman and Diplomat, 1830–1915*. New York: Putnam's, 1916.
Soanes, Catherine, and Sara Hawker. *Compact Oxford Dictionary of Current English*. Oxford: Oxford University Press, 2005.
Speed, James. *Opinion of the Constitutional Power of the Military to Try and Execute the Assassins of the President*. Washington, DC: Government Printing Office, 1865.
Starr, Stephen Z. *Colonel Grenfell's Wars*. Baton Rouge: Louisiana State University Press, 1971.
Steers, Edward, Jr. "General Conspiracy." In Edward Steers, ed., *The Trial*. Lexington: University Press of Kentucky, 2003.
Steiner, Bernard C. *Life of Reverdy Johnson*. Baltimore: Norman Remington, 1914.
Story, Joseph. *Commentaries on the Constitution of the United States*. Durham: Carolina Academic Press, 1987.
Summers, Anthony. *The Arrogance of Power*. New York: Penguin, 2001.
Thomas, Benjamin P., and Harold M. Hyman. *Stanton: The Life and Times of Lincoln's Secretary of War*. New York: Alfred A. Knopf, 1962.
Tidwell, William A. *April '65*. Kent: Kent State University Press, 1995.
Tidwell, William A., with James O. Hall and David W. Gaddy. *Come Retribution: The Confederate Secret Service and the Assassination of Lincoln*. Jackson: University Press of Mississippi, 1988.
Trial of John H. Surratt. Washington, D.C.: Government Printing Office, 1867.
Trindal, Elizabeth Steger. *Mary Surratt: An American Tragedy*. Gretna, LA: Pelican, 1995.
Turner, Thomas R. *Beware the People Weeping*. Baton Rouge: Louisiana State University Press, 1982.
Wallace, Lew. *An Autobiography*. New York: Harper, 1906.
War of the Rebellion: A Compilation of the Official Records of the Union and Confederate Armies. Washington, D.C.: Government Printing Office, 1899.

Warner, Ezra J. *Generals in Blue.* Baton Rouge: Louisiana State University Press, 1964.
Washington, City and Capital. Washington, D.C.: Government Printing Office, 1937.
Weichmann, Louis J. *A True History of the Assassination of Abraham Lincoln and of the Conspiracy of 1865.* Ed. Floyd E. Risvold. New York: Alfred A. Knopf, 1975.
Whiteman, Maxwell, ed. *While Lincoln Lay Dying.* Philadelphia: Union League of Philadelphia, 1968.
Wilson, James Grant, and John Fiske, eds. *Appleton's Cyclopedia of American Biography.* New York: D. Appleton, 1887.
Winthrop, Major W., ed. *Digest of Opinions of the Judge Advocate General of the Army.* Washington, D.C.: Government Printing Office, 1868.
Wright, Anthony. *Citizens and Subjects: An Essay on British Politics.* London: Routledge, 1994.

Articles

Bates, Edward. "Diary." *Annual Report of American Historical Society* 4 (1930).
Bradford, Gamaliel. "Union Portraits, 5. Edwin M. Stanton." *Atlantic Monthly* 116, no. 2 (August 1915).
Brennan, John C. "More on the Three Versions of the 1865 Trial Testimony." *Surratt Courier* 11, no. 2 (February 1986).
———. "The Three Versions of the Testimony in the 1865 Conspiracy Trial." *Surratt Society News* 8, no. 3 (March 1983).
Carnahan, Burrus. "The Role of Military Commissions." *Surratt Courier* 27, no. 3 (March 2002).
Chaconas, Joan. "Historic Fort McNair." *Surratt Society News* 9, no. 6 (June 1984).
Christensen, Christine. "Finding Frederick." *Lincoln Herald* 112, no. 2 (Summer 2011).
Cooney, Charles F., ed. "At the Trial of the Lincoln Conspirators." *Civil War Times Illustrated* 12, no. 5 (August 1973).
Clampitt, John W. "The Trial of Mrs. Surratt." *North American Review* 131, no. 298 (September 1880).
Curran, John W. "Lincoln Conspiracy Trial and Military Jurisdiction Over Civilians." *Notre Dame Lawyer* 9, no. 1 (November 1933).
Curry, Andrew. "Liberty and Justice." *U.S. News & World Report*, December 10, 2001.
De Young, Karen. "Ex Secretaries Suggest New War Powers Policy." *Washington Post*, July 9, 2008.
"Defends Mrs. Surratt." *Washington Post*, January 7, 1908.
"The Execution." *Washington Evening Star*, July 7, 1865.
Fahrenthold, David A. "House Reprimands Obama Over Military Effort in Libya." *Washington Post*, June 4, 2011, p. A-3.
———. "Legislators Call Obama's Actions on Libya Illegal." *Washington Post*, May 26, 2011, p. A-6.
Finn, Peter. "Terror Detainee Largely Acquitted." *Washington Post*, November 11, 2010.
———, and Anne E. Kornblut. "Verdict in Terror Case a Setback for Advocates of Civilian Trials." *Washington Post*, November, 19, 2010.
Ford, John T. "Behind the Curtain of a Conspiracy." *North American Review* 148, no. 389 (April 1889).
"Frederick A. Aiken." *Washington Post*, December 24, 1878.
Gambone, Joseph G. "*Ex parte Milligan*: The Restoration of Judicial Prestige?" *Civil War History* 16, no. 3 (September 1970).

George, Joseph, Jr. "The Conspiracy Trial's 'Suppressed Testimony.'" *Lincoln Herald* 111, no. 2 (Summer 2009).
———. "The Days Are Yet Dark." *Records of the American Catholic Historical Society of Philadelphia* 95, nos. 1–4 (1984).
———. "H.B. Ste. Marie and His Role in the Arrest of John H. Surratt." *Lincoln Herald* 85, no. 4 (Winter 1983).
———. "Military Trials of Civilians Under the Habeas Corpus Act of 1863." *Lincoln Herald* 98, no. 4 (Winter 1996).
———. "Subornation of Perjury at the Lincoln Conspiracy Trial?" *Civil War History* 38, no. 3 (September 1992).
Gray, John A. "The Fate of the Lincoln Conspirators." *McClure's Magazine* 37, no. 6 (October 1911).
Grover, Leonard. "Lincoln's Interest in the Theatre." *The Century Magazine* 77, no. 6 (April 1909).
Hall, James O. "An Interview with James O. Hall." *Journal of the Lincoln Assassination* 4, no. 2 (August 1990).
———. "John M. Lloyd: Star Witness." *Surratt Society News* 2, no. 3 (March 1977).
———. "The Mercy Recommendation for Mrs. Surratt." *Surratt Courier* 15, no. 8 (August 1990).
———. "The Prop Knockers." *Surratt Courier* 11, no. 9 (September 1986).
———. "Why John M. Lloyd Was in Upper Marlboro." *Surratt Society News* 5, no. 9 (September 1980).
Hsu, Spencer S. "Holder Criticizes Exclusive Use of Military Commissions." *Washington Post*, April 16, 2010.
Isacsson, Alfred. "The Status of Weichmann Studies." *Surratt Courier* 11, no. 1 (January 1986).
Jehl, Douglas. "CIA Chief Orders 'Curveball' Review." *New York Times*, April 8, 2005.
Johnson, Carrie. "Terror Trials by Military Flawed, Too." *Washington Post*, March 14, 2010.
"Judge Hall's Decision." *Wilmington* (Delaware) *Gazette*, November 23, 1866.
Kauffman, Michael W. "Fort Leslie McNair and the Lincoln Conspirators." *Lincoln Herald* 80, no. 4 (Winter 1978).
———. "John Wilkes Booth and the Murder of Abraham Lincoln." *Blue & Gray Magazine* 7, no. 4 (April 1990).
Keys, Thomas Bland. "Were the Lincoln Conspirators Dealt Justice?" *Lincoln Herald* 80, no. 1 (Spring 1978).
"L.J. Weichmann Goes to Rest." *Anderson* (Indiana) *Herald*, June 6, 1902.
Lardner, George. "Nazi Saboteurs Captured!" *Washington Post Magazine*, January 13, 2002.
Marquis de Chambrun. "Personal Recollections of Mr. Lincoln." *Scribner's Magazine* 13, no. 1 (January 1893).
Mauncy, Albert. "The Gibraltar of the Gulf of Mexico." *The Florida Historical Quarterly* 21, no. 4 (April 1943).
McNamara, George. "History Again: The Rehearing of Dr. Samuel A. Mudd." *Journal of the Lincoln Assassination* 7, no. 1 (April 1993).
Messmer, Joseph E. "Sanford Conover—Charles A. Dunham—Forger." *Civil War History* 4, no. 4 (December 1958).
"Military and Martial Law." *North American Review* 102, no. 211 (April 1866).
Miller, Greg. "Iraq War Helps Fund Al-Qaeda, Officials Say." *Washington Post*, May 20, 2007, p. A-10.
Miller, Stephen G. "Roll Call for the Garrett's Farm Patrol." *Surratt Courier* 19, no. 9 (September 1994).

"A New Version of the Greatest Manhunt." *New York Times Magazine*, December 7, 1930.
O'D, A. "Thirty Months at the Dry Tortugas." *The Galaxy* 7, no. 2 (February 1869).
Peckham, Howard H. "James Tanner's Account of Lincoln's Death." *The Abraham Lincoln Quarterly* 2, no. 4 (December 1942).
Pincus, Walter. "Bush Memoir Makes Selective Use of Iraq Data." *Washington Post*, November 16, 2010.
Porter, Lorie Ann. "Not So Strange Bedfellows: Thomas Ewing II and the Defense of Samuel Mudd." *Lincoln Herald* 90, no. 3 (Fall 1988).
Rice, Allen Thorndike, ed. "New Facts About Mrs. Surratt." *North American Review* 147, no. 380 (July 1888).
Steers, Edward, Jr. "Judge Friedman's Ruling in the Case of Dr. Mudd." *Surratt Courier* 24, no. 1 (January 1999).
Storey, Moorfield. "Dickens, Stanton, Sumner, and Storey." *Atlantic Monthly* 145, no. 4 (April 1930).
Surratt, John H., Jr. "Lecture." *Washington Evening Star*, December 7, 1870.
"Tanner Also Present." *Washington Post*, April 16, 1905.
Turner, Thomas R. "Public Opinion and the Assassination of Abraham Lincoln." *Lincoln Herald* 78, no. 1 (Spring 1976).
Verge, Laurie. "That Man Lloyd." *Surratt Courier* 13, no. 4 (April 1988).
Warren, Louis A., ed. "Edwin McMasters Stanton." *Lincoln Lore* 990, March 29, 1948.
———. "A $100,000 Reward." *Lincoln Lore* 314, April 15, 1935.
———. "Stanton at Lincoln's Bedside." *Lincoln Lore* 575, April 15, 1940.
Warrick, Joby. "Warnings on WMD 'Fabricator' Were Ignored, Ex CIA Aide Says." *Washington Post*, June 25, 2006.
Welles, Gideon. "Lincoln and Johnson." *The Galaxy* 14, nos. 4 and 5 (April and May 1872).
"Why No War Declaration?" and "Why Declaration 'Seems Undesirable': The Official View." *U.S. News & World Report*, May 22, 1967.
Williams, Frank J., and Nicole J. Benjamin. "Military Trials of Terrorists: From the Lincoln Conspirators to the Guantánamo Inmates." *Northern Kentucky Law Review* 39, no. 4 (2012).

Newspapers

Albany (New York) *Argus*
Anderson (Indiana) *Herald*
Baltimore American
Boston Journal
Detroit Free Press
Harper's Weekly
London Times
New York Daily News
New York Evening Post
New York Herald
New York Times
New York World
Philadelphia Inquirer
Washington Evening Star
Washington National Intelligencer
Washington Post
Wilmington (Delaware) *Gazette*

Documents

Constitution of the United States of America
Letter, E.M. Stanton to A. Johnson, February 15, 1867, Department of Justice Archives
U.S. Army Center of Military History, Historical Resources Branch, Letter to author, November 5, 2012, Frederick Hatch Papers
U.S. House of Representatives, Report No. 23, 39th Congress, 2nd session

Collections

Army Board for Correction of Military Records, Transcript of Hearing in the Matter of Samuel A. Mudd, M.D., Department of the Army
Bureau of Military Justice Records, War Department Files, National Archives
David Rankin Barbee Papers, Lauinger Library, Georgetown University, Washington, D.C.
Frederick Hatch Papers
Investigation and Trial Papers Relating to the Assassination of Abraham Lincoln, National Archives Microcopy 599 (Washington, D.C.: National Archives and Records Service, General Services Administration, 1965)
James O. Hall Papers, J.O. Hall Research Center, Surratt Society, Clinton, Maryland
Judge Advocate General's Files, War Department Records, National Archives
Lincoln Assassination Reward Files, National Archives Microcopy 619
Oldroyd Manuscripts, Lilly Library, Indiana University, Bloomington, Indiana
Richard D. Mudd Papers, Lauinger Library, Georgetown University, Washington, D.C.
War Department Records, National Archives

INDEX

Adams, John 155
Afghanistan 169
Aiken, Frederick A. 39, 73, 80, 104, 111, 114
Allen, Ethan 20
al Qaeda 162, 164, 166
American Civil Liberties Union 154, 164–165
American Revolution 45
Amnesty for Southerners 78
Army Board for the Correction of Military Records 139–144
Arnold, Samuel Bland 39–40, 47, 60–61, 66, 69, 74, 77, 101, 118, 130
Arsenal, Washington 38–39
Articles of War 46, 48, 146, 151–152, 209, 211
Ashley, James M. 135
Attainder, Bill of 183–184
Atzerodt, George Andrew 25, 27, 39–41, 60–62, 66–67, 72–73, 81, 83, 85, 91, 101, 110–117
Atzerodt, John C. 72
Augur, Christopher C. 19, 25, 63

Bailey, F. Lee 138
Bainbridge, Absalom R. 136
Baker, James A. 161
Baker, Joseph Stannard 23
Baker, Lafayette Charles 20–24, 56
Baker, Milo 21
Balance of Power 53, 161, 178
Barbary Pirates War 156
Bates, Edward 44–45, 146, 177–181
Beckwith, Samuel H. 27, 81
Bell, William H. 60
Ben-Hur 32
Biddle, Francis 150–151, 154
Bingham, John Armor 29, 43, 45, 47–49, 77–78, 100, 105, 106

Black, Hugo L. 174
Black, Jeremiah S. 15, 123
Blackstone, Sir William 10
Blair, Montgomery 22
Bloyce, Julia Ann 79
Booth, John Wilkes: associates 40, 61, 83; burial 39; Canada visit 59, 61; capture and death 60; Confederate connection 29, 64, 81, 102; escape route 25, 60, 86; evidence against 20, 28, 61, 102; identifying remains 56; motives 11, 204; rewards for capture 25–27
Booth, Junius Brutus, Jr. 21
Bowles, William A. 123
Boynton, Thomas J. 127, 130
Bradley, Joseph H., Jr. 105
Brandegee, Frank 149
Breyer, Stephen G. 174
Briscoe, Washington 76
Brophy, John P. 91, 110–111
Browning, Orville Hickman 70
Bryant, William L. 136
Buchanan, James 15, 30
Bureau of Military Justice 30, 65, 199
Burnett, Henry Lawrence 29, 51, 56–58, 72, 80, 92, 98, 100, 119
Burnside, Ambrose E. 109
Burroughs, Joseph 42, 63
Bush, George H.W. 143, 168
Bush, George W. 162, 166
Butler, Benjamin F. 123, 135
Butler, John George 113, 115

Caesar, Julius 195
Caldera, Louis 142
California Gold Rush 21
Cameron, Simon 16
Canada 22, 29, 58–59, 61, 91, 102, 119, 134
Carland, Louis J. 76, 92, 136

229

Carroll Prison *see* Old Capitol Prison
Carter, Jimmy 141–142, 161
Cato 195
Cerone, John P. 165
Chaconas, Joan 81
chains, handcuffs, restraints 67
Chamlee, Roy Z., Jr. 91–92
Chandler, Zachariah 16
Chase, Salmon P. 13, 126
Chase, Samuel 155
Chester, Samuel Knapp 64
Christopher, Warren 161–162
Cicero 197
Clampitt, John W. 39, 68, 73, 81, 104, 111
Clark, Joseph 71
Clark, William D. 40–41, 143
Clay, Clement Claiborne 29
Clayton, John M. 156
Cleary, William W. 29, 59, 134
Clendenin, David Ramsey 30, 37
Clinton, William J. 143–144
Clinton, MD 42
Cold War 187
Collier, Daniel L. 14
commander-in-chief, president as 50, 127–129, 146–147, 156–157, 169, 178–179, 184–189
Comstock, Cyrus Ballou 30, 36–37
Confederate States of America 12–13, 28, 29, 58–60, 64, 68, 77–78, 80, 90, 102, 119, 134, 149
Conger, Everton Judson 27, 60
Congress, U.S. 11, 16, 27, 44, 47, 128–131, 146, 151, 155–170, 191
Conover, Sanford *see* Dunham, Charles A.
conspiracies 48
Cooper, John Sherman 158–159
Cortes, Herman 33
Cottingham, George 96
courts martial 146, 152, 188, 211
Cox, Walter S. 39, 73–75
Cox, Walter T. 138
Coxshall, William E. 114
Craig, George 77
Creighton, H.J. 99
Crimean War 119
Crook, George 36
Crown Dam, NY 59
Curry, Jennie 21

Daggett, Albert 20
Dana, Charles A. 13, 90
Dasch, George John 150, 152
Davis, Jefferson 21, 29, 64, 78, 149
Dean, Mary Apollonia 63

Declaration of Independence 70, 146
Declaration of War 155, 157, 168
DeWitt, John 153
Dodd, Levi A. 114
Doherty, Edward P. 60
Doster, William E. 39, 72–73, 76–77, 81
Douglas, Adele C. 111
Douglas, Henry Kyd 67
Douglas, John Jay 138
Douglas, Stephen Arnold 68, 111
Douglas, William O. 154–155
Dry Tortugas, FL 118
Dunham, Charles A. 59, 134, 137
Dyer, Sarah Frances *see* Mudd, Sarah Frances Dyer

Early, Bernand J. 77
Early, Jubal Anderson 32–33, 36
Eckert, Thomas T. 96
Edmonds, Sibel 163
Eisenhower, Dwight D. 175
Eisenschiml, Otto 51
Elcin, James Adams 30, 37, 87, 98, 105
Elston, Susan 33
Everett, Robinson O. 138
Ewing, Thomas, Jr. 39, 43, 47, 51, 69–72, 75, 78–79, 82, 125, 138, 174
Ewing, Thomas, Sr. 69
ex post facto laws 164, 184
Execution of Conspiracy Suspects 104–105, 108–117

The Fair God 33
Federal Bureau of Investigation 150, 163
The Federalist 128
Field, David D. 123
Fisher, George P. 98
Fitzpatrick, Honora 36, 62–63, 80
Ford, Gerald R. 160
Ford, John Thompson 41–42, 75, 92–93, 96, 107, 137
Ford's Theatre 18–19, 27, 36, 42, 63, 75–76
Fort Jefferson 57, 118–120
Foster, John A. 91–92, 94
Foster, Robert Sanford 30, 35–36, 92, 105
Founding Fathers 3–4, 133–134, 145, 157–158, 168, 171, 173
Franklin, Benjamin 172
Fremont, John Charles 31
French, E.B. 136
Friedman, Paul L. 142
Fulbright, J. William 158–159

Gaddafi, Muammar el 170
Garfield, James A. 123

Garrett Farm 60
Geneva Conventions 164, 167
German spies 150
Gerry, Elbridge 146
Ghailani, Ahmed 167–168
Gifford, James J. 76
Gillette, Abram D. 112, 115
Gleason, Daniel H.L. 89–90
Goldsmith, Jack 167–168
Graham, Lindsey O. 168
Grant, Ulysses S. 13, 34, 37, 63
Greeley, Horace 45
Grenfell, George St. Leger 57, 119–120
Grover, Leonard 17
Guantanamo Bay, Cuba 167
Guerrilla War 166–167, 209
Gulf of Tonkin Resolution *see* Tonkin Gulf Resolution

habeas corpus 6, 10–12, 46, 112, 122, 124, 146, 148, 164, 168, 177–183
Habeas Corpus Act 11, 52–53, 124, 130
Hague Conferences 149
Hall, Charles B. 77
Hall, Willard 129–130
Halleck, Henry W. 23, 46, 48, 132–133, 208
Hamilton, Alexander 48, 128, 175, 185
Hancock, Winfield Scott 73, 107–110, 114
Hansen, Emerick W. 28
Harlan, James 106
Harper, George 29
Harris, Clara Hamilton 27
Harris, Thomas Maley 30, 36, 67, 87
Hartranft, John F. 67, 98, 109
Harvard University 11
Haslett, Joseph B. 114
Hebert, F. Edward 157
Henderson, James B. 77
Henry, Patrick 143
Henry, Patrick (founding father) 197
Herold, David Edgar 25–27, 39, 41, 60, 66, 70–83, 91, 101–102, 110–117
Hitt, Robert R. 50
Holder, Eric H., Jr. 168
Holt, Joseph 14–15, 27, 29–30, 38, 43, 51, 53, 55, 57, 81–82, 87, 97–98, 100, 104–108, 127, 131–133, 206–209
hoods worn by prisoners 67
Hoover, J. Edgar 150
Horsey, Stephen 123
Hotchkiss, Giles Waldo 27
House Where Lincoln Died *see* Petersen House
Howe, Albion Parris 30, 36

Howell, Augustus S. 80, 90
Hudspeth, Mary 135
Humphreys, Andrew 123
Hunter, David 30–32, 105
Hutchinson, Ellen 15

Ickes, Harold L. 154
impeachment 125, 181, 189
Instructions for the Government of Armies of the U. S. in the Field 48–50, 147–149, 189, 210–212
intelligence, wartime 22
Iraq War 162, 169–170

Jackson, Robert H. 152, 174, 187
Jackson, Thomas J. "Stonewall" 36
Japanese-American internment 153–155, 186–187
Jefferson, Thomas 146, 156, 175
Jenkins, John S. 138
Jett, William Storke 60
Johnson, Andrew 13, 25, 30, 41, 44, 61, 67, 73, 76, 78, 104–108, 111, 119, 125, 135, 141–142
Johnson, Lyndon B. 138–139
Johnson, Reverdy 34–35, 36, 39, 45–46, 67–68, 73, 112, 125
Jones, John Paul 138
Judiciary Act 10, 131
jurisdiction of military commission 43–50, 70, 73, 123–127, 164, 191, 211
justice 4, 121, 175

Kauffman, Michael W. 81–82
Kautz, August Valentine 30, 34–35, 67, 98, 101–105
Kelly, William D. 21, 98
Key, Francis Scott 15
Key, Philip Barton 15
Keys, Thomas B. 130
kidnap conspiracy 40–41, 60, 64, 91, 102
Kirkwood House 25
Knights of the Golden Circle 57
Knott, Joseph T. 80, 95, 136
Kohut, Andrew 166
Ku Klux Klan 183

Lamb, James 75–76
Lamson, Mary A. 14
law: Anglo-American 65, 121; different from justice 4; English 12, 50, 146–147; martial 45–47, 65, 122, 146–150, 190–205, 210–211; military 29, 44–45, 65, 72, 104, 122, 127, 144–150, 189–205; of nations 44, 145, 148, 191–205;

of war 44, 145, 151–152, 164, 187, 191–205, 207, 211
Leahy, Patrick J. 165
Lee, John 61
Lee, Robert E. 78, 139
L'enfant, Pierre Charles 38
Leon, Juan Ponce de 118
Lewis, Lloyd 97
Libya 170
Lieber, Francis 147–149, 189, 210–212
Lincoln, Abraham: assassination 9, 18–20, 27–28, 77–78; commander-in-chief of military forces 50, 127–129, 146–147, 189; criticism 68; death 20, 28, 44; funerals 13, 68; habeas corpus, suspension of writ 6–7, 50, 122, 147–149, 156, 177–181; inaugural journey (1861) 31; kidnap, conspiracy 40–41, 60, 64, 91, 102; Mexican War, oppositon 156; military commissions defended 52, 122; personality 1; powers assumed 45–46, 156; reaction of public to murder 1, 9, 12, 19; Stanton, relationship with 15–17; threats against 59–63
Lloyd, John Minchin 60, 63, 80, 83–89, 136–137
Lusby, James 80

Madison, James 48, 146, 165, 175
Magna Carta 50
martial law *see* law, martial
Massachusetts Bill of Rights 146
Mathews, John 64
McAlister, Samuel 76
McCall, William H.H. 114
McClellan, George B. 16, 22
McConnell, Mitch 167
McDonald, Joseph E. 123
McKim, Samuel A.H. 75
McLemore, Henry 153
McNamara, Robert S. 157–159
McPhail, James L. 74, 98
Meade, George G. 108
Meigs, Montgomery C. 118
Merrick, Richard T. 125
Merritt, James B. 137
Mexican War 14, 31, 33, 45, 50, 156
military commissions 30, 45, 48, 50, 52, 65, 122–123, 150, 163, 188, 190–209
Military-Industrial Complex 175
military law *see* law, military
Milligan, Lambdin P. 57, 122–144
Milligan decision 53, 57, 122–144, 147, 151, 183, 208
Mohammed, Khalid Sheikh 168

Montgomery, Richard 59, 136–137
moot court 138
Morgan, John Hunt 34, 119
Morse, Wayne L. 158–159, 168–169
Morton, Oliver H.P.T. 33, 57
Mosby, John Singleton 41
Mudd, George 79
Mudd, Mary Clare 79
Mudd, Richard Dyer 139–140, 143–144
Mudd, Samuel Alexander 39, 41, 47, 60–62, 64, 66, 69–82, 88, 101–102, 118, 125, 130, 138–144
Mudd, Sarah Frances Dyer 41, 70
Mudd, Thomas B. 140
Murphy, Dennis F. 50
Murphy, Edward 77
Murphy, Edward V. 50
Murphy, Francis W. 154
Murphy, James J. 50, 71

Napoleon Bonaparte 149
National Detective Bureau 22
National Hotel 61, 77, 88, 135
National Theatre 17
Navy Yard, Washington 41
Nevins, Allan 125
Nichols, Charles H. 76–77
9/11 attacks 162
9/11 Commission 162–163
Nixon, Richard M. 159
Nokes, James 75
Northwest Conspiracy 57, 119, 123
Norton, Marcus P. 61, 79

oath 67–68
Obama, Barack 169–170
O'Beirne, James Rowan 24–25
O'Crowley, Philomena 97, 99
Odem, William 166
O'Laughlen, Michael 39, 41, 47, 60–61, 66, 69, 73–75, 77, 101, 118
Old Capitol Prison 22, 63, 92–93, 112, 137
Oldroyd, Osborn H. 98–99
Olds, Rev. 113, 115
Orders of American Knights 123
Oxford Research Group 166

Paine, Payne *see* Powell, Lewis T.
Petersen House 18–20, 25
Peterson Brothers transcript 51
petition for Mrs. Surratt 33, 36, 56–57, 102–105
Pew Research Center 166
Philippine Insurrection 149, 183
Pierrepont, Edwards 106

Pinkerton, Allan 22
Pitman, Benn 50–51, 106
Pitman, Isaac Newton 50
Pitman Method of Shorthand 50, 84
Plutarch 195
Polk, James K. 156
Poore, Benjamin Perley 51
Porter, Fitz John 32
Porter, George L. 117
Porter, Horace 30, 37
Powell, Lewis Thornton 25, 28, 36, 41, 59–60, 62, 66–67, 72–82, 85, 91, 101–102, 109–117, 135
president as member of armed forces 157, 185
presidential power 45–46, 146, 156, 158–159, 169, 178–189
prisoners of war 211
Purdy, Robert 135

quasi war with France 155
Quinn, Richard 152
Quinn Decision 151–153

Radical Republicans 44, 125
Rand Corporation 166
Randall, James G. 130–131
Randolph, Edmund J. 192
Rath, Christian 110–117
Rathbone, Henry Reed 27
Raynor, Gilbert J. 89
Re, Edward D. 138
Reagan, Ronald 142, 161, 166
reporting trial in news media 64–65, 79
rewards for assassins 25–27
Rice, Condoleezza 162–163
Richards, Almarin C. 91, 98
Richter, Ernest Hartman 76
Ridenour, J.W. 96
Ritterspaugh, Jacob 63, 76
Roberts, Owen J. 154
Robinson, George Foster 28, 60
Roosevelt, Franklin D. 150–154, 163, 186–187, 189
Ruggles, Mortimer B. 136

sabotage 150–151, 153
St. Albans, VT, raid upon 59
Ste. Marie, Henri B. 89
"Sam Letter" 61
Sanders, George Nicholas 29, 59, 134–135
Scott, Winfield 21, 50
secrecy at trial 51
sedition 149

Seward, Augustus Henry 28, 60
Seward, Frederick William 17–18, 28
Seward, William Henry 10, 13, 17–18, 21, 25–28, 41, 60, 73, 86, 102, 106
Sheridan, Philip 35–36
Sherman, William T. 69
Shoup, Daniel F. 114
Sickles, Daniel 15
Simms, Joe 63
Simms, Mary 61
slavery 68–69
Smith, Joseph Sim 118
Spangler, Edman 39, 41–42, 47, 60, 63, 66, 69, 75, 91, 101, 118, 130
Spanish-American War 120
Speed, James 43, 106, 112, 123, 145, 190–205
Speed, Joshua Fry 44
Stanbury, Henry 123
Stanton, David 61
Stanton, Edwin L. 14
Stanton, Edwin McMasters: attorney general 15; criticism of 45, 65; early life 14–17, 55; health 14; informs nation of assassination 9–10, 27–28; money for witnesses 136; plot to assassinate 13, 74–75, 77; powers assumed by 10, 16; reconstruction plan 17, 44; relationship with Lincoln 15–17; releases prisoners 126; secretary of war 16; silence decreed in Mrs. Surratt's case 56; threatens witnesses 91–92; tragedies 14, 19; trial, involvement in 38, 43, 58, 102, 151
Steele, Candida E.S. 138
Steinacker, Henry von 59
Stevens, Thaddeus 125
Stone, Frederick 39, 70–71, 75
Stone, Thomas 70
Story, Joseph 11, 185
Stryker, Augustus 115
Stuart, James E.B. 119
Sumner, Charles 13
Supreme Court, U.S. 12, 57, 67, 123–126, 153–155, 157, 168, 183–184
Surratt, Anna 36, 42, 62–63, 90, 109–117
Surratt, Isaac Douglas 42
Surratt, John Harrison, Jr. 27, 29, 42, 59–61, 63, 79–80, 83–86, 88–91, 93–95, 97, 104, 129, 137
Surratt, John Harrison, Sr. 42
Surratt, Mary Elizabeth 33, 35–36, 39, 42, 45, 56–57, 60–82, 84–117, 137
Surrattsville, MD 42, 60, 80, 89
Sutton, Richard 50

Taney, Roger B. 183
Tanner James 20
Tappan, Benjamin 14
Taylor, George F. 114
Taylor, Zachary 69
terrorism 162, 166
Thomas, Daniel J. 61, 78
Thomas, John C. 78
Thompson, Jacob 29, 59
Tine, Mary van 61
Tod, David 34
Tompkins, Charles Henry 30, 37, 105
Tonkin Gulf Resolution 157, 169
Townsend, Edward Davis 27
transcript of trial 50, 106
treason 77–78, 133, 157, 189
trial of John Surratt 63, 104
Truman, Harry S. 187–188
Trumbull, Lyman 122
Tucker, Nathaniel Beverly 29
Turley, Jonathan 165

Uniform Code of Military Justice 163–164, 168
United Nations 162
U.S. Constitution 2, 5–6, 10, 45, 47, 53–54, 127–134, 145, 150, 156, 164, 168–169, 171–172, 174–175, 178–205

Vallandigham, Clement L. 131
Vietnam War 149, 155, 157, 170

Wade, Benjamin F. 16
Wallace, David 33
Wallace, James Watson *see* Dunham, Charles A.
Wallace, Lewis 30, 32–34, 87, 98

Walsh, Francis J. 75
Walter, Jacob A. 110
War Department, U.S. 16, 144, 149
War of 1812 38–39
"War on Terror" 162
War Powers 128, 133, 145–146, 156, 159, 167–170, 187–189
War Powers Act 157–162, 170
Warren, Earl 153
Washington, George 123, 129, 146, 172
Washington, Melvina 61
Washington, DC 44, 46, 190
weapons of conspirators 60, 80–81, 83–84, 86, 88–89, 93–94, 96
Weichmann, Frederick C. 99
Weichmann, Louis J. 36, 58, 62–64, 80–83, 86–100
Weichmann, Tillie 97, 99
Welles, Gideon 17, 44, 106
Wells, Henry H. 81, 94
Wharton, John W. 77
Wheeler, Joseph 119
Whiskey Rebellion 123, 129
Whitehurst, Daniel W. 118
Wiget, Bernardine F. 80–81, 110
Williams, Frank J. 168
Wilson, Woodrow 149–150, 188–189
Wirz, Henry 34, 132, 207
Wood, William P. 88–89, 96
World War I 120, 149
World War II 150–155, 183, 186–187
Wylie, Andrew B. 112

Yellow Fever 118–119
Yellow Fever Plot 59
Young, George 29

www.ingramcontent.com/pod-product-compliance
Ingram Content Group UK Ltd.
Pitfield, Milton Keynes, MK11 3LW, UK
UKHW041942140426
5217IPUK00014B/617